Two Kingdoms

The Battle for Man's Soul

Graham Powell

Sovereign World

Sovereign World Ltd
PO Box 777
Tonbridge
Kent TN11 0ZS
England

Unless otherwise stated, Scripture quotations in this volume are from the New American Standard Bible, Copyright The Lockman Foundation, 1960, 1962, 1963, 1971, 1973, 1975, La Habra, California.

Other Scripture quotations are from the Amplified New Testament (AMP), Copyright ©, The Lockman Foundation 1954, 1958.

ISBN 1 85240 306 3

The publishers aim to produce books which will help to extend and build up the Kingdom of God. We do not necessarily agree with every view expressed by the author, or with every interpretation of Scripture expressed. We expect each reader to make his/her judgement in the light of their own understanding of God's Word and in an attitude of Christian love and fellowship.

Typeset by CRB Associates, Reepham, Norfolk.
Printed in the United States of America.

Author's note

Two Kingdoms is really two books in one. The first part describes how a person can be delivered from the power of sin, and the second part, from the power of evil spirits. My suggestion is that you read the book from beginning to end as one unit. In order to be delivered from demonic bondage and to maintain a life of freedom, an understanding of both sections is crucial.

Graham Powell

Other books by the author

Christian Set Yourself Free
(Sovereign World Ltd, Tonbridge, England)

This best-selling book is written from personal experience and shows how a Christian can become free from demonic oppression through personal praying and the application of biblical truth. *Christian Set Yourself Free* is used world-wide as a balanced and practical teaching resource for the body of Christ. It has helped many to become free from bondages which seemed impossible to overcome.

Fear Free
(New Wine Press, Chichester, England)

The author exposes the 'spirit of fear' that cripples the lives of multitudes and shows how a person can come into freedom through the power of Christ.

Contents

Chapter 1

The Seen and the Unseen

Two worlds influence us at the same time, whether we realise it or not. One is the seen world, the other the unseen world. We are all familiar with the seen world, but usually not so familiar with the unseen. Because of the importance of these worlds in our lives, it is imperative that we have an understanding of them both. We are then able to make informed choices about how we want to live. If we make wise decisions, a whole new dimension of living will open up before us.

The Bible clearly tells us all we need to know about these two worlds and will therefore be the source of reference for this book. To live only for the things that are seen is folly, and yet this is how most people conduct their lives. As we will see, this is because of spiritual blindness, causing an inability to recognise and therefore understand things pertaining to the unseen world.

Imagine how you would feel if you were to lose the ability to see! Last summer I spent some time with a man who suffers from night blindness. During the day he sees as well as most of us, but when darkness comes he can see nothing at all unless lights are on. Consequently, he is only able to drive his car during the day. However, he can make his way around the streets of his community at night because he has memorised the number of steps and turns he needs to take from his front door to where he wants to go.

How sad to be in such a plight! His condition is mild, however, to what most people live with. The Bible says that the god of this world has blinded the minds of those who do not believe in Jesus Christ, so that they cannot see or understand the things pertaining to God's kingdom. All unbelievers, then, are spiritually blind.[1] Many Christians have only partial sight, and need to allow God's Word to grant them greater insight or better vision. Jesus said that if we would continue in His Word, we would know the truth and the truth would make us free.[2] The purpose of this book is to declare the truth that will enable the Holy Spirit to work in our lives, and to bring people into the freedom that Jesus spoke about. In Hebrews 11:3 we read:

> *'By faith we understand that the worlds were prepared by the word of God, so that what is seen was not made out of things that are visible.'*

In 2 Kings chapter 6 is the story of an army sent by the king of Syria to capture the prophet Elisha, who had been telling the king of Israel the plans of the opposing Syrian army. Elisha knew about these plans because God had revealed them to him. When Elisha's servant rose early one morning he was alarmed to see a great army with horses and chariots circling the city of Dothan. In trepidation he informed Elisha what was happening, only to be told not to be afraid, because there were more with them than with the Syrians. Elisha's servant could count. There were probably hundreds, if not thousands, of Syrians, and only two of them! How could Elisha say such a thing? He was soon to find out, for Elisha prayed and said, *'O Lord, I pray, open his eyes that he may see.'*[3]

There is a seen world, but there is also an unseen world. Just because we do not see into this realm does not mean it does not exist. The servant's eyes were opened, that is, his spiritual eyes, *'and behold, the mountain was full of horses and chariots of fire all around Elisha.'*[4] Angels had come to their rescue and now he could see them. He was no longer limited to natural sight alone, but could see into two worlds at the same time. As a result of angelic intervention and the supernatural events that followed, Elisha and his servant experienced a great deliverance.[5]

Earthly and heavenly

Another way of talking about the seen and unseen worlds is to refer to the earthly and the heavenly realms. That is, the things of the earth and the things beyond the earth.

In Psalm 113:5, 6 we read,

> *'Who is like the Lord our God, who is enthroned on high, who humbles Himself to behold the things that are in heaven and in the earth?'*

I remember reading these verses as a young Christian. Suddenly I became aware of the greatness of God and the smallness of man. I saw, as it were, God holding not only planet earth, but also the entire universe in the palm of his hand. All that made up the heavens and the earth was compressed into a mass no larger than a grain of sand. It was overwhelming to see things as they really are. From our perspective, this earth is very large and the size of the universe beyond our comprehension, and yet God is beyond them both, humbling Himself even to consider the things of the heavens and the earth.

Talking of sand, there are as many or more stars in the universe than the number of grains of sand on all the seashores of this world combined. And remember that these grains of sand are compressed together, whereas the stars in the universe are often hundreds of millions of light years apart. With light travelling at 186,000 miles (about 300,000 kilometres) per second, the extent of the heavens above is beyond our ability to fully comprehend. Astronomers have penetrated some 12 billion light years into space and still have not found the full expanse of the universe. The Creator of course, is much greater than His creation. How great He is! If that were not enough, the message of Christianity is that this God of greatness came down to our level, taking on a human form and walking among us as a man – but with one difference: He was without sin.

In the first chapter of the gospel of Matthew, we read that when Joseph discovered his fiancée was pregnant, he was greatly troubled and considered breaking the engagement. After an angelic messenger told him in a dream that Mary had conceived through the Holy Spirit, he changed his mind. The angel then revealed that the Son she would bear was to be called Jesus, and that He would save His people from their sins. This, the angel said, was the fulfilment of Isaiah's prophecy,

> *'Behold, the virgin shall be with child, and shall bear a Son, and they shall call Him Immanuel, which translated means, "God with us."'*   (Matthew 1:23)

Our planet has a unique place in the plans and purposes of God. Isaiah declared on behalf of the Lord,

> *'Heaven is My throne, and the earth is My footstool.'*
>   (Isaiah 66:1)

The prophet goes on to talk of the Temple that was built for the Lord. At the dedication of this Temple in Jerusalem, Solomon declared:

'Will God indeed dwell on the earth? Behold heaven and the highest heaven [literally, "heaven of heavens"] *cannot contain Thee, how much less this house which I have built.'*

(2 Chronicles 6:18)

Solomon knew that God could not be confined to the limitations of the Most Holy Place, where He would manifest His presence. His own father, David, had rejoiced:

'Sing to God, O kingdoms of the earth; sing praises to the Lord, to Him who rides upon the highest heavens [literally: "heaven of heavens"], *which are from ancient times.'*   (Psalm 68:32–33)

The Bible speaks often about the heavens, and as we look more closely we discover reference to the third heaven. Logically, we can conclude, if there is a third heaven there must also be a second and first heaven. There is no reference in the Bible to a seventh heaven. Paul talks of being caught up to the third heaven, which he also calls Paradise.[6] This is the immediate presence of God, where all genuine believers in Jesus Christ are taken by angelic transportation upon physical death.[7]

Paul also talks of the resurrection body that believers will one day be clothed with, and of the struggles we have with our mortal bodies. He says it is preferable to be absent from the body and present with the Lord.[8] All true believers have the certain hope of entering the third heaven when their earthly sojourn is over.

While the third heaven ushers us into the immediate presence of God, the second heaven, as I understand it, refers to the realm above us that we see such a small part of on a clear night and that extends billions of light years into space. The first heaven, then, refers to the atmosphere around our earth where the clouds float and the birds fly. One thing is without dispute: God's creation is awesome and God Himself is high above it all.

Under the earth

While looking around us and above us we have usually failed to look beneath us. Although the Bible has much to say of the heavens and the earth, it also speaks of the realm beneath the earth. In the heart of the earth is a place called Sheol in Hebrew, Hades in Greek, which is the place of departed spirits.

Everybody is going somewhere when they physically die. To say that when death comes everything is over, is a fallacy without biblical foundation. Man was made to live forever. We are eternal souls and have an eternal destiny. While the physical body returns to dust or ashes until the time of resurrection, the spirit and soul of man (referred to from now on simply as man's spirit) move on to another realm. This destiny is determined while we are living on earth, in time, through our response or lack of response to Jesus Christ, God's Son.[9]

In Luke chapter 16 we have an account of two men and their divergent destinies after death. Jesus Himself told this story of one man who was rich in earthly wealth but a pauper in regard to the heavenly, and the other who was a pauper in earthly wealth but rich in regard to the heavenly. The rich man lived in a mansion, enjoying all that money could buy, while at his gate sat a beggar who longed to be fed even with the crumbs that would fall from the rich man's table. Dogs licked his open sores and he was to be pitied in every way. Eventually they both died and went to different places, not as a result of poverty or riches, but because of the spiritual condition of their heart. One had a genuine faith in God, the other had not.

The place of departed spirits

Let us first consider what happened to people who died in the era before Jesus Christ was crucified and rose from the dead. The spirits of both believers and unbelievers went down into Sheol or Hades, in the heart of the earth. There were two exceptions: Enoch and Elijah, who were both caught up to the third heaven before they could experience physical death.[10] Everyone else went down to Sheol, not to the same location, but to different parts of Sheol.

Jesus described this place in Luke 16 as being divided into two distinct sections, with a great chasm between them making it impossible for anyone on either side to pass to the other.[11] One section, called Abraham's bosom, was for true believers in God, a place of comfort and hope; the other was for unbelievers, a place of torment and despair. The rich man found himself in the place of torment, the poor man in the place of comfort. The rich man cried out to Abraham that the poor man, named Lazarus, might bring him water to quench his thirst because of the agony he was in. Abraham replied that this was not possible. The rich man then pleaded that someone be sent to warn his five brothers back on earth about the reality of hell, but he was told by Abraham,

*'If they do not listen to Moses and the Prophets, neither will they
be persuaded if someone rises from the dead.'*   (Luke 16:31)

Why, you may ask, was it necessary for true believers in God to
go down into Sheol and not up into the third heaven on death?
The answer is simple. The blood shed through the Old Covenant
sacrifices could never fully deal with sin. Only through the death
of Jesus, God's Passover Lamb, could God's justice be satisfied and
sin be dealt with once and for all.[12]

Also, there had been a defiling of the heavenly sanctuary in
former days through the rebellion of Lucifer and the numerous
angels who joined him.[13] The heavenly sanctuary had to be
cleansed before believers could come directly into God's presence.
(Of these matters, we have only been given partial understanding
in God's Word; there is much yet to be revealed.) This cleansing
would only take place after the Son of God had been crucified;
after the Father had raised Him from the dead; and after He had
sprinkled His blood in the heavenly sanctuary. Then, and only
then, could the Son present before the Father the believers who
had died in centuries past, as well as those who would die from the
time of His resurrection onward.[14]

Jesus tasted death

Hebrews 2:9 says,

*'But we do see Him who has been made for a little while lower
than the angels, namely, Jesus, because of the suffering of death
crowned with glory and honor, that by the grace of God He might
taste death for everyone.'*

A few verses later we read:

*'Since then the children share in flesh and blood, He Himself
likewise partook of the same, that through death He might render
powerless him who had the power of death, that is, the devil; and
might deliver those who through the fear of death, were subject to
slavery all their lives.'*   (Hebrews 2:14–15)

When Jesus came to earth He did so primarily to offer Himself
up for our sins, by dying on a Roman cross and pouring out
His blood for us. As a perfect and sinless sacrifice, He was able
to present Himself to the Father, taking our place and the

punishment that we rightly deserved for breaking the laws of God.[15]

When Jesus triumphantly cried from the cross, *'It is finished!'* He was declaring to both the seen and unseen worlds that the purpose of His coming to the earth had been perfectly fulfilled.[16] The power of sin had been broken over mankind and the originator of sin, Lucifer, soundly defeated. Three days after His death, Jesus rose from the dead, bearing with Him the keys of death and Hades. The power of death had been gloriously overcome. Lucifer, now known as Satan or the Devil, had been stripped of his authority over the human race. Freedom had been won for mankind. However, it would only come into effect when individuals called on the name of Jesus, and chose to turn from darkness and to walk in the light of God.[17]

Three days and three nights

When Jesus died, His body was taken and placed in a tomb. But what happened to Jesus Himself? The physical body is just a house for man's spirit to reside in. Where did the spirit of Jesus go? Jesus foretold His crucifixion and rising from the dead three days later, but He also foretold where He would be during those three days and three nights.

> *'An evil and adulterous generation craves for a sign; and yet no sign shall be given to it but the sign of Jonah the prophet; for just as Jonah was three days and three nights in the belly of the sea monster, so shall the Son of Man be three days and three nights in the heart of the earth.'* (Matthew 12:39, 40)

Jesus went down into Sheol. He experienced the 'tasting' of death in three ways.

First, He experienced spiritual death. On the cross, as He identified with mankind's sinfulness by becoming our sin offering, the Father turned His back on the Son. That is why Jesus cried out, *'My God, My God, why hast Thou forsaken Me?'* (Matthew 27:46). Spiritual death is separation from God, and Jesus was separated from the Father when He took upon Himself the sin of the world.

Second, He experienced physical death, which is the natural consequence of spiritual death. Physical death is the separation of man's spirit from his body. From the cross, Jesus cried, *'"Father, into Thy hands I commit My spirit." And having said this He breathed His last'* (Luke 23:46).

Third, He experienced eternal death, as He went down to Sheol carrying away our sins. In Isaiah 53 we read that Jesus bore and carried away our iniquities, our griefs (literally: 'malady, disease, sickness'), and our sorrows (literally: 'anguish, affliction, grief, pain, sorrow'). This he did to fulfil the type or Old Testament example of the scapegoat (literally: 'goat of removal'). According to the Old Testament, on the annual Day of Atonement two male goats were presented before the Lord at the tent of meeting. Lots were cast to determine which animal would die as a sin offering for the people, and which would become the scapegoat. After the sin offering was slain and its blood sprinkled in the Tabernacle, the live goat was taken.

> *'Then Aaron shall lay both of his hands on the head of the live goat, and confess over it all the iniquities of the sons of Israel, and all their transgressions in regard to all their sins; and he shall lay them on the head of the goat and send it away into the wilderness by the hand of a man who stands in readiness. And the goat shall bear on itself all their iniquities to a solitary land; and he shall release the goat in the wilderness.'* (Leviticus 16:21–22)

Jesus fulfilled both the type of the sin offering and the type of the scapegoat, as He tasted death for everyone. He died that we might live. He was rejected by the Father so that we might be accepted by the Father. On His 'release in the wilderness' Jesus made proclamation to the spirits in prison in the unrighteous section of Sheol, to those who had been disobedient during the days of Noah.[18] This was not to save their souls, for once physical death has been experienced it is too late for a person to be reconciled to God. He also went to the righteous section of Sheol, since He said to one of the thieves who had been crucified alongside Him and had called upon Him, *'Truly I say to you, today you shall be with Me in Paradise'* (Luke 23:43). Paradise was another name for the righteous section of Sheol.

Let us take a short digression. Have you ever wondered about the timing of the death and resurrection of Jesus? We are usually told that Jesus died on Good Friday and rose again on Easter Sunday, but this does not allow for three days and three nights (72 hours) to be fulfilled. There has to be another explanation.

We need to understand that during the week of the crucifixion there were two sabbaths. The regular weekly sabbath commenced at sunset on Friday and continued until sunset on Saturday, and the Passover or High Day sabbath commenced at sunset on the

Thursday and continued until sunset on the Friday. We can now see how the order of events unfolded to fit the scriptural criterion.[19] The Last Supper took place on Tuesday, the crucifixion on Wednesday, the burial before sunset on Wednesday, and the resurrection before sunset on Saturday. This gives a full three days and three nights or 72 hours.

A glimpse of Sheol

Years ago, when Shirley and I were leading an evangelistic team of young men and women in Hamilton, New Zealand, a couple who were new Christians joined our team. One day the husband came to me greatly concerned about his mother's physical and spiritual condition. She was in the intensive care unit of Waikato Hospital. After experiencing a heart attack she had gone into a coma for four-and-a-half-hours. When she regained consciousness in hospital, she told her gathered family what she had seen during the coma. As a result, I was asked by her son to visit her and share the way of salvation, as she was not a Christian.

This woman told me what she had told her family. I will never forget her simple yet profound words. She said that she had found herself falling, falling, falling, and knowing that she was not going up, but going down. Finally, she came to a place where she recognised family members who had died before her. One was an uncle, an ungodly man who had died two years earlier. Another was her grandmother, who cried out to her, 'Go back, go back. Do not come to this place! Do not come to this place!'

Realising she was facing eternity unprepared, she cried out to God to save her. Graciously the Lord responded, and she regained consciousness on the hospital bed, eager to experience the forgiveness of sins and come into a right relationship with God. She had seen into the unrighteous section of Sheol. It was so easy to talk with her about God's plan of salvation. I told her of how our sin has separated us from God, and of God's rescue plan for man through the sending of His Son Jesus to die on a cross in our place. Of how Jesus was raised from the dead, and that He lives today to save all who call upon Him from the consequences of sin; and then of the new life to be found in knowing Jesus and walking with Him every day.

I explained that in order to come into a right relationship with God she had to be willing to confess her sin to God, turn from her lifestyle of independence from God, and be willing to confess Jesus Christ as her Lord. That is, to come under God's rule and be willing to live a life in obedience to God's Word. Frankly, I did not know if she would live long, but I spoke to her as if she had many days ahead. Gladly she prayed a simple prayer from her heart, confessing her sin, acknowledging Jesus as the Son of God, and His death on a cross and rising from the dead. Upon confessing Jesus as her Lord, she had a life-changing encounter. The peace of God filled her heart, the burden of her sin was taken away, and she received the gift of eternal life. Jesus had become very real to her.

The following day I visited her once again to find that she was out of intensive care and in another ward. As I walked to her bedside she greeted me with these simple words, referring to her readiness to face death: 'Next time I know I am going up. I know I am not going down.' Even though she lacked understanding of the Scriptures, she was bearing witness to spiritual reality. As a believer in Jesus Christ, she would be ushered into the immediate presence of God when it was time for her to die. She would be going up, not down.

Jesus our great High Priest

When Mary lingered outside the empty tomb some hours after Jesus had risen from the dead, Jesus Himself drew near and asked her whom she was seeking. Thinking she was talking to the gardener, she asked that if he had removed the body she wanted to know where it was, so that she might take it away. As soon as Jesus spoke her name she realised she was indeed in the presence of the risen Christ. With great joy Mary embraced her Lord to hear Jesus say to her,

> *'Stop clinging to Me, for I have not yet ascended to the Father; but go to My brethren, and say to them, "I ascend to My Father and your Father, and My God and your God."'*   (John 20:17)

Just as each year the High Priest entered the Most Holy Place of the earthly tabernacle on the Day of Atonement to sprinkle the animal blood of the sin offerings, so Jesus, as our great High Priest, had yet to ascend to the true tabernacle in the heavens and sprinkle His blood in the heavenly sanctuary. In doing this He would fulfil the Old Testament types.[20] Through the sprinkling of the blood of animal sacrifices, the earthly tabernacle was cleansed. Through the sprinkling of the blood of Jesus, the heavenly tabernacle was to be cleansed. Once this had been accomplished,

Jesus could then lead the Old Testament believers from the righteous section of Sheol into the immediate presence of the Father, to His throne in the third heaven or Paradise.[21]

As a result of the new and living way Christ has made for us to enter into the Father's presence when physical death is experienced, New Testament believers no longer go down into Sheol, but up to Paradise. We can say as believers that we know we are going up, not down! Hallelujah![22]

Where do unbelievers go at death?

Before the cross, all unbelievers went down into the unrighteous section of Sheol on physical death. Since the cross, unbelievers continue to go down into Sheol, there to await the day of resurrection and judgment that most assuredly is to come.[23] Paul warned the Athenians:

> *'God is now declaring to men that all everywhere should repent, because He has fixed a day in which He will judge the world in righteousness through a Man whom He has appointed, having furnished proof to all men by raising Him from the dead.'*
>
> (Acts 17:30–31)

The great white throne

The Apostle John foresaw some amazing and terrible things that were yet to come, as recorded in the book of Revelation. In chapter 20 he describes seeing a great white throne and the One who sat upon it. So awesome was His presence that the earth and heaven fled away. What a day this will be!

Standing before the throne were those who had died over the centuries, now raised up from their temporary abode in Sheol and required to give an account of the lives they had lived on earth. Books were opened with detailed records, not only of their outward deeds, but also of the inward motives of their hearts. Another book, the Book of Life, was opened, and if their names were not recorded in it they were thrown into the lake of fire, known also as the second death.[24] This is what the Bible calls eternal judgement – separation from God forever.

There is a seen world but there is also an unseen world. In reality, the unseen world is more important than the seen world, for the seen is temporal, but the unseen is eternal.

Chapter 2

The Temporal and the Eternal

Most people today invest their time and energies into matters temporal rather than matters eternal. Our materialistic societies place ever more demands on us to have this or that in order to be considered successful and secure. In all our pursuits to obtain the things that we must one day leave behind, there is no mention of the most important issue of life. Surely this has to do with the very reason for our existence? We have been made by God, for God, and not to live self-centred lives rejecting our Creator.[1] James, in his Epistle, warns the rich man of the temporary nature of life:

> 'Let the rich man glory in his humiliation, because like flowering grass he will pass away. For the sun rises with a scorching wind, and withers the grass; and its flower falls off, and the beauty of its appearance is destroyed; so too the rich man in the midst of his pursuits will fade away.' (James 1:10–11)

The Bible is not against prosperity, but warns us of living only for the things of this world.[2] Later in his letter, James, under the inspiration of the Holy Spirit, says,

> 'Come now, you who say, "Today or tomorrow, we shall go to such and such a city, and spend a year there and engage in business and make a profit." Yet you do not know what your life will be like tomorrow. You are just a vapour that appears for a little while and then vanishes away. Instead, you ought to say, "If the Lord wills, we shall live and also do this or that."' (James 4:13–15)

This way of thinking, of living for the eternal and not just for the here and now, is foreign to the average person.

Eat, drink and be merry

Jesus told the parable of a rich man whose land was very productive, so that he considered building larger barns to store all his grain and goods. Feeling secure in his temporal assets he spoke to himself, saying,

> '*"Soul you have many goods laid up for many years to come; take your ease, eat, drink and be merry." But God said to him, "You fool! This very night your soul is required of you; and now who will own what you have prepared?" So is the man who lays up treasure for himself, and is not rich toward God.'*   (Luke12:19–21)

The literal rendering of verse 20 reads in part, '*You fool! This very night they are demanding your soul from you...* ' Who are 'they'? In order to understand this we have to look into the unseen world. Fortunately, John gives us the answer in Revelation chapter 6.

▶ *Angel of war*

John witnessed the opening of a book that was sealed with seven seals. With the opening of each seal he saw the unfolding of certain events. For instance, as recorded in verses 3 and 4, he saw a red horse with a person sitting on it:

> '*...and to him who sat on it, it was granted to take peace from the earth, and that men should slay one another; and a great sword was given to him.'*

John looked into the heavenlies and witnessed something happening in that realm that was to have a major impact on the peoples of the earth. He saw an angel of war, a spiritual power in the unseen world that influenced people to kill one another. I wonder what we would see happening over a nation gripped with war if our spiritual eyes were opened to the unseen realm? There may be many natural reasons why people rise up to kill one another, but would we consider any spiritual reasons?

▶ *Angel of famine*

In verses 5 and 6 John witnesses a person riding on a black horse, with a pair of scales in his hand.

> '*And I heard as it were a voice in the centre of the four living creatures saying, "A quart of wheat for a denarius, and three*

quarts of barley for a denarius; and do not harm the oil and the wine."'

He saw an angel of famine, a spiritual power whose assignment was to cut off the food supply. Again, there may be many natural reasons why there would be lack of provision in a nation, but would we consider any spiritual reasons?

►   *Angels of death and Hades*

As he continued looking, John saw an ashen horse with a person riding on it called Death. Following closely behind Death was Hades.

> *'And authority was given to them over a fourth of the earth, to kill with sword and with famine and with pestilence and by the wild beasts of the earth.'*

Not only is there a state of death, but there is an angel of death. Not only is there a place called Hades (Sheol), but there is an angel of Hades. These angelic beings work closely together. The angel of death seeks to cut short a human life-span, while the angel of Hades takes the spirit of a person, at death, to the place of Hades. There may be many natural reasons as to how and when a person dies, but could there also be spiritual reasons?

Jesus made the statement that, *'If anyone keeps My word he shall never see death'* (John 8:51). Those to whom He spoke were all to die sooner or later, so what did He mean? He was stating that those who truly followed Him – and that would be evident because they obeyed His teaching, would never encounter the angel of death. Nor the angel of Hades, for that matter, because they were not going down, but up, when physical death came.

The Day of the Lord

Again and again in our present society we are cautioned to care for our environment, and rightly so. Some, however, go to extremes on environmental matters. Whatever our position may be, it is sobering for us all to realise that not only is our stay on planet earth very temporary, but the earth itself is temporary. It will not be here forever.

In 2 Peter 3:8–13 we are told of God's great desire to see people turn from their sin and come to know Him, but that there are limitations on God's willingness to wait forever for man to repent. A day of judgement is coming.

> *'But the day of the Lord will come like a thief, in which the heavens will pass away with a roar and the elements will be destroyed with intense heat, and the earth and its works will be burned up.'* (2 Peter 3:10)

The old order will be destroyed to make way for the new.

> *'But according to His promise we are looking for a new heavens and a new earth, in which righteousness dwells.'* (2 Peter 3:13)

To be a part of God's purposes now and in the future, we need to be people who choose righteousness. That is, to be rightly related to God and to walk before Him in a way that is pleasing to Him. This we cannot do in our own strength and our own resources. It is impossible for anyone to attain righteousness without God's help. To all who trust in Jesus Christ, God gives the gift of righteousness, the gift of eternal life, and the gift of the Holy Spirit.

> *'For by grace you have been saved through faith; and that not of yourselves, it is the gift of God; not as a result of works, that no one should boast.'* (Ephesians 2:8–9)

On the edge of eternity

When Shirley and I lived in Sydney, Australia, the work we were part of would send a team to conduct evangelistic meetings on the beaches of a holiday resort over the Christmas holidays. Two weeks before our team arrived, one of our staff would go ahead and finalise arrangements. One year when I was doing this, the widow in whose home I was staying asked me to visit the man next door and talk to him about Christ, because he was dying of cancer. She was unable to do this because he was very unfriendly, an agnostic who shunned his neighbours, all of whom were Christians.

Looking over the fence, I saw a very thin man lying on a bed on the back verandah of his home. His earthly sojourn was almost over, for not only was he very ill but he was eighty-nine years of age. I purposed to talk to him about his need of getting right with God before he moved into eternity. As I approached his bedside and introduced myself, he said, 'I am almost at the end of my journey.' Realising it would not be wise to talk immediately about spiritual issues, I tried to establish a friendship with him. As we talked he kept saying, 'But of course, I am not afraid to die.' The more he repeated these words the more I realised he was terrified of dying. Although his body was very frail, his mind was fully alert and we had a good time conversing. At the appropriate moment I steered the conversation towards the spiritual. 'When I came to your bedside today you said to me, "I'm almost at the end of my journey," but have you considered the fact that your journey is really only about to begin?'

With that introduction I talked about the brevity of life, the reality of eternity, the certainty of accountability, of God's great love for a fallen humanity, and the purpose of Jesus coming from heaven to earth to be mankind's Saviour. He listened intently and asked many questions. I urged him to call upon Jesus to save him from his sin and to receive the gift of eternal life, and thus be ready to meet God. Although interested, he was not yet at the place of surrendering his life to Christ. He was happy for me to pray with him, and I said I would visit him when I came back in ten days time.

On returning to the widow's home, the first thing I did was to look over the fence to see if the ailing man was on his verandah. He was not. Not only that, the windows were closed and the house appeared to be empty. Our hostess said that her neighbour had died a few days after I had spoken with him. My heart sank, but was lifted up when she told me he had died a believer. It was a wonderful story! Days after I had spoken with him, he had had a vision of the coming day of judgement. Perhaps he saw that day as the Apostle John records it in the book of Revelation.[3] Not only that, the Lord Jesus Himself had appeared to him, and as a result of these merciful encounters the man had trusted in Jesus and became a Christian. Not only were his sins forgiven, but he received the gift of eternal life. He was now ready to face eternity. He was now assured of going 'up' to heaven upon death and not 'down' to Hades.

The Christians in the street now had a new and friendly neighbour. With the fear of death gone, this new believer was eager to talk of what he had experienced. One morning he said to them, 'Did you hear the choirs of angels singing last night?' They had not. Around 2.30 a.m. that morning he had heard the glorious sounds of the angelic hosts praising Almighty God. He was seeing and hearing the realities of the eternal world of God's kingdom. Within hours he had passed on.

When I visited his eighty-six-year-old widow, she took me into the bedroom where he had been at the moment of death. She had been standing alongside him, when suddenly a momentary surge of strength caused him to sit up in amazement. 'Can you see the two men dressed in white at the end of the bed?' he exclaimed. 'Can you see the two men dressed in white?' She looked, but saw nothing. His body then slumped back. He had died. Thank God he was ready for that moment, because he had trusted in Jesus Christ. Two angels of the Lord had come to escort him to his heavenly home.[4] He had been saved on the edge of eternity.

The promise of a new body

Just as the physical body of Jesus was resurrected or raised up and He was clothed with a new body, so the promise of a new body awaits all believers in Christ.[5] Jesus is coming back again to this earth with a spectacular entrance. When He comes He is bringing with Him all the believers who are in heaven.

> 'For if we believe that Jesus died and rose again, even so God will bring with Him those who have fallen asleep in Jesus. For this we say to you by the word of the Lord, that we who are alive, and remain until the coming of the Lord, shall not precede those who have fallen asleep. For the Lord Himself will descend from heaven with a shout, with the voice of the archangel, and with the trumpet of God; and the dead in Christ shall rise first. Then we who are alive and remain shall be caught up together with them in the clouds to meet the Lord in the air, and thus we shall always be with the Lord.'   (1 Thessalonians 4:14–17)

There will be a raising up of the body that returned to dust or ashes.

> 'So also is the resurrection of the dead. It is sown a perishable body, it is raised an imperishable body; it is sown in dishonour, it is raised in glory; it is sown in weakness, it is raised in power; it is sown a natural body, it is raised a spiritual body. If there is a natural body, there is also a spiritual body.'
>   (1 Corinthians 15:42–44)

Our spirit will one day be clothed with a completely new body perfectly suited to our new environment.

Mr Eternity

On New Year's Eve, 1999, the city of Sydney, Australia, put on an impressive fireworks display to usher in the New Year. More than two billion people around the world were able to watch this spectacular event, thanks to television coverage. As a finale, the word 'ETERNITY' appeared in massive copperplate writing across the most visible inner-city landmark, the Sydney Harbour Bridge. Welcoming a new Millennium, 'ETERNITY' lit up the night sky and lingered for all to see. But why was such a word chosen?

To understand this, we need to know something of the mystery that remained unsolved for twenty-four years in Sydney. Over that time, and for a further thirteen years – thirty-seven in all – the word 'Eternity' had appeared in chalk on the city pavements in elegant copperplate handwriting, always with a flourish on the 'E' and underlined by the tail of the 'y'. Written when most people were sleeping, the author was never revealed until 1956, when the pastor of the Burton Street Baptist Church discovered Arthur Stace kneeling on the pavement writing the now famous word. Arthur, who worked as a cleaner in the church, was caught in the act, and acknowledged that he was the originator of the word 'Eternity'.

Arthur Stace was born in 1884 in Balmain, Sydney. His father and mother, his two brothers and two sisters, were all alcoholics. His sisters were brothel operators. Raised in abject poverty, he fended for himself from an early age and became a ward of the state at twelve years of age. He received no education and was in and out of prison from the age of fifteen. During World War I he served in France as a stretcher-bearer and drummer. Shell-shocked, partially blind in one eye and suffering the effects of mustard gas, he returned to Australia and was discharged. From then until the middle of the Great Depression he resorted to alcohol, gambling and crime, drinking methylated spirits and living on handouts as well as feeding out of garbage cans.

On August 6, 1930, he attended a men's meeting run by Archdeacon R.B.S. Hammond at St Barnabas' Anglican Church on Broadway, where he heard a gospel presentation and was given a rock cake and a cup of tea. After the meeting he went to Sydney University Park and, under a large fig tree, fell to his knees and amidst tears of repentance cried out, 'God, be merciful to me, a sinner!' At that moment, God heard Arthur's cry and he became of child of God. He later testified that, 'I went in to get a cup of tea and a rock cake, but I met the Rock of Ages!' He found he was then able to stop drinking and get regular employment.

In November, 1932, he heard the Rev. John Ridley preaching at the Burton Street Baptist Tabernacle in Darlinghurst, where he was attending. This preacher made some statements that deeply impacted this former alcoholic. 'Eternity! Eternity! I wish I could sound or shout that word to everyone in the streets of Sydney. Eternity! You have to meet it. Where will you spend eternity?'

Arthur Stace recalled that meeting. ' "Eternity" was ringing through my brain, and suddenly I began to cry and felt a powerful call from the Lord to write "Eternity". I had a piece of chalk in my pocket and outside the church I bent down right there and wrote it. The funny thing is, that before I wrote it I could hardly write my own name. I had no schooling and I couldn't have spelled "eternity" for a hundred quid. But it came out smoothly in a beautiful copperplate script. I couldn't understand it, and I still can't,' he said. That word changed his life. No doubt the lives of many others too, as the Spirit of God used it to alert beholders to the temporal nature of time and the prospect of entering eternity. Thus began thirty-seven years of sidewalk evangelism.

Arthur died on 30 July, 1967 at the age of eighty-three, but the word 'Eternity' lived on in the public mind. Today if you visit Sydney Square, you can see that one-word sermon gleaming in wrought aluminium letters nearly 21 centimetres high. Arthur Stace still speaks in time – about eternity! So when 'ETERNITY' lingered for the world to see at the ushering in of a new Millennium, Arthur Stace's message touched, in moments, more people than he could ever have imagined.

Seeing Him who is unseen

In the midst of a world so full of uncertainties, how incredible it is to enjoy walking daily with a loving Saviour. To experience not only peace with God, but the peace of God. To be ready to go into eternity whenever that moment comes.

Moses was a man who had much going for him as far as this world was concerned. Adopted by Pharaoh's daughter, he could have lived a life of ease and pleasure, but when he grew older he chose to identify with his people, the Jews. As the Scripture says:

'Choosing rather to endure ill-treatment with the people of God, than to enjoy the passing pleasures of sin; considering the reproach of Christ greater than the treasures of Egypt; for he was looking to

the reward. By faith he left Egypt, not fearing the wrath of the king; for he endured, as seeing Him who is unseen.'

(Hebrews 11:25–27)

Seeing Him who is unseen – that is where our focus needs to be. Paul wrote an encouraging word to the Corinthian church to remind them of their rightful focus:

'Therefore we do not lose heart, but though our outer man is decaying, yet our inner man is being renewed day by day. For momentary, light affliction is producing for us an eternal weight of glory far beyond all comparison, while we look not at the things which are seen, but at the things which are not seen; for the things which are seen are temporal, but the things which are not seen are eternal.'   (2 Corinthians 4:16–18)

Are you living only for the temporal, or are you also living for the eternal?

Chapter 3

Creatures of the Unseen World

God has an everlasting kingdom, and in this kingdom are created spirit-beings. Scripture talks about cherubim, seraphim, archangels and myriads of angels.[1] There are about three hundred references in the Bible to angels or 'messengers'. In our contemporary society, many people believe in and are fascinated by angels. Numerous movies have been made around the theme of an angel or angels. None can accurately portray what they are like, as the angels of secular movies bear little or no semblance to the angels of Scripture.

Archangels

Hebrew tradition says there are twelve archangels, and twelve is the number of Divine government, but the Scripture names only three that are generally accepted as archangels. The Greek prefix *arch* means 'principal', so an archangel is a principal or chief angel, of a higher order than an angel. Let us look at these three archangels for a moment.

▶ Lucifer

Lucifer means 'day star', 'light bearer' or 'son of the morning'. He was the archangel associated with the throne of God, who once led the worship of God among the angelic hosts. We read of him in the book of Isaiah.[2]

▶ Michael

Michael is specifically called an archangel and his name means, 'who is like God' or 'God-like'. There are five accounts of his activity in the Bible,[3] and he is always seen in connection with warfare with Satan and with the resurrection of the body. Many

Bible expositors believe he is the archangel who will come with the Lord Jesus at His Second Coming, associated with the resurrection of believers.[4]

▶ *Gabriel*

Gabriel means 'strength of God'. It seems that Gabriel is a prophetic angel, the messenger and interpreter of the prophetic word concerning Christ. Four passages of Scripture speak of him.[5]

Multitudes of angels

There are multitudes of angels living and active in the unseen world. How many, the Bible does not tell us. The Apostle John had a vision of the throne of God surrounded by many angels.[6] In fact, he said their number was myriads of myriads and thousands of thousands. A myriad is ten thousand. Ten thousand times ten thousand, equals one hundred million – and thousands of thousands. What an awesome sight and sound as he he heard them praising Jesus, the Lamb of God!

> *'And every created thing which is in heaven and on the earth and under the earth and on the sea, and all things in them I heard saying, "To Him who sits on the throne, and to the Lamb, be blessing and honour and glory and dominion forever and ever."'*
>
> (Revelation 5:13)

Note the three dimensions: heaven, earth and under the earth, to which John adds, the sea. The day is fast approaching when all creatures in every realm of God's creation will acknowledge who Jesus Christ is. Because of the Son of God's willingness to lay aside His heavenly splendour and take on Himself the form of a man and suffer death on a cross, God the Father has highly exalted Him. Jesus has been given the name which is above every other name:

> *'that at the name of Jesus every knee should bow, of those who are in heaven, and on earth, and under the earth, and that every tongue should confess that Jesus Christ is Lord, to the glory of God the Father.'*
>
> (Philippians 2:10–11)

The nature of angels

Angels are created beings. As such, they are finite and dependent beings and were probably created early in creation, as we read of them singing and shouting for joy when the earth was being created.[7] The Bible also tells us that angels are:

- Spiritual beings. We are limited by the restrictions of a physical body, whereas angels are pure spirit and not confined to natural limitations.[8]
- Immortal. Because they do not have a flesh and blood body, they are not subject to physical death.[9]
- A people, but not a race. That is, they neither marry or procreate as we humans do.[10]
- Innumerable. Multitudes of angels form the angelic creation.[11]
- A higher order of creation than man.[12]
- A free-will creation. Power of choice has been given to them, as it has to the human race.[13]
- Personalities. No mere impersonal influences, they have intelligence and will.[14]
- Invisible. As they live in the unseen world, we do not see them unless our spiritual eyes are opened.[15]

Angelic visitations

The Bible is full of encounters between angels and humans. Daniel had been fasting and praying for three full weeks when an angelic messenger appeared to him on the bank of the Tigris River. So glorious was his countenance, and so overwhelming his presence, that Daniel lost all strength and fell to the ground trembling.[16]

David came under God's judgement because of his numbering of Israel and relying on his own resources rather than God's. He saw an angel of the Lord standing between earth and heaven, with a drawn sword stretched out over Jerusalem to destroy it. After David had repented and offered sacrifices to the Lord, he witnessed the angel put his sword back into its sheath and Jerusalem was spared. So terrified was David that he was afraid to enquire further of the Lord at that time.[17]

Peter was in prison awaiting death at the order of king Herod, but the believers fervently prayed to God for his release. He was bound in chains and sixteen soldiers had been assigned to guard him. The night before his execution, an angel of the Lord suddenly appeared and a light shone in the cell. The angel commanded him to get up, and as he did so the chains fell off his hands. Following the angel, he passed the various guards up to the iron gate of the prison, which opened by itself. Peter found himself free on the streets of the city and the angel disappeared.[18]

Angels, as we have said, are messengers and carry out the will of God.

> *'Are they not all ministering spirits, sent out to render service for the sake of those who will inherit salvation?'*   (Hebrews 1:14)

Not all angelic encounters are as dramatic as those just mentioned, and it is possible to have dealings with an angel without realising it at the time. The book of Hebrews exhorts believers not to neglect hospitality to strangers, for in so doing people have sometimes unknowingly entertained angels.[19]

Some Christians have been supernaturally protected and rescued in times of calamity and probable death, by angels appearing not as Daniel, David or Peter saw them, but in the normal clothes of the culture in which these Christians were serving as missionaries. Only after they were rescued did it become fully apparent that their survival had been through angelic intervention.

Elect and fallen angels

There are two kinds of angels: the elect or chosen, and the fallen.[20] Although in the beginning all angels were created perfectly and without sin, they were created with free will. A time of testing came, and Lucifer decided he no longer wanted to be in subservience to God and rebelled against his Maker. It seems that one third of the angelic host joined him in this rebellion, which divided the angels into one of two camps. Those who remained faithful to God are called elect or chosen angels, while those who rebelled against Him are known as fallen angels.[21]

What a tragic decision Lucifer made! From what heights he fell. The Bible tells us that he was perfect in the day he was created, a being of great beauty and endowed with great wisdom. A master musician, it appears he was leader of heaven's worship. But he was lifted up with pride in his God-given wisdom, anointing and beauty, and in exalting himself came under condemnation:

'How you have fallen from heaven,
O star of the morning, son of dawn!
You have been cut down to the earth,
You who have weakened the nations!
But you said in your heart,
"I will ascend to heaven;
I will raise my throne above the stars of God,
And I will sit on the mount of assembly
In the recesses of the north.
I will ascend above the heights of the clouds;
I will make myself like the Most High."'   (Isaiah 14:12–14)

Such arrogance! This self-exalting and self-deifying behavior brought a swift reaction from the throne of God. A mere creature was no match for his Creator.

What was God's response?

'Nevertheless, you will be thrust down to Sheol, to the recesses of the pit.'   (Isaiah 14:15)

A study of the phrase 'stars of God' shows that it refers to the angels of God.[22] When Lucifer exalted himself, he was cast out from the immediate presence of God in the third heaven, into the heavenlies, the sphere of the second and first heavens, and gained access to and influence over planet earth.

▶ *As quick as lightning*

One night around midnight, while visiting Texas, I was about to have a shower. I could hear a storm rolling closer and decided to open the bathroom window and watch the lightning as I was showering. Within moments a bolt of lightning struck nearby. Knowing that water is a conductor of electricity, I quickly turned it off and waited till the storm had passed. The lightning strike was sudden and, because of its closeness, scary.

Jesus said, *'I was watching Satan fall from heaven like lightning'* (Luke 10:18). This exalted creature, Lucifer, was cast out of heaven as quickly as lightning strikes, and the eternal Son of God witnessed it happening. Lucifer also had a name change to Satan, which means 'adversary, hater, opponent' or 'enemy'. He seeks to oppose God and everything God's kingdom stands for. His opposition is particularly vented against true Christians; those who love and serve Jesus Christ.

The nature of Satan

Satan's names aptly describe his nature and his function. Here are
30 of them:

- Satan (Job 1:6–12)
- Devil (John 8:44)
- Serpent (Revelation 12:9)
- Dragon (Revelation 12:3–17)
- Beelzebub (Matthew 12:24)
- God of the Age (2 Corinthians 4:4)
- Ruler of this World (John 14:30)
- Prince of the Power of the Air (Ephesians 2:2)
- Lucifer (Isaiah 14:12)
- Belial (2 Corinthians 6:15)
- The Enemy (Matthew 13:39)
- The Tempter (1 Thessalonians 3:5)
- The Wicked One (1 John 5:18–19)
- Angel of Light (2 Corinthians 11:13–15)
- Accuser of the Brethren (Revelation 12:10)
- Antichrist (1 John 4:1–4)
- Adversary (1 Peter 5:8)
- Murderer (John 8:44)
- Liar (John 8:44)
- Sinner (1 John 3:8)
- Abaddon or Apollyon (Revelation 9:11)
- Roaring Lion (1 Peter 5:8)
- Wolf (John 10:12)
- Thief (John 10:10)
- Wicked One (Matthew 13:19)
- Fowler (Psalm 91:3)
- King of a Kingdom (Colossians 1:13)
- Angel of the Bottomless Pit (Revelation 9:11)
- Leviathan (Isaiah 27:1)
- Son of Destruction (2 Thessalonians 2:1–12)

Satan's activity

Satan is not omnipresent as God is, but through his followers he seeks to influence people all over the world at the same time.

▶ *He seeks to oppose*[23]

As his name indicates, he is in the opposing business. Sometimes I have heard young Christians say it was easier being a non-Christian. By this they meant that before becoming a Christian they did not experience the battles they were now going through. Before coming to Christ they walked according to the course of this world, according to the prince of the power of the air, influenced by a spirit of disobedience that was working in them.[24] They were 'going with the flow', living a life of independence from God and fulfilling the desires of their sinful natures.[25] This is the popular way that most people choose, but is the pathway that leads to destruction.[26] And when the Scripture talks of destruction, as in Ephesians 2:1–2, it is not talking of annihilation, but of eternal loss. Now, as the young Christians endeavoured to live a righteous life, they were discovering pressures, both within and without, which made life a struggle at times.

▶ *He seeks to tempt*[27]

Jesus was baptised in water, giving all who believe in Him an example to follow. As He came up out of the water He was baptised in the Holy Spirit, again leaving us an example to follow. He was then led by the Holy Spirit into the wilderness, where He was tempted by Satan for forty days. Although greatly tempted, Jesus did not succumb to these temptations. We also are tempted, and with the help of the Lord we can overcome, as He overcame.[28] Remember, temptation is not sin, and does not have to be confessed as sin. It is only as we yield to the temptation that it leads us into sin and requires confession and the cleansing of the blood of Jesus.[29]

▶ *He seeks to defile*[30]

All sin leads to the defiling of our lives, and creates a barrier between ourselves and God until it is removed through repentance, confession and cleansing. Continuing in sin leads to the possibility of demonic intrusion in our lives, and all evil spirits defile.

► *He seeks to drive* [31]

Restlessness is usually a sign of a person needing deliverance from evil spirits. Many people are driven in their lives and cannot slow down and stop. For many years, before and after becoming a Christian, I was very restless. Holidays were often difficult, because when I had time to rest I was unable to relax. Today, having experienced deliverance in my life, I simply love holidays and days of rest. There is a rest we can enter into in Christ.

► *He seeks to condemn* [32]

'Devil' (*diabolos*) means accuser, slanderer, whisperer. He constantly seeks to condemn God's people, and does a very good job of it. As one constantly ministering to believers, I am only too well aware of how many struggle with feelings of condemnation and unworthiness. For years, even as an evangelist, I lived under a burden of condemnation. The harder I tried to live a holy life, the more unholy I felt. It seemed that I was confessing 'sins' hundreds of times a day to the Lord. No sooner had I lifted one prayer of confession to God, than I was ready to ask for forgiveness for something else. So many of the wrong thoughts in my mind I confessed as sin, not realising that they were often placed there by evil spirits who immediately condemned me for having them in my mind.

► *He seeks to deceive* [32]

To deceive means 'to cause to believe what is not true; to mislead; to lead astray by deliberate misrepresentation or lies'. For years I was deceived by the enemy into constantly confessing sin. What I should have done was to resist and rebuke the enemy who was the source of so many of my thoughts. Today I enjoy a mind at rest, free from the years of turmoil. When I need to confess sin I do so, but no longer is Satan able to play mind games with me as in the past.

► *He seeks to bind* [34]

Satan will bind us in any way he can. We may be bound and know it, or we may be bound and not know it. In a later chapter we will look at how we can tell if an evil spirit is binding our life or not.

► *He seeks to torment* [35]

One can be tormented in body, or tormented in mind. I experienced torment in both areas for many years, particularly in the mind. As a young Christian I prayed some foolish prayers, asking the Lord to let me have physical pain rather than mental anguish. When it was morning I often wished it was evening, and when it was evening I often wished it was morning. Then one day I realised this indicated a curse at work in my life.[36]

▶ *He seeks to steal*[37]

As a thief, Satan is out to rob us of all he can, even the joy of being alive. So many find life a burden, and are constantly wishing they had not been born or that they could die. Life is not meant to be a burden, but a wonderful adventure! I once had a saying on my wall: 'Life is either a daring adventure or nothing at all.' Because of the freedom Jesus has brought into my life, I can say that life is indeed a wonderful adventure and no longer a burden.

▶ *He seeks to destroy*[38]

One of Satan's names in Greek is Apollyon, which means 'destroyer'. All around us we see destruction: people destroying themselves, destroying others. Whether in movies or video arcades, it is kill, kill kill; punch, punch, punch; kick, kick, kick; shoot, shoot, shoot. No wonder these fantasies are played out in real life. And behind it all, in the unseen world, spiritual powers are at work instigating and encouraging such activities.

▶ *He seeks to damn*[39]

Knowing that his own fate has been determined, Satan nevertheless continues to resist every purpose of God, and do all he can to prevent people from being reconciled to God.

Satan's judgement assured

Satan is limited in location: he is not omnipresent as God is, and he is also limited in knowledge and power. What he thought would be his greatest triumph – the crucifying of Jesus Christ – turned out to be the instrument of his eternal defeat.[40]

God's judgement of Satan has been progressive ever since he rebelled against God in the third heaven. He was cast out of Paradise, out of the immediate presence of God, into the heavenlies; he was judged in Eden's earthly Paradise when he caused Adam and Eve to sin; and he was soundly defeated by Jesus through His death on the cross and resurrection from the dead.[41] As Christians proclaim the good news of Jesus and in His name cast out demons holding people in captivity, a further judgement is carried out on the satanic hosts. Then, at the close of the age, Satan and his angels are to be cast out of the heavenlies into the earth during the time of the tribulation; and from there into the bottomless pit in the heart of the earth for a period of one thousand years.[42] On being loosed from the bottomless pit for a season, Satan and his angels will be cast into the lake of fire to suffer eternal judgement.[43]

Chapter 4

The Battle for Man's Soul

As we have glimpsed the reality of the unseen world and been reminded of the temporary nature of our earthly sojourn, it is obvious that man is the centre of a struggle between two opposing powers. On the one hand, God, who created the human race for His own purposes, on the other hand, Satan, who covets for himself the allegiance and worship of mankind.

God is motivated by love, and a desire for people to be set free; Satan is motivated by hatred, and a desire that people be brought into bondage. The outcome of this battle for man's soul has eternal consequences, as it deals with the issues of eternal life and eternal judgement. While man is at the centre of this struggle, he is by and large oblivious to the drama being played out in the unseen world, because he is spiritually blind and spiritually dead.[1] Focused almost entirely on the interests and pursuits of time, he lives in a world full of conflict, selfishness, bitterness, injustice, suffering, poverty, sorrow, despair, sickness and death.[2] The list of negatives could go on. But why?

Back to the beginning

Man is a created being, made in the image and likeness of his Creator.[3] At the dawn of human history, Adam and Eve were placed in a beautiful garden, where they enjoyed daily communion with God. Because they walked in a relationship of obedience to God, they experienced a life full of harmony and happiness. Like Lucifer and the angelic creation, they had free will.[4] All the trees of the garden and their fruits were before them to partake of, but there was one tree – the tree of life – whose fruit they were forbidden to eat. If they chose to disobey God's directive, the consequence would be death.[5]

Into the garden came Satan. He approached Eve and put doubts into her mind about what God had said. Having sown doubt he went on to sow denial, and, deceived, she tasted the forbidden fruit. Eve then gave some of the fruit to Adam and he ate it as well. As a consequence they both died.[6] Neither fell to the ground and physically expired, but they experienced spiritual death, that is, they became separated from God. Corrupting powers immediately began to work in their lives, bringing a deterioration in their bodies. Adam died physically at the age of 930 years. Had he not sinned, he would not have died.[7]

Because Satan had instigated man's fall, God put a curse on him. The Lord also prophesied to Satan of a day to come when, through the seed of the woman, a child would come forth who would rise up and crush Satan's head. God also said that Satan would crush the heel of the woman's seed.[8]

In spite of their rebellion, the Lord immediately reached out to Adam and Eve, desiring a restoration of relationship with them and through the slaying of animals provided them with clothing. However, they were driven out of the earthly Paradise; cherubim were stationed at the east of the garden and a flaming sword protected the tree of life. Life would never be the same again.[9]

Despite a restored relationship with God, Adam and Eve continued to reap the consequences of their initial rebellion. Not only did they now have a sinful nature to contend with, their children also had sinful natures. Cain, their first-born son, chose not to walk in God's ways, whereas Abel, their second-born, chose to do so. One day in a fit of anger, Cain rose up and killed his brother, and the earth suffered its first murder.[10] Generation after generation of men tilled the soil that was now cursed and – as God had foretold – women brought forth children in the midst of pain. Every person had to make a choice whether to follow God's way or to walk in his or her own way. Some chose God's way, some their own way, and it is the same today.[11]

God's foreordained plan

The fall of Adam and Eve did not take God by surprise. In eternity past, even before the creation of the world, God in His foreknowledge knew what would unfold, and formulated a rescue plan or plan of salvation. This would provide, for all who wanted to walk with God, a way of being brought back into a right relationship with Him.[12] This plan was to unfold in two distinct stages and be progressive in its outworking. The stages involved God making two major covenants with man, which we know as the Old Covenant and the New Covenant.[13] A covenant was an agreement entered into by two parties and secured through the blood of a sacrificial offering. The very word covenant in Hebrew speaks of 'a cutting', and according to Strong's Exhaustive Concordance of the Bible, means 'a compact made by passing between pieces of flesh.' A 'compact' is simply an agreement or a covenant.

God's desire has always been that people would choose to love and serve Him, not as programmed robots with all the correct responses but no heart relationship, but with willing hearts, seeking and serving Him because they wanted to. People are free to choose to be in a covenant relationship with God.[14]

In those early years of human history God communicated His ways to those who wished to follow Him. Even with Cain and Abel, the Lord made known what kind of offering was acceptable and what was not. Cain brought an offering of the fruit of the ground that God had cursed, whereas Abel brought an offering of the firstfruits of his flock and of their fat portions that required the shedding of blood. The very reason Cain killed Abel was that God received Abel's offering but rejected his own – the fruit of the soil which God had cursed. Abel did it God's way, Cain did it his way. Cain became jealous and angry and murdered his brother over the issue of acceptable worship.[15]

The call of Abram

God looked for a man who would walk in His ways and be willing to play a crucial part in the unfolding of His plan for the redemption of mankind. In the land of Chaldea, known today as Iraq, lived a man called Abram. God called Abram to leave his homeland and set out for a destination that God would later show him.[16] Following in simple obedience, Abram was led to the land of Canaan, which God then promised to give to him and to his descendants. God also promised that Abram's descendants would be great in number.[17] Although Abram and his wife Sarai had no children, Abram continued to believe God's promise that his descendants would be many. Because of his faith, the Lord changed Abram's name to Abraham, meaning 'father of a multitude'. Sarai's name was changed to Sarah, or 'princess'. The Lord then entered into a covenant with Abraham, which required the slaying of sacrificial animals.[18]

By the time Abraham was eighty-five years of age and Sarah had still not conceived, he decided, on her advice, to take his Egyptian maid Hagar as a wife and father a child in this way. This was the custom of the day when a wife was barren and it was not considered immoral.[19] Hagar conceived and bore a son to Abraham, whom he called Ishmael. But Ishmael's arrival brought strife into the family. God's promise to Abraham was not to be fulfilled through him, but through another son yet to be born.[20] When Abraham was one hundred years of age and Sarah ninety years, the son of God's promise was born through Sarah, and they named him Isaac.[21]

The rise of a nation

With the birth of Isaac, God's purposes continued to unfold. Abraham walked in the ways of God and taught his son Isaac to do likewise. Isaac married, and his wife Rebekah had twins, Esau and Jacob. Esau was the first-born, yet he despised his birthright and became a godless and immoral man. Jacob, on the other hand, valued a relationship with God.[22] As mankind multiplied on the earth, individuals continued to make decisions either to trust in God and walk in His ways, or to follow the dictates of their own sinful hearts and walk in rebellion.

One night, Jacob had a life-changing encounter with God that resulted in his name being changed to Israel. His twelve sons married and formed twelve tribes, who together formed the nation of Israel. Thereafter, God called Himself the God of Abraham, Isaac and Jacob, or the God of Israel.[23] It was through the descendants of Israel that a nation would arise with whom God would enter into a covenant relationship. God would teach this people His ways, and as the nation followed Him it would be a living witness to the surrounding nations of the one true God and His ways.[24]

Giving of the Law

Volumes have been written about the history of the nation of Israel, and all I can do is to touch one or two highlights. After the people of Israel had experienced a supernatural deliverance from slavery in Egypt under the leadership of Moses, God called Moses to the top of Mount Sinai and gave him the Ten Commandments. These commandments were to be the foundation of Israel's spiritual and moral life.[25]

The first commandment declared,

'You shall have no other gods before Me.'   (Exodus 20:3)

All around Israel were nations worshipping many gods, fashioning them out of wood, stone and other materials. As the people bowed down, giving allegiance and offerings to these gods, they were in reality bowing down to Satan.[26] How great was the spiritual darkness filling the hearts and minds of these people! How far mankind had fallen from the original purpose and plan of God.[27]

The Tabernacle of Moses

Not only did God give to Moses the Ten Commandments, but many other laws governing the way the people were to live in order to remain in a right relationship with Himself and to know His presence in their midst.[28] The Lord also told Moses to build a Tabernacle or tent, and gave him clear instructions about the materials it was to be constructed of and the furnishings to be placed in it. Again and again, Moses was commanded to make this Tabernacle according to the pattern shown him on the mountain.[29] The reason for this insistence is clearly seen in the book of Hebrews in the New Testament. There is a heavenly tabernacle, and the earthly tabernacle was to be a copy or shadow of this true tabernacle in the heavens. God was teaching His people the way of approach to His presence.[30]

The Tabernacle was divided into three parts. First, the Outer Court, surrounded by a linen fence and lit by daylight. Entering the Outer Court, one came upon a bronze altar where sacrificial animals were slaughtered and their blood flowed down. Beyond that was a bronze laver, where the priests would wash themselves in water before going about their sacred duties in the Tabernacle.[31] A veil divided the Tabernacle into two parts: the larger area was called the Holy Place and the smaller the Most Holy Place.[32] Entering the veil into the Holy Place one would see the table of shewbread, with its twelve loaves of unleavened bread, and wine to be poured out in drink offerings. On the other side was a seven-branched candlestick, which gave light to this enclosed sanctuary. Before the second veil, screening the Most Holy Place, was the altar of incense.

In the Most Holy Place itself was the Ark of the Covenant, which contained the Ten Commandments, a pot of manna and Aaron's rod that had budded. On the mercy-seat, which was the lid of the

Ark of the Covenant, two cherubim bowed toward each other, their extended wings covering the mercy-seat. Into this inner sanctuary only the High Priest could enter, and that only on one day of the year, the Day of Atonement. Anyone else would instantly die.[33] It was here that God spoke audibly to the High Priest. God's presence could be seen over the tabernacle in a pillar of cloud by day and a pillar of fire by night, throughout the wilderness wanderings of the children of Israel.[34]

Sacrificial offerings

Death was the result of Adam's sin: spiritual death that led to physical death, physical death that led to eternal death, unless a way of dealing with the devastating power of sin could be found. Yet from the very beginning of God's dealings with fallen man, God Himself instituted a way of dealing with the sins of individuals. It was the way of substitutionary sacrifices. Instead of the sinner dying for his sin, an animal would take the sinner's place. The animal would die so that the sinner could live. Certain kinds of animals were specified as substitutes, and certain criteria were required of the animals being sacrificed – for instance, they had to be in top condition and not sick or blemished.[35]

When an Israelite sinned, he brought his offering to the priest. If the offering proved acceptable, the sinner laid his hands on the head of the sacrificial offering and a transference of his sin took place. The priest did not look at the sinner, but at the sacrifice. If the sacrifice was acceptable, the sinner was acceptable. The animal then died, because the penalty for sin is death. The sinner was forgiven and his relationship with God was restored, but only because a substitutionary sacrifice had been offered.

Apart from the individual sacrifices – and they were multitudinous – there were daily morning and evening sacrifices on behalf of the nation, when the priests offered up a male lamb as a burnt offering, along with a grain offering and a libation or drink offering. In addition, every sabbath two male lambs were offered as a burnt offering with accompanying grain and libation offerings. At the beginning of each month two bulls, one ram, and seven male lambs were offered as burnt offerings along with the grain and libation offerings for each animal.

Of the five kinds of offerings the Lord commanded, four involved the shedding of blood; three were freewill offerings and two were obligatory.[36]

The feasts of Israel

God also required of Israel to keep three feasts each year: the Feast of Passover in the first month, the Feast of Pentecost in the third month, and the Feast of Tabernacles in the seventh month. On these feast days numerous bulls, lambs, rams and goats were offered to the Lord, as He Himself had specified. All the feasts and all the sacrifices pointed to their fulfilment in Jesus, God's Son. They were the types and shadows: Jesus was the substance and reality. Over the centuries, as the people of Israel walked with God, millions upon millions of sacrificial animals died to cover the sins of the people, thus enabling God's presence to continue with His people and God's favour to be poured out among them.

High times and low times

Because of the special relationship Israel enjoyed with God, one would think that the people would always walk in ways pleasing to Him. This was not so, however, and the history of Israel was beset with many a low time, when the people were backslidden, rising to many a high time when Israel kept its covenant with the Lord.[37] When Israel walked with God it experienced much blessing and victory over its enemies, but when the people turned their back on God, the nation experienced numerous cursings and came into captivity to its enemies. God raised up prophets to speak His word to the people, and godly leaders and kings to govern them.[38]

Ever at work behind the scenes, Satan and his hosts did all they could to influence the leaders and the people to turn away from God and follow the ways of the heathen nations on their borders. During the low times, people turned to worshipping idols and even offered their children to the god Molech.[39] In the high times, as in much of king Solomon's reign, the fame of Israel and its God were known afar.[40]

A very low period in Israel's history was its captivity in Babylon, when most who survived the invading Assyrian armies were transported far from their homeland. The issue was always the people's willingness, or lack of willingness, to walk in the ways of the living God. As it was then, so it is now.[41] On one occasion, Joshua, one of Israel's great leaders, challenged the people:

> '*Now, therefore, fear the Lord and serve Him in sincerity and truth; and put away the gods which your fathers served beyond the River and in Egypt, and serve the Lord. And if it is disagreeable in your*

*sight to serve the Lord, choose for yourselves today whom you will
serve: but as for me and my house, we will serve the Lord.'*

(Joshua 24:14–15)

Moses had said to the fledgling nation,

*'I call heaven and earth to witness against you today, that I have
set before you life and death, the blessing and the curse. So choose
life in order that you may live, you and your descendants, by loving
the Lord your God, by obeying His voice, and by holding fast to
Him.'*   (Deuteronomy 30:19, 20)

Behind the scenes

As the drama of human life is outworked on the stage of time, we
see very clearly what was happening behind the scenes, in the
unseen world, in the life of a man who loved God, called Job. We
are told that Job was blameless, upright, feared God and turned
away from evil. He was wealthy, rich in sons and daughters, and in
livestock and servants. Job continually stood before the Lord on
behalf of his children.[42]

Scripture tells us that one day Satan came before the throne of
God, having been roaming around the earth. Here we are made
aware of what was happening behind the scenes. Satan had
noticed the prosperity of Job, and taunted God that Job only
served Him because God had blessed him, and that if Job was to
suffer loss he would curse God to His face. Having obtained divine
permission, Satan went out to prove his case, but was forbidden to
touch Job himself. God in His wisdom allowed Job to go through a
time of extreme testing.[43] In quick succession, four tragedies
struck. The Sabeans attacked and killed Job's servants tending the
oxen, and took Job's oxen and donkeys. Fire fell from the sky and
burned up the sheep and the servants with them. The Chaldeans
raided the camels, capturing them and killing their keepers, and,
worst of all, a great wind struck the house where Job's sons and
daughters were, causing it to collapse and killing them all.[44]

Today, some would call such tragedies 'acts of God', but we
know they were, in fact, 'acts of Satan'. Such was Job's trust in
God, however, that on hearing news of these calamities he tore his
robe, shaved his head, fell to the ground and worshipped his
Lord.[45] Again Satan came before God's throne and again we see
behind the scenes. God boasted of His servant Job, who still held
fast his integrity even in the midst of great loss. Satan again

taunted God, saying that if Job's body was touched he would curse God. The Lord gave Satan permission to touch Job, but not to take his life.[46] Satan went out from the presence of the Lord and smote Job with terrible boils, from the soles of his feet to the crown of his head. As Job scraped himself with a fragment of broken pottery, his wife provoked him to curse God and die. Even under such pressure Job did not sin with his mouth. Truly, there was a battle for Job's soul, as Satan tried to turn Job against His God.[47] Satan failed.

When God's purposes had been fulfilled in allowing such a testing, God restored the fortunes of Job two-fold. His livestock numbers doubled and he had seven more sons and three more daughters. To add to this blessing, his daughters were the fairest in the land! [48]

In the fullness of time

Every passing year brought one special day just a little closer. The prophet Isaiah had prophesied of a day of unparalleled significance:

> '*Therefore the Lord Himself will give you a sign: Behold a virgin will be with child and bear a son, and she will call His name Immanuel.'*   (Isaiah 7:14)

And again:

> '*For a child will be born to us, a son will be given to us; and the government will rest on His shoulders; and His name will be called Wonderful Counsellor, Mighty God, Eternal Father, Prince of Peace.'*   (Isaiah 9:6)

The word that God spoke to Satan, of a day when his head would be crushed, would come to pass at the appointed time. It was to happen in a way that even Satan did not anticipate.

Chapter 5

The Coming of Jesus

Zacharias was startled, for there to the right of the altar of incense, stood Gabriel himself. God's angels are His messengers, and Gabriel had a very special announcement to make to this priest of the Lord, who was faithfully fulfilling his priestly duties. Zacharias's prayers over many years had been heard, and his wife Elizabeth was to have a son, whom he was to call John.[1] The angel spoke of the joy this boy would bring and of the uniqueness of God's call on his life. John would be filled with the Holy Spirit while yet in his mother's womb, and be used of God to turn many of the Israelites back to a right relationship with God. Indeed, John would be the forerunner of the promised seed of the woman, the Messiah or Anointed One.[2]

After this announcement Elizabeth conceived, but kept herself in seclusion for five months. During her sixth month of pregnancy, Gabriel came again with a message from God, not to Elizabeth, but to a young woman called Mary, who was engaged to Joseph, a carpenter in Nazareth.[3] Gabriel told her that she was favoured of God and would conceive and bear a son, whom she was to call Jesus. This Jesus would be great and would be called the Son of the Most High and would have a kingdom that would have no end.[4] Mary responded that she was a virgin, and therefore wondered how this would come about. Gabriel said,

'The Holy Spirit will come upon you, and the power of the Most High will overshadow you; and for that reason the holy offspring shall be called the Son of God. And behold, even your relative Elizabeth has also conceived a son in her old age; and she who was called barren is now in her sixth month. For nothing will be impossible with God.' (Luke 1:35–37)

Filled with excitement, Mary hastened to the home of Zacharias and greeted Elizabeth. The moment she did so, Elizabeth felt her baby leap in her womb for joy, as both she and the baby were filled with the Holy Spirit. Mary then stayed with her for nearly three months.[5]

Joseph's dilemma

The time came when Mary approached her fiancé with the news that she was pregnant. Joseph was shocked, because he thought that Mary had been unfaithful and had had sexual relations with another man. Being kindly, he did not want to disgrace her and pondered what to do. Before he could take any action Joseph was visited by an angel, who said to him in a dream:

'Joseph, son of David, do not be afraid to take Mary as your wife; for that which has been conceived in her is of the Holy Spirit. And she will bear a Son; and you shall call his name Jesus, for it is He who will save His people from their sins.'

(Matthew 1:20–21)

Joseph awoke from the dream, assured that Mary was indeed a righteous woman, and had been specially favoured by God to fulfil Isaiah's prophecy, that a virgin would conceive and bear a son who would be called Immanuel – God with us. He then married Mary, but had no sexual relations with her until after the baby was born.[6]

The promised One

Joseph and Mary journeyed from Nazareth to Bethlehem to register for the census decreed by the emperor Caesar Augustus. While there, Mary gave birth to Jesus. The entrance into human history of the God of creation in the form of a man took place in the obscurity of a stable where animals were sheltered, because all the inns of Bethlehem were full.[7] In the nearby fields, shepherds were caring for their sheep, when an angel of the Lord suddenly appeared to them and declared:

'Do not be afraid; for behold, I bring you good news of a great joy which shall be for all the people; for today in the city of David there has been born for you a Saviour, who is Christ the Lord.'

(Luke 2:10–11)

The angel told the shepherds where the baby was to be found, and multitudes of angels appeared with them, praising God. The shepherds hastened to the stable, where they saw for themselves this unique child and shared with Mary and Joseph what the angel had said. Returning to their flocks, they glorified and praised God for all they had seen and heard.[8]

Satanic destruction

After Jesus was born, some magi from the east arrived in Jerusalem and sought out Herod the king, to ask where the King of the Jews had been born. These wise men said that they had seen His star and had come to worship Him.[9] Herod was greatly troubled by their words and gathered all the chief priests and scribes to enquire of them where the Messiah was to be born. On discovering that the prophet Isaiah had said it would be Bethlehem in Judah, Herod told the magi and asked them, on finding the child, to inform him so that he too could come and worship Him.[10]

Following the star, the magi came to where Jesus was and fell down and worshipped Him. Warned by God in a dream not to return to Herod, they went home another way. Joseph also had a dream from the Lord, commanding him to take Mary and Jesus to Egypt, because Herod intended to seek the child and kill Him.[11] When Herod realised that he had been tricked by the magi, he was filled with anger and sent soldiers to Bethlehem and its surrounding areas to put to death all boys two years old and under.[12] Although this genocide was carried out by human hands, we know from the Scriptures that there are unseen satanic powers seeking to influence people to kill one another. Surely this was an action of Satan himself, through human agents, to destroy the One whom he was told would crush his head.[13]

The childhood of Jesus

The Scriptures tell us little about the childhood of Jesus, but we know He was raised according to Jewish customs of the day. Luke simply states,

> *'And the Child continued to grow and become strong, increasing in wisdom; and the grace of God was upon Him.'*   (Luke 2:40)

He then tells of the incident when Jesus was twelve years old and in Jerusalem with His family for the Feast of Passover. Joseph and Mary went a day's journey home, thinking Jesus was with friends or relatives. Realising that He was not with the caravan, they returned to Jerusalem to find Him in the Temple, sitting among the teachers, listening to them and asking questions.

When Mary expressed the anxiety that she and His stepfather had felt, Jesus replied that He had to be about the things of His Father, but Mary and Joseph did not understand this. Jesus returned home and continued in submission to them, increasing in wisdom and stature and in favour with God and men.[14]

The forerunner

Not only did Jesus grow and mature, so did His cousin John. This son of Zacharias became strong in spirit and lived in the desert until the day of his public appearance to Israel. At the appointed time, John began his public ministry, preaching a baptism of repentance for the forgiveness of sins.[15] He was a fearless preacher, calling one and all to change their minds about the way they had been living, and turn to God and live for Him. To certain people who came to be baptised in water he would say, *'You brood of vipers, who has warned you to flee from the wrath to come?'* (Luke 3:7). He knew that eternal judgement would befall all those who did not repent and walk in the ways of righteousness. When people wondered whether he was the Christ or not, John said plainly,

> *'As for me, I baptise you with water; but One is coming who is mightier than I, and I am not fit to untie the thong of His sandals; He will baptise you with the Holy Spirit and fire. And His winnowing fork is in His hand to thoroughly clear His threshing floor, and to gather the wheat into His barn; but He will burn up the chaff with unquenchable fire.'* (Luke 3:16–17)

One day Jesus appeared and asked John to baptise Him in water, but John responded that he needed Jesus to baptise him! However, Jesus persuaded John – not because He had any sin to confess or turn from, but as an act of righteousness, setting an example for all who were to believe in Him to also be immersed in water. Baptism symbolises death to the old life of sin and self, and a rising in newness of life to live for God and in God's strength.[16]

When Jesus was baptised in water, the Spirit of God descended on Him in the form of a dove, and He was filled with the Holy Spirit. At that moment, His Father spoke from heaven, acknowledging to all that Jesus was His beloved Son in whom He was well-pleased.[17] The ministry of John as the forerunner to Jesus was almost over. He would soon find himself in prison as a consequence of reproving king Herod for taking Herodias, his brother's wife. Eventually Herod would have him beheaded.[18]

The temptation of Jesus

After being baptised in water and in the Holy Spirit, Jesus was led by the Holy Spirit into the wilderness, to be tempted by the devil.[19] During the forty days of His fasting in the wilderness, Satan came to tempt Him, seeking to make Him fall. In the beginning, Satan had been successful in causing Adam and Eve to sin, and he now sought to seduce the second Adam.[20] It is important to remember that when Jesus came to earth as a man, He walked this earth as a man, totally dependent on His Father to keep Him through the power of the Holy Spirit.[21] Philippians 2:6–7 says:

> *'Although He existed in the form of God, did not regard equality with God a thing to be grasped, but emptied Himself, taking the form of a bondservant, and being in the likeness of man.'*

In two of the three temptations, Satan sought to put doubt in the mind of Jesus by challenging whether He really was the Son of God. Satan also quoted Scripture and tried to turn it to his own purposes, but Jesus used the Word of God as a sword and drove him back on each attack. Jesus prevailed.[22]

The Scripture is fulfilled

Jesus returned to Galilee from the time of temptation in the power of the Holy Spirit.[23] On the sabbath, He entered the synagogue in Nazareth, and when the book of the prophet Isaiah was handed to Him, He opened it at chapter 61 and began to read:

> *'The Spirit of the Lord is upon Me, because He anointed Me to preach the gospel to the poor. He has sent Me to proclaim release to the captives, and recovery of sight to the blind, to set free those who are downtrodden, to proclaim the favourable year of the Lord.'*

He went on to say,

> *'Today this Scripture has been fulfilled in your hearing.'*
>
> (Luke 4:18–21)

All in the synagogue spoke well of Him, but as He began to expound the Scriptures they were filled with rage. This was to be the experience of Jesus in the next three-and-a-half years as He ministered in Israel. He either made people glad or mad as He ministered among them. So angry were the people on this occasion that they cast Him out of the city to the brow of a nearby hill, to throw Him off the cliff to His death. However, it was not the time for Jesus to die, nor the way in which He was to die, and He simply passed through their midst to safety.[24] Again Satan had influenced people to destroy Jesus, but did not succeed.

Calling of the twelve

At the beginning of His public ministry, Jesus called twelve men to be His close companions. Into these twelve He would pour understanding about the kingdom of God, and prepare them to assume leadership after His departure.

> *'And He appointed twelve, that they might be with Him, and that He might send them out to preach, and to have authority to cast out the demons.'* (Mark 3:14–15)

Four were fishermen and one a tax-gatherer. None were religious leaders, but all had a strong desire to know and serve God, and quickly responded to the invitation of Jesus to follow Him. There was Simon, James (the elder), John, Andrew, Philip, Bartholomew, Thomas, Matthew, James (the younger), Thaddaeus, Simon and Judas. Later Jesus was to call seventy others as well – indeed, He called all to follow Him.[25] But He did not make it easy for people to become His disciples. What He was longing to see was people truly having a change of mind and heart in regard to their way of life. As a result, their relationship with God would be restored and the blessings of God could be poured into their lives.[26]

Repent and believe

'Repent, for the kingdom of heaven is at hand,' was the familiar call of Jesus to the people.[27] Many were religious and caught up in forms of godliness, but their hearts were not right with God. Hundreds, even thousands, would gather as He preached and taught the Word of God. The common people received Him gladly. Never before had they heard someone speak with such authority. But, as ever, He dealt with issues of the heart.[28]

'If anyone wishes to come after Me, let him deny himself, and take up his cross, and follow Me. For whoever wishes to save his life shall lose it; but whoever loses his life for My sake shall find it.'

(Matthew 16:24, 25)

It was to be an all-or-nothing commitment. To take up a cross and follow Jesus meant a willingness to die to one's own way and yield to God's way. Jesus went on to say:

'For what will a man be profited, if he gains the whole world, and forfeits his soul? Or what will a man give in exchange for his soul? For the Son of Man is going to come in the glory of His Father with His angels; and will then recompense every man according to his deeds.'

(Matthew 16:26–27)

Knowing well the brevity of life and the judgement to come, He urged His hearers to consider seriously the consequences of living only for temporal gain and not preparing themselves for eternity. His greatest enemies were the religious leaders, to whom He showed no mercy. He called the Pharisees hypocrites, blind guides, fools, sons of hell, whitewashed sepulchres, lawless ones, robbers and sons of murderers. No wonder they wanted to kill Him.[29] Jesus loved people dearly, but He hated the religious system that brought people into bondage and deceived them into believing they were right with God when they were not. Some Pharisees, however, believed in Jesus.[30]

Miracles, miracles, miracles

Everywhere Jesus went miracles occurred. Such was His compassion for people and such was the power of the Holy Spirit on Him, that supernatural manifestations were a natural consequence. Some of His miracles recorded for us include:

▶ *Water changed to wine*

When wine ran out at a wedding feast, Jesus commanded that six stone water jars each containing twenty or thirty gallons be filled with water, which He then turned to wine (John 2:1–11).

▶ *Great catch of fish*

After fishermen had been fishing all night and caught nothing, He commanded them to put down their nets in deep water. Such was the catch that the nets were breaking and the boats threatened to sink (Luke 5:1–11).

▶ *Demonised man in the synagogue*
A man bound by evil spirits is set free in the Capernaum synagogue (Mark 1:21).

▶ *Cleansing a leper*
A needy leper, an outcast of society, calls on Jesus for healing. He heals him (Matthew 8:1–4).

▶ *Withered hand healed*
A man with a withered hand has his hand wholly restored at a simple command (Matthew (12:9–14).

▶ *Widow's son raised*
Coming upon a funeral procession, Jesus raises from the dead the only son of a widow (Luke 7:11–17).

▶ *Tempest stilled*
Caught on the lake in a violent storm, Jesus commands the wind and waves to be still and they obey Him (Mark 4:35–41).

▶ *Blind men healed*
Two blind men call on Jesus for mercy. He touches their eyes and they are healed (Matthew 9:27–31).

▶ *Feeding thousands*
Five thousand men and probably as many or more women and children are fed with five barley loaves and two fishes, after Jesus gives thanks for the food (John 6:1–14).

▶ *Deaf-mute cured*
After putting His fingers into the ears of a deaf-mute and touching his tongue with saliva, Jesus commands that the man's ears be opened. The man hears and speaks (Mark 7:31–37).

▶ *Tribute money provided*
Jesus commands Peter to go to the sea, throw out a line, take the first fish that comes up, open its mouth and find a stater (Roman coin) to pay their taxes (Matthew 17:24–27).

► *Lazarus raised from the dead*

A friend of Jesus is raised from the dead after being dead for four days (John 11:1–46).

Two kingdoms

There are two kingdoms: the kingdom of God and the kingdom of Satan.[31] Both influence the inhabitants of the earth, and each of us belongs to one or other of these kingdoms. Only through believing in Jesus Christ, and living a life in obedience to Him, can we claim to belong to the kingdom of God. Jesus said to Nicodemus, a Pharisee,

> *'Truly, truly, I say unto you, unless one is born again, he cannot see the kingdom of God.'*   (John 3:3)

Nicodemus tried to understand what Jesus was saying but could not, and questioned how a man could enter his mother's womb and be born a second time. He tried to understand spiritual things with his natural mind. Jesus replied,

> *'Truly, truly, I say to you, unless one is born of water and the Spirit, he cannot enter into the kingdom of God. That which is born of the flesh is flesh, and that which is born of the Spirit is spirit.'*   (John 3:5–6)

Jesus was saying that flesh gives birth to flesh, but the Holy Spirit gives birth to man's spirit. Through a natural birth we receive physical life, but through a spiritual birth we can receive spiritual life. This impartation of God's life, this coming alive spiritually, happens the moment a person turns from their sin and confesses Jesus Christ as Lord. By submitting to the rulership or authority of Jesus, who is the king of God's kingdom, we become recipients of the life of the kingdom. When we trust in Christ something wonderful happens, as Colossians 1:13–14 tells us:

> *'For He delivered us from the domain of darkness, and transferred us to the kingdom of His beloved Son, in whom we have redemption, the forgiveness of sins.'*

Have you been born again?

God's Kingdom is:

- A kingdom of light
- A kingdom of holiness and righteousness
- A kingdom of healing and health
- A kingdom of truth
- A kingdom of joy and life

Satan's Kingdom is:

- A kingdom of darkness
- A kingdom of sin and unrighteousness
- A kingdom of sickness and disease
- A kingdom of deception
- A kingdom of sorrow and death

Which kingdom do you belong to?

Clash of kingdoms

As Jesus preached the Word of God, cast out demons and healed the sick, there was a profound clash of kingdoms. Because God's kingdom is a kingdom of light, it exposed the darkness in people's hearts. Many who did not want to come into the light criticised and opposed Jesus, but He knew that this opposition was not only flesh against flesh, but the powers of darkness venting their resistance through human vessels.[32]

The Bible calls Satan the god of this world, who has blinded the minds of unbelievers so that they do not understand who Jesus is and do not receive the good news about His kingdom.[33] It also says that, without Christ, people are dead in their trespasses and sins and walk according to the course of this world, according to the prince of the power of the air. An evil spirit, the Scripture says, works in those who walk in disobedience.[34]

No wonder there was a clash of kingdoms! Those who preferred their own ways were very much convicted of sin by the teaching of Jesus. However, multitudes believed He was their Messiah and trusted Him fully. Those bound by sin, Jesus forgave. In so doing He was overcoming Satan, the author of sin.[35] Those bound by evil spirits, Jesus set free. In so doing He was overcoming Satan, the ruler of demons.[36] Those bound by sickness and disease, He healed. In so doing He was overcoming Satan, the author of sickness and disease.[37] Those bound by death, He raised. In so doing He was overcoming Satan, who held the power of death.[38] Jesus came to destroy the works of the devil and bring new life to all who believed in Him.[39]

Betrayal

Satan was losing ground on every side, as people believed in Jesus and transferred their allegiance to Him. It was imperative to find a way of destroying this miracle worker. Then the idea came into his corrupted mind that perhaps he could influence one of the twelve disciples of Jesus to work against his Lord.

Judas Iscariot was in charge of the finances. Although Jesus was aware that Judas had been taking money from the common purse, He had not confronted him. This sin gave Satan a door by which he could enter Judas's life. The Scripture simply says,

> *'And Satan entered Judas who was called Iscariot, belonging to the number of the twelve.'*   (Luke 22:3)

Judas then went to the chief priests and officials and discussed how he might betray Jesus. They were greatly pleased, and agreed to pay him for this despicable deed. Jesus of course, was fully aware of what was unfolding.[40] During the last meal Jesus was to have with His disciples before His betrayal and crucifixion, He took some bread, gave thanks and broke it, saying,

> *' "This is My body which is given for you; do this in remembrance of Me." He then took a cup of wine and continued speaking, "This cup which is poured out for you is the new covenant in My blood." '*
> (Luke 22:19–20)

Through these actions He spoke of His imminent death and the ushering in of a new covenant – the second phase in God's rescue plan for mankind. In the course of this same meal, Jesus said to His disciples that one of them was about to betray Him. When the disciples wondered who this might be, Judas said, *'Surely it is not I, Rabbi?'* Jesus responded, *'You have said it yourself'* (Matthew 26:25).

Capture and trial

After their last meal together, Jesus and the eleven disciples went to a garden near Jerusalem, where He prayed to the Father. It was to this garden that Judas led a large group of people armed with swords and clubs to capture Jesus. Judas identified his master with a kiss. Jesus was then led to the priest Annas and then to Caiaphas, the High Priest, at whose house the scribes and elders had gathered.[41] The chief priests and the full Jewish Council tried to obtain false testimony against Jesus in order to have Him put to death, but could find none. They accused Him of blasphemy, because He said He was the Son of God, and He was beaten and spat on before being sent to Pontius Pilate, the Roman governor.[42]

Before Pilate, the Jewish leaders brought false accusations against Jesus and also said He was a king, which they thought would arouse Pilate's condemnation. After Jesus answered affirmatively that He was the King of the Jews, Pilate sent Him to Herod Antipas, who had jurisdiction over Galilee, because Jesus was a Galilean. At that time Herod was visiting Jerusalem.[43] He had heard much about Jesus and wanted to meet Him, hoping to see a miracle, but Jesus would not answer even one of his questions. After Herod and his soldiers had treated Jesus with contempt, they dressed Him in a resplendent robe and sent Him back to Pilate.

Pilate found nothing wrong with Jesus and wanted to release Him, but when he summoned the chief priests and rulers of the people they insisted that Jesus be put to death. It was the custom for a prisoner to be released at this time of year, and when Pilate suggested that it be Jesus, both the leaders and the people insisted that Jesus should be crucified, and Barabbas, an insurrectionist, robber and murderer, released instead.[44] In the midst of this turmoil, Pilate's wife warned her husband to have nothing to do with Jesus, who was a righteous man, as she had suffered terribly in a dream the night before because of Him.[45] Pilate ignored his wife's counsel. If only he could have seen into the future! This prominent man, who at the time held the power of life and death in his hands, would himself eventually be put on trial before the emperor in Rome in connection with the slaughter of some Samaritans. He would then be banished to Vienne in southern France, where he would commit suicide.[46]

On the insistence of the gathered multitude that Jesus be crucified, Pilate publicly washed his hands before them, declaring that he was innocent of the blood of Jesus. The crowd then cursed themselves as they cried out, 'His blood be upon us and on our children' (Matthew 27:25). Barabbas was released to the people, while Jesus was taken and scourged before being led to crucifixion.[47] The Jews had a law prohibiting more than forty lashes, and it was strictly enforced. Jesus would have experienced the

customary thirty-nine lashes. Scourging was a brutal punishment
in those days:

> 'Romans used a scourge of cords or thongs with pieces of lead
> or brass, or small, sharp pointed bones attached to the lashes.
> The victim was stripped to the waist and bound in a stooping
> position, with the hands behind the back, to a post or pillar.
> The suffering under the lash was intense. The body was
> frightfully lacerated. The Christian martyrs at Smyrna about
> A.D. 155 were so torn with the scourges that their veins were
> laid bare, and the inner muscles and sinews, and even the
> entrails were exposed.' [48]

After He was scourged, a purple robe was put on Jesus and a
crown of thorns placed unceremoniously on His head. A reed was
put in His right hand and many bowed before Him, saying
mockingly, *'Hail, King of the Jews!'* The reed was then used to strike
blow after blow on Jesus's face and head. Spittle from His taunters
dripped on Him.[49] From this scene of humiliation, He was led
away to be crucified.

Crucifixion

Crucifixion is the torture and execution of a person by fixing them
to a cross. At the site of the crucifixion an upright post was secured
in the ground, while the condemned person was forced to carry the
heavy cross-arm from the prison to the place of death. Weakened
by the inhumane treatment and resulting loss of blood, Jesus
struggled to carry the cross-arm, which cut into His lacerated flesh.
Simon of Cyrene, a bystander, was made to carry it for Him.[50]

At about nine o'clock in the morning, at the place of crucifixion,
nails were driven through the hands of Jesus as He was secured
to the cross-arm, which was then lifted and fastened to the top of
the post. A nail was driven through His feet, securing them to the
cross. Above His head, the soldiers put up the charge against Him,
which read, *'This is Jesus the King of the Jews.'*[51] Around noon, a
darkness settled on the land as the sufferings of Jesus intensified.
Excruciating as the physical pain must have been, there was the
added dimension of spiritual pain, as Jesus, our sin offering – our
substitute – took on Himself the sin of a fallen humanity and the
punishment for that sin.

About three o'clock in the afternoon Jesus cried out with a loud
voice, *'My God, My God, why hast Thou forsaken Me!'* (Matthew

27:46). Taking our place necessitated the Father turning His back on His Son. We will never be able to comprehend the agony of that rejection. Jesus was rejected by the Father that we might be accepted by the Father.[52] Shortly after, Jesus cried out with a loud voice, *'It is finished!'* This was a triumphant declaration that the work He had come to earth to accomplish had been perfectly fulfilled.[53]

The second phase of God's rescue plan for mankind had now commenced. The Old Covenant had given way to a New Covenant. The 'once for all' sacrifice of Jesus, God's Passover Lamb, fulfilled the Old Covenant types and brought to a conclusion the former way of dealing with sin – the continual offering up of animal sacrifices and the sprinkling of their blood.[54] Now the sinner could look directly to God and declare his or her trust in what Jesus had accomplished through His death, in their place, on the cross. Only the blood of Jesus could be relied on for the cleansing of sin.[55]

Burial

Two thieves were crucified alongside Jesus. In order that their bodies would not be on the crosses the next day, a sabbath, the Jews asked Pilate if the legs of those crucified could be broken. The restriction placed on the lungs through the sagging weight of the body, meant that those being crucified would push up with their feet in order to fill their lungs with oxygen. With broken legs and lack of breath, death came quickly. The soldiers broke the legs of the two thieves, but when they came to Jesus they saw that He was already dead. One soldier thrust a spear into His side, and out came blood and water. This flow of blood and the water fluid from the sac around the heart indicated that Jesus had died of heart failure, due to shock and constriction of the heart by fluid in the pericardium, and not of suffocation like the thieves.[56]

Joseph of Arimathea, a secret disciple of Jesus, requested Pilate that he might take the body of Jesus for burial. Permission was granted, and he and Nicodemus the Pharisee placed the body in a new tomb that Joseph had prepared for himself. After binding it in linen wrappings and spices, they rolled a large stone over the entrance to the tomb. Mary Magdalene and Mary the mother of Jesus looked on.[57] The next day the chief priests and Pharisees expressed their concern to Pilate about Jesus's prediction that He would rise from the dead after three days. With Pilate's approval, a guard was stationed at the tomb and its entrance sealed.[58]

Descent

While the physical body of Jesus lay for three days and three
nights in the tomb, Jesus Himself descended into Hades (Sheol) in
the heart of the earth. Bearing our sins and diseases away to a
'solitary land', He fulfilled the type of the scapegoat spoken of in
Leviticus 16. Romans 10:6–7 puts it this way:

> 'But the righteousness based on faith speaks thus, "Do not say in
> your heart, 'Who will ascend into heaven?' (that is, to bring Christ
> down), or 'Who will descend into the abyss?' (that is, to bring
> Christ up from the dead)."'

The word 'abyss' in the Greek language of the New Testament
can be rendered 'depthless, infernal abyss, deep, or bottomless pit'.
Jesus 'tasted' death for everyone so that no-one need experience
the horror of the eternal consequences of sin. In Psalm 88 a
prophetic voice is heard:

> 'I am reckoned among those who go down to the pit;
> I have become like a man without strength,
> Forsaken among the dead,
> Like the slain who lie in the grave,
> Whom Thou dost remember no more,
> And they are cut off from Thy hand.
> Thou hast put me in the lowest pit,
> In dark places, in the depths.
> Thy wrath has rested upon me,
> And Thou hast afflicted me with all Thy waves.'
>
> (Psalm 88:4–7)

After further utterings of distress, questions are asked which
demand an answer:

> 'Wilt Thou perform wonders for the dead?
> Will the departed spirits rise and praise Thee?
> Will Thy lovingkindness be declared in the grave,
>   Thy faithfulness in Abaddon?
> Will Thy wonders be made known in the darkness and
>   Thy righteousness in the land of forgetfulness?'
>
> (Psalm 88:10–12)

To each of these questions the answer is a resounding **Yes!**

Resurrection

When the three days and nights had been fulfilled, a severe earthquake shook Jerusalem, and an angel from heaven came and rolled away the stone to the entrance of the tomb. His sudden appearance and shining countenance brought such overwhelming fear on those guarding the tomb that they fell to the ground as dead men.[59] This supernatural act was not to let Jesus out, but to let people in. Jesus was no longer bound by the limitations of an earthly body, and in His resurrection body was able to pass through physical walls and appear at will, as He did that evening to His disciples, who were behind closed doors.[60]

Thomas was not with the disciples on that occasion and would not believe their report:

> *'Unless I shall see in His hands the imprint of the nails, and put my finger into the place of the nails, and put my hand into His side, I will not believe.'*   (John 20:25)

Eight days later, Thomas was with his fellow disciples when Jesus suddenly appeared to them. Once again they were behind locked doors. Jesus beckoned Thomas to touch His hands and side, but Thomas did not need to do so. With his own eyes he saw his Lord and with his own ears heard His voice. Jesus indeed had risen from the dead.[61] For forty days Jesus made numerous appearances to those who were His followers. Whether it was to one, or to more than five hundred at the same time, many saw for themselves that He truly was alive.[62]

Ascension

Jesus's time on earth was limited, however, as He purposed to ascend back into heaven so that the Holy Spirit could be poured out on His followers. After commanding the apostles not to leave Jerusalem, but to await the outpouring of the Holy Spirit, Jesus told them that they would then be His witnesses not only in Jerusalem, Judea and Samaria but in the remotest parts of the earth.[63] After saying this, He began to rise from the ground. While the disciples watched in awe, He ascended until a cloud hid Him from sight. Suddenly two angels stood alongside them and pronounced:

'Men of Galilee, why do you stand looking into the sky? This Jesus,
who has been taken up from you into heaven, will come in just
the same way as you have watched Him go into heaven.'

(Acts 1:11)

Jesus had ascended to the third heaven to sit at the right hand of
His Father on the throne of God. From this place of exaltation He
would intercede to the Father for those who believed in Him. And
He would await the Father's command to return to the earth.[64]

Coming again

Jesus had often talked to His followers about going away and
coming back again, but this had not made sense to them. It was
only after He had been crucified, resurrected and had ascended to
heaven that full understanding dawned.[65] Soon the Holy Spirit
would empower them to take the message of God's kingdom to
the nations. Jesus had previously told them that His coming again
would be preceded by many and varied signs, culminating in the
'good news' of God's salvation being proclaimed to every part of
the world.[66]

'This gospel of the kingdom shall be preached in the whole world
for a witness to all the nations, and then the end shall come.'

(Matthew 24:14)

When Jesus does come again, it will not resemble in any way His
First Coming. This was in humility and obscurity – born in an
animal shelter and cribbed in a feeding trough. His Second
Coming will be dramatic and glorious.[67] Accompanied by all
believers who have died over the centuries, whether under the
Old or New Covenants, and by myriads of angels, He will appear in
the clouds above the earth. A heavenly trumpet will sound. An
archangel will shout in triumph. The whole earth will see Him and
tremble before this awesome King of kings and Lord of lords. Jesus
will descend to stand on the Mount of Olives in Jerusalem, the
very mountain on which He was betrayed, captured and led to
trial and crucifixion.

When He comes, the bodies of believers, long turned to dust or
ashes, will be supernaturally raised, and God's people who come
with Him, as well as those living at that time on the earth, will
each receive a new resurrection body.[68] When He comes, the
nations will be gathered before Him and judgement passed. Some

people will be assigned to eternal life, but many will be assigned to the eternal fire prepared for the devil and his angels.[69]

But we are looking ahead. For the disciples at the time of the ascension of Jesus, it was imperative that they return to Jerusalem to await the fulfilment of His words concerning the Holy Spirit. An encounter with the power of God was coming that would enable them to fulfil the Lord's commission, for this great task was not to be accomplished by mere human ability, but by men and women divinely endued with supernatural power.[70]

Chapter 6

Commitment to Jesus Christ

Before explaining how we can come into freedom from demonic bondages, it is important that we first have a clear understanding of how an individual can experience forgiveness of sins and peace with God. I am aware that some reading this book have not yet experienced a personal relationship with Jesus Christ and do not know how it can happen. There are also those who have previously opened their lives to Jesus but are not presently walking closely with Him – you are unable to say in all truthfulness that Jesus is Lord of your life. To all of you, God is giving an opportunity to meet with Him. After going through the steps below, a prayer is offered that you can make your very own, and as you pray it with understanding, and in faith, the Lord Jesus will reveal Himself to you and a transformation will take place in your life. Those who are already Christians will be reminded afresh of the steps to salvation by which you can lead others to Christ.

1. Sin and its consequences

When he rebelled against God, Adam experienced separation from God. His choice was wilful and its consequences have affected all of us:

> 'Through one man sin entered into the world, and death through sin, and so death spread to all men, because all sinned.'
> (Romans 5:12)

Our sin has temporal consequences. Spiritually blind and spiritually dead, man pursues his own course in life, living independently from God. Because he is a sinner he keeps on sinning, making life hard for himself and for others.[1]

'For we also once were foolish ourselves, disobedient, deceived, enslaved to various lusts and pleasures, spending our life in malice and envy, hateful, hating one another.' (Titus 3:3)

Our sin has eternal consequences. God keeps a record of everyone's sins. A day of accountability has been set aside, when every person is to stand before God and give an account of the life that he or she lived on earth.

- Judgement will be according to truth (Romans 2:1–2)
- Judgement will be according to one's deeds (Romans 2:6)
- Judgement will be without partiality (Romans 2:11)
- Judgement will be according to light (Romans 2:12)

'God is now declaring to men that all everywhere should repent, because He has fixed a day in which He will judge the world in righteousness through a Man whom He has appointed, having furnished proof to all men by raising Him from the dead.'
(Acts 17:30–31)

Without a Saviour, man is without God and without hope.[2] Eternal judgement most certainly awaits all who walk in their own ways. In regard to the Second Coming of Jesus, the Scriptures declare:

'The Lord Jesus shall be revealed from heaven with His mighty angels in flaming fire, dealing out retribution to those who do not know God and to those who do not obey the gospel of our Lord Jesus. And these will pay the penalty of eternal destruction, away from the presence of the Lord and from the glory of His power, when He comes to be glorified in His saints on that day, and to be marvelled at among all who have believed.'
(2 Thessalonians 1:7–10)

2. Man's inability to save himself

There is absolutely nothing – no human endeavour – that a person can do to save himself from the coming judgement and to reconcile himself with God. Man cannot lift himself up by his own bootstraps!

> *'For all of us have become like one who is unclean, and all our righteous deeds are like a filthy garment.'*   (Isaiah 64:6)

God calls 'dead works' anything we do that we are relying on to save ourselves, including religious activities:

> *'Therefore leaving the elementary teaching about the Christ, let us press on to maturity, not laying again a foundation of repentance from dead works and of faith toward God.'*   (Hebrews 6:1)

Grace alone is the means by which a person is reconciled to God. Grace has been defined as the unmerited favour of God toward the undeserving and ill-deserving. It can also be defined as God's enabling, through which we can be all that He wants us to be and accomplish all that He wants us to do.

> *'For by grace you have been saved through faith; and that not of yourselves, it is the gift of God; not as a result of works, that no one should boast.'*   (Ephesians 2:8–9)

It is what God has done that we must rely on. If man could save himself, God would not, under the Old Covenant, have instituted animal sacrifices. If man could save himself, the Son of God would never have had to come from heaven and endure the terrible agony of the cross in order to usher in a New Covenant. Salvation depends on God's mercy and grace alone, and not on man's good works.

3. God's love expressed in Christ

From before the creation of mankind, God desired to enjoy an intimate relationship with Adam and Eve and their descendants. His heart is very much toward us, and it grieved Him greatly that we should turn our backs on Him and go our own way.

> *'Then the Lord saw the wickedness of man was great on the earth, and that every intent of the thoughts of his heart was only evil continually. And the Lord was very sorry that He had made man on the earth, and He was grieved in His heart.'* (Genesis 6:5–6)

In spite of man's sin God still loved us, and we have seen how He provided a way to deal with sin and restore fellowship under two successive covenants.

'And you were dead in your trespasses and sins, in which you formerly walked according to the course of this world, according to the prince of the power of the air, of the spirit that is now working in the sons of disobedience. Among them we too all formerly lived in the lusts of our flesh, indulging the desires of the flesh and of the mind, and were by nature children of wrath, even as the rest.

But God, being rich in mercy, because of His great love with which He loved us, even when we were dead in our transgressions, made us alive together with Christ (by grace you have been saved), and raised us up with Him, and seated us with Him in the heavenly places, in Christ Jesus, in order that in the ages to come He might show the surpassing riches of His grace in kindness toward us in Christ Jesus.' (Ephesians 2:1–7)

The familiar words from John's Gospel put it succinctly:

'For God so loved the world, that He gave His only begotten Son, that whoever believes in Him should not perish, but have eternal life. For God did not send the Son into the world to judge the world, but that the world should be saved through Him.'
(John 3:16, 17)

God's love has been extended to the world – and that includes you. No matter where you have been or what you have done, there is forgiveness and reconciliation through the blood of Jesus Christ:

'God demonstrates His own love toward us, in that while we were yet sinners, Christ died for us. Much more then, having now been justified by His blood, we shall be saved from the wrath of God through Him.' (Romans 5:8–9)

4. Repentance and faith

As John the Baptist prepared the way for the coming of Jesus, he cried out again and again to the Israelites, *'Repent, for the kingdom of heaven is at hand'* (Matthew 3:2).

When Jesus began His public ministry He likewise declared, *'Repent, for the kingdom of heaven is at hand'* (Matthew 4:17). When the twelve disciples went out at the bidding of Jesus, they too preached repentance.[3] It is not enough to have faith or belief in God; this believing must be preceded by repentance.[4] Repentance means simply to change one's mind. A genuine change of mind leads to a change of direction and brings the fruit of repentance.

This fruit indicates that there truly has been a change of mind, the result of turning from ungodliness and embracing a godly life-style.[5]

> *'But when he [John] saw many of the Pharisees and Sadducees coming for baptism, he said to them, "You brood of vipers, who warned you to flee from the wrath to come? Therefore bring forth fruit in keeping with repentance."'*   (Matthew 3:7–8)

When a person is willing to agree with what God says about sin and accept what God has done to provide a way of salvation, then they are ready to exercise faith in God. To believe or have faith in Jesus (the two expressions mean the same) is not just a mental exercise, but involves a wholehearted relying on or trusting in the Lord. It is to come under the lordship or rulership of Jesus. He is King of a kingdom and we need to acknowledge His rightful place in our lives as our Creator, Redeemer and Lord.[6]

5. Confessing Jesus as Lord

> *'If you confess with your mouth Jesus as Lord, and believe in your heart that God raised Him from the dead, you shall be saved; for with the heart man believes, resulting in righteousness, and with the mouth he confesses, resulting in salvation.'*
>   (Romans 10:9–10)

The Greek text says that we believe 'to righteousness' and confess 'to salvation'. Believing in the heart is to be followed by confession with the mouth that Jesus is Lord. As we confess with the mouth what we believe in the heart, there is a confirming in the heart.

> *'The one who believes in the Son of God has the witness in himself ... He who has the Son has life; he who does not have the Son of God does not have life.'*   (1 John 5:10–12)

The moment we believe in our hearts and confess with our mouths that Jesus is Lord, we receive forgiveness of sins and the gift of eternal life.[7] Jesus, through the Holy Spirit, comes to indwell our heart or spirit, and we are born again. A spiritual birth takes place. Our spirit is made alive with the life of God. Remember what

Jesus said to Nicodemus, that unless a person is born again he cannot see and cannot enter into the kingdom of God:

> *'That which is born of the flesh is flesh, and that which is born of the Spirit is spirit.'*   (John 3:6)

I well remember the night I surrendered my life to Christ some thirty-eight years ago. On turning from my own way and yielding to Jesus, I suddenly felt clean on the inside. A great weight lifted off me and I just knew that my sins had been forgiven and I had received the gift of eternal life. That night, as I read the Scriptures, they came alive to me. Next morning, when I went to check on the birds in my aviary, even they appeared different. The nearby mountains, the clouds above – the creation all around me was somehow much more alive and beautiful. The Creator was now my Heavenly Father. I was at peace with God and could appreciate the magnificence of His creation in a greater way than ever before.[8]

To confess Jesus as Lord is to acknowledge that we have come under the rulership of Jesus, the King of kings and Lord of lords. It is not just to say some nice-sounding religious words. It means that from now on we are committed to obeying God and being led by His Holy Spirit, and no longer want to continue in our own independent lifestyle.

6. Entering into a right relationship with God

For those of you desiring to come into a right relationship with God, the following prayer made personal and coming from the heart, will enable this to happen. Right now, wherever you are, you can pray. I encourage you to speak this prayer out loud:

> 'Dear God, I sincerely desire to be in a right relationship with You. I now turn from going my own way and I choose to start following Your way. Please forgive me all the sin I have committed over my lifetime. I acknowledge that I cannot save myself and need You to save me. I acknowledge that You have provided the only way of salvation through sending your Son Jesus to die on a cross for me. I believe Jesus took upon Himself my sin and the punishment I deserved for it. I believe that You raised Him from the dead three days after He was crucified and that He is now seated at Your right hand in heaven.

With all of my heart I now surrender my life to Jesus. Lord
Jesus Christ, I welcome You into my heart. I gladly confess
You to be Lord of my life. Thank you for forgiving me all of
my sin. Thank you for giving me the gift of eternal life.
Thank you that I am now a member of Your family.'

7. Walking with Jesus and His people

The moment we turn from our sin and surrender our life to Jesus as
Lord, we are born again and indwelt by the Holy Spirit. Thus the
Christian life begins. In order to grow spiritually we need nourish-
ment to become spiritually strong. As in the natural, so in the
spiritual: babes must be fed and cared for to develop properly.

My childhood love of birds continues and recently I had a few
pairs of canaries sitting on eggs or rearing young. One day a young
mother hatched four offspring the same day. As I looked into the
nest, the newborns all stretched out their necks with open
mouths, anticipating being fed. Next day when I looked they were
all dead. On checking their crops, I discovered they were empty.
The young mother had failed to feed them and they had died of
starvation. Immediately I considered what happens to some
newborn Christians. It is one thing to be brought to birth, another
to start growing, and another to develop and mature as believers
in Christ. The following are some important pointers to assist your
spiritual growth.

▶   *Develop a relationship with Jesus*
The Christian life is all around Jesus. It is not following people,
programmes or man-made regulations, but following the person
of Christ. Now that we have begun to know God, we can talk to
Him and anticipate Him talking to us. It takes time to develop
relationships with other people, and so it is with God. The more
time you spend with somebody the more you get to know them.
Jesus said,

> *'My sheep hear My voice, and I know them, and they follow Me,
> and I give eternal life to them...'*   (John 10:27–28)

▶   *Develop relationships with other Christians*
When we become a Christian we are automatically joined to other
believers in Christ. We become part of what the Bible calls the
church or body of Christ. Church or *ekklesia* means 'called-out
ones'. Having been called out of darkness into God's marvellous

light, we are spiritually joined to all other believers. The Scripture refers to a body of many members with Christ as its head.[9] God has called and gifted many men and women in His church to strengthen and encourage His people. If we do not join ourselves to other believers, we miss out on all the benefits associated with fellowship.

> *'And He gave some as apostles, and some as prophets, and some as evangelists, and some as pastors and teachers, for the equipping of the saints for the work of service, to the building up of the body of Christ; until we all attain to the unity of the faith, and of the knowledge of the Son of God, to a mature man, to the measure of the stature which belongs to the fullness of Christ.'*
>
> (Ephesians 4:11–13)

▶ *Renew your mind with the Word of God*

It is imperative that we begin to allow God's Word, the Bible, to renew our minds so that we begin to think and understand as God does. The present world system is dominated by Satan, and is contrary to God and His standards of righteousness. Only by God's Word, made alive and understandable to us through the Holy Spirit, can our minds be changed.[10]

Just as food nourishes our physical body, so the Word of God nourishes our spirit. Without food, the body becomes malnourished and eventually ceases to function properly. Jesus said that man should not live on bread alone, but on every word that proceeds from the mouth of God.[11] As we begin to develop the habit of reading the Bible regularly and pondering on it, we discover what an awesome book it is and what a source of life and strength to us.

> *'And do not be conformed to this world, but be transformed by the renewing of your mind, that you may prove what the will of God is, that which is good and acceptable and perfect.'*
>
> (Romans 12:2)

▶ *Be filled with the Holy Spirit*

To be filled with the Holy Spirit is to be filled with the life of God. Only as we are filled with God's Word and Spirit can we follow and serve Jesus as we should. When Jesus rose from the dead, He breathed on His disciples and imparted to them the life of the Holy Spirit. At that moment they were born again and the Holy Spirit came to dwell within them. Wonderful as that experience was, they were still not empowered to bear witness to their faith at home and abroad.[12] Just before Jesus ascended back into heaven, He urged His disciples to wait in Jerusalem for the promise of the Father, called the baptism in the Holy Spirit. This was to empower them to be His witnesses. When the Day of Pentecost came, the Holy Spirit filled them with the presence of Jesus.

> *'And suddenly there came from heaven a noise like a violent, rushing wind, and it filled the whole house where they were sitting. And there appeared to them tongues as of fire distributing themselves, and they rested on each one of them. And they were all filled with the Holy Spirit and began to speak with other tongues, as the Spirit was giving them utterance.'*   (Acts 2:2–4)

Jesus is the one who fills us with the Holy Spirit.

When we recognise our need of God's power to follow and serve Him, and God's provision of this through the Holy Spirit, we can then ask Jesus to fill us with the Holy Spirit. For some this is a dynamic experience, for others a quiet receiving by faith. Whichever way we receive this enduement, it is life-changing.

▶ *Experience deliverance from demonic bondages*

The second section of this book will focus on recognising demonic bondages and becoming free from them. Suffice to say here that Jesus wants to set everyone free from the invisible chains that entangle their lives.

> *'The Son of God appeared for this purpose, that He might destroy the works of the devil.'*   (1 John 3:8)

▶ *Become a servant*

When God became a man, He came to this earth to serve. As followers of Jesus, we are led to see beyond our own little world and to reach out into the worlds of others. Sin causes us to be self-centred, but as we look to our Saviour and Lord we find ourselves becoming more 'other-focused'. God blesses us so that we, in turn, can be a blessing to others. Jesus spoke about how the rulers of the Gentiles loved to rule over the lives of others. This way, He said, was not the way of His kingdom:

> *'It is not so among you, but whoever wishes to become great among you shall be your servant, and whoever wishes to be first among you*

shall be your slave; just as the Son of Man did not come to be served,
but to serve, and give His life a ransom for many.'

(Matthew 20:26–28)

Our ultimate goal as Christians is not to get to heaven but to become more like Jesus. As we receive more from God, let us purpose to share His goodness with others.

Chapter 7

Personal Testimony

A battle was raging within me. I was pulled in two directions at once. Somehow I was aware that this was the most important moment in my life, and my decision would have eternal consequences.

In the days leading up to this moment, I had on three occasions visited a church near my home and prayed to God that He would forgive me my sin. I had been alone in the building and it seemed that God was nowhere to be found. My prayers seemed to reach no higher than the ceiling. A sense of urgency was upon me. Here I was, wanting to find peace with God, but not knowing how. On the third visit, I prostrated myself on the floor and told God I would do anything if He would only forgive my sin. Looking back, I see how I was being humbled before Almighty God. This rebellious, independent, Christ-blaspheming young man had at last come to a place where he was willing to turn from his own way and follow Jesus.

Knowing that missionaries were good people sent out by churches to other countries to help others, I told God I would even be a missionary if only He would forgive me my sin. There was no response. It seemed that God had not heard my cry – yet He had! Perusing the local newspaper, I saw that Youth for Christ was conducting a series of meetings led by a musical team from the USA. The evangelist was a former big band leader and his wife also was an accomplished musician. Although I was just concluding my training to be a schoolteacher, my real ambition was to be a professional musician and to lead my own big band one day. The advertisement drew me to the meetings, but God was drawing me to Himself.

Moment of decision

The musical programme was excellent and was followed by the evangelist speaking from the Bible on the Second Coming of Jesus, a topic I had never heard of. I knew about the First Coming, but not the second. My heart and mind were gripped by the truth of Scripture. Even before the evangelist concluded his message and challenged those present to give their lives to Christ, God was challenging me to make a total surrender of my life to His Son. I felt that if I rejected this offer of salvation, I would never have the opportunity to respond to Jesus again. It truly was the most important moment of my life.

A voice was telling me not to be a fool; that if I surrendered my life to Christ, I would be miserable. Another voice was speaking as well; somewhat quieter and yet more appealing. It said that I could reject all I had heard and continue to live for myself, but that a day of accountability was coming, and if I was wise I would give my life to Jesus. With the evangelist still preaching and the battle still raging within, I prayed simply, from my heart, asking God to forgive me all my sin and telling Jesus I wanted Him to take over my life. I was surrendering to Him as Lord. The moment I prayed, a great weight lifted off me and I felt clean on the inside. I just knew that God had answered the cry of my heart and that my sins were forgiven![1] I just knew that I had received the gift of eternal life, and that Jesus had indeed risen from the dead and was very much alive. And, would you believe it, I felt God calling me to be a missionary!

When the meeting was over I walked forward to inquire how I could get involved in serving God. Also, I was saying to myself, that now that I knew God, I had someone to turn to with my problems. Ever since I could remember, I had had difficulties in breathing freely and was allergic to many things. As well, I was gripped daily by debilitating fears that sapped a great deal of my energy. I was even afraid of being afraid.

Transformation

From the moment I surrendered my life to Jesus, radical changes became evident – changes that were a testimony to all my non-Christian friends. I was eager to tell them what Jesus had done for me and what He could do for them. As a believer, I discovered I was part of a very large family. New friends came into my life and I found myself being drawn into involvement in evangelism. Jesus was real, the Bible had become a living book and a new sense of purpose filled my life. The old desires for sinful activities had left me, and all I wanted to do was to know Jesus and make Him known.

A few weeks after I became a Christian, Ken Wright, one of the members of the Youth for Christ committee, talked to me about being filled with the Holy Spirit. Being ignorant of the Scriptures, everything was new to me, including the truth that Jesus baptises with the Holy Spirit. Ken and his wife Shirley lived near my family home and the next day I went to their house for prayer. As they laid their hands on me, I asked Jesus to baptise me with the Holy Spirit. He did! An empowering of the Holy Spirit came upon me that thrust me into a new dimension of Christian living and serving.

As a Christian I had, as it were, been swimming in a river. Now, filled with the Holy Spirit, it was as if I was swimming in the ocean, a vast area without the confines of river banks. The Lord Jesus became even more real and the Scriptures even more alive. For the first time I began to lead others to Christ.

Disappointment with God

After being filled with the Holy Spirit I experienced a spiritual high for about one week. It seemed as if all the problems in my life had gone away and I felt wonderful. Unfortunately, this euphoria came to an end and I realised that my problems were still there. I became disappointed with God. As the years unfolded, I continually struggled with this. Why God did not answer my earnest cries for freedom I did not understand.

After being baptised in the Spirit, it seemed that in many ways my life was getting better and better and yet in other ways it was getting worse and worse. The conflicts within me began to increase rather than decrease, and I did not understand what was happening. As a result of the growing turmoil, I found it necessary to seek God even more earnestly. My times of prayer and reading the Scriptures increased until I averaged about four hours every day just seeking the Lord. This pattern continued for years. There were days in which I could do nothing else but pray, because of the conflicts. It was not that I was a spiritual giant, but my desperation compelled this intense seeking. Without time with God I could not function properly.

Three years after becoming a Christian I married Shirley Garratt of Wellington, New Zealand. Shortly after our marriage we became full-time evangelists with Open Air Campaigners, the organisation we had been associated with as voluntary workers. A few years ago, I was invited by OAC to return to New Zealand to speak at the annual conference of the evangelists and their wives. While at this conference, Bob McNaughton, the former New Zealand Director of OAC, expressed something to me that was a real surprise. He said that when I came on staff, the evangelists commented among themselves about the amount of time I spent seeking God, and that God would surely use me because of this. He said that neither he nor the others knew of the internal conflicts in my life until years later, when they read *Christian Set Yourself Free*, a book I had written on spiritual warfare and deliverance and that contained my testimony.

Years of struggle

Very few people were aware of my needs, because I did not make them known to many. From time to time I sought counsel, opening my heart to various pastors and to ministries visiting my country. No one seemed to understand what was happening inside me, nor did I understand myself. I was always a mystery case to those trying to help me. As I continued to seek God daily, regularly memorising Scripture, serving Him wholeheartedly, and seeking the help of others, with nothing ever happening to bring change, disappointment with God remained constant. It was not that no positive things were happening in my life, but when the struggles were very intense they overshadowed everything.

Not only did I pray a lot, I also fasted and prayed. Pressures would build inside me until they became unbearable. The only way I knew of getting relief was to fast. The longer I fasted the better I felt, but also the hungrier I became. When I started to eat again the pressures would build and build until I would resort to fasting for relief. Every so often I would tell Shirley I needed to be alone. Seeking the face of God, I would be lost for words as my heart cried out to Him for help. Groanings and sighings would come forth and I would weep and weep until there were no more tears to shed. How I longed to be free from these daily torments, but all my seeking seemed to no avail. One year followed another.

On one occasion I received prayer from an evangelist in his home. This man saw marvellous results in his ministry with healings and deliverances abounding. When he prayed for me he tried to cast out demons. As I knelt in his kitchen and he fervently commanded demons to leave me, nothing happened on the inside. All was calm. Consequently, it was not long before I began to think to myself what a ridiculous situation I was in, with this man thinking I had demons in me! But this evangelist was the only person to that time who recognised the source of my conflicts as rooted in evil spirits. Even I did not recognise what I was bound by, and in my great ignorance I mocked him in my heart.

After a time of earnest prayer on his part, with no freedom resulting, he suggested I visit a psychiatrist friend of his in the city of Auckland. Little did he know that one of my fears was that of going insane. There was no way I would go to see his friend. I thought to myself that if this evangelist could not help me, no one else I knew of could, and I resolved never to seek counsel again. I would just keep on seeking God.

Time of crisis

As time went by, I am sure Shirley and I would have been considered successful by those in authority over us. Every year we reached thousands of non-Christians with the gospel message and people regularly responded and surrendered their lives to Christ. Yet in the midst of all these blessings, I continued to struggle daily on the inside. How I longed to be free!

Unknown to me, a personal crisis was looming that would reveal in a very clear way the source of my lifelong problems. For some time I had been struggling with some policies of the evangelistic work we were in that I felt were limiting the organization's effectiveness. Out of frustration I wrote a letter of resignation to my director, Noel Gibson. Noel and his wife Phyl were wonderful people, greatly used by God. Calling me to his office, Noel inquired about the guidance the Lord had given me to resign. To my surprise I did not have any, but I did have many frustrations and a good deal of immaturity. On his questioning me, I reluctantly shared my long-standing inner conflicts. When I had finished talking, he made a statement that shocked me: 'Graham, I believe you need deliverance from evil spirits!'

If only I knew then what I know now. What a difference the understanding would have made. However, God was to allow Shirley and me to go through a time of intense trial in which we would be granted many insights into the workings of evil spirits. As time went on, we were to be given understanding of how to break free from the bondages of the enemy. Many of these insights are revealed in the following chapters.

Chapter 8

The Commission of Jesus

A commission is a mandate: a command to be obeyed, a task to be completed. Jesus made it quite clear what He wanted His followers to do. He told them to preach the gospel of the kingdom of God throughout the whole world (Matthew 24:14). After He had risen from the dead He again said,

> *'Go into all the world and preach the gospel to all creation.'*
> (Mark 16:15)

Jesus wanted those who believed in Him to tell others of God's love and how they too could experience God's forgiveness and receive eternal life. The inward faith experienced by those trusting in Jesus was then to be expressed in an outward act of obedience – baptism in water:

> *'He who has believed and has been baptised shall be saved; but he who has disbelieved shall be condemned.'* (Mark 16:16)

As people believed in Christ and began to walk in obedience to Him, four signs would be in evidence as they ministered to others in the power of Jesus's name:

1. Supernatural authority – the ability to cast out demons.
2. Supernatural languages – the ability to speak in unlearned languages.
3. Supernatural protection – the ability to be kept safe in times of danger.
4. Supernatural power – the ability to heal the sick.

> *'And these signs will accompany those who have believed: in My name they will cast out demons, they will speak with new tongues; they will pick up serpents and if they drink any deadly poison it shall not hurt them; they will lay hands on the sick and they will recover.'*   (Mark 16:17–18)

The Christians in the early church fulfilled this commission. Jesus wants us to do likewise (Mark 16:19–20). Note that the supernatural sign heading the list is the casting out of demons. Looking at other passages of Scripture where Jesus commissions His disciples, we notice again the emphasis on casting out demons. I will focus later on this aspect of the signs that follow the preaching of the good news of the kingdom of God.

> *'And having summoned His twelve disciples, He gave them authority over unclean spirits, to cast them out, and to heal every kind of disease and every kind of sickness.'*   (Matthew 10:1)

> *'And He appointed the twelve, that they might be with Him, and that He might send them out to preach, and to have authority to cast out the demons.'*   (Mark 3:14–15)

> *'And He summoned the twelve and began to send them out in pairs; and He was giving them authority over the unclean spirits ... and they went out and preached that men should repent. And they were casting out many demons and were anointing with oil many sick people and healing them.'*   (Mark 6:7, 12, 13)

> *'Now after this the Lord appointed seventy others, and sent them two and two ahead of Him to every city and place where He Himself was going to come ... And the seventy returned with joy, saying, "Lord, even the demons are subject to us in Your name."'*   (Luke 10:1, 17)

There can be no mistaking these clear commands to set people free from the power of evil spirits. Because the modern church, particularly the Western church, has by and large neglected to do this, millions of Christians struggle with inner conflicts caused by demonic influences in their lives. The lack of obedience to this clear command is usually due to ignorance and unbelief. For some, though, it is an unwillingness to do what they know they should do. The Bible calls this rebellion. For the sake of clarity, when I refer to demons and evil spirits I am talking about the same spiritual beings – demons are evil spirits, evil spirits are demons.

Early in His public ministry Jesus attended the synagogue in Nazareth, where He was handed the scroll of the prophet Isaiah. Finding the following words, He began to read:

> *'The Spirit of the Lord is upon Me, because He anointed Me to preach the gospel to the poor, He has sent Me to proclaim release to the captives, and recovery of sight to the blind, to set free those who are downtrodden, to proclaim the favourable year of the Lord.'*
>
> (Isaiah 61:1, 2)

It was now the time for this messianic prophecy to be fulfilled. From Nazareth Jesus went to Capernaum, where we read of Him teaching, casting out demons and healing (Luke 4:31–43). Everywhere He went, He fulfilled these words and commanded His disciples to do likewise.

From children to adults

No age group is exempt from demonic attack or the need to be set free. In the following accounts, we see Jesus ministering in compassion to those in desperate need of His delivering power.

▶ *A Boy*

A distraught father brought his son to Jesus after the disciples had been unable to set him free. The demonic power within the boy had constantly gripped him, throwing him into convulsions, screaming out through him, mauling him and causing foaming at the mouth. Jesus rebuked the spirit and set the boy free. An overjoyed father now had a son who was healed (Luke 9:37–42).

▶ *A Girl*

A Syrophoenician woman had a daughter troubled by an unclean spirit. Hearing of Jesus, she sought Him out and begged that He cast out the demon from her child. Because of her persistence and faith, Jesus set the girl free, and the mother returned home to find her daughter lying on her bed healed (Mark 7:24–30).

▶ *A Man*

A man who lived among the tombs, tormented day and night, mutilating himself and exerting supernatural power to snap the chains restraining him, a man bound by many spirits, came to Jesus. After the demons had been cast out, he became normal in every respect. Totally transformed, wearing clothing again, free from restlessness and with his mind restored, Jesus told him to return to his people and bear testimony of what the Lord had done for him (Mark 5:1–20).

▶ *A Woman*

For eighteen long years a woman had been bent over double, unable to straighten up, with a sickness caused by a spirit. Jesus cast out the demonic presence and healed her. Her first response was to praise God for His great salvation (Luke 13:10–17).

Casting out demons

Ekballo is the Greek word translated 'cast out' in English. Its meaning, according to Strong's Bible Concordance, is to 'bring forth, cast forth, cast out, drive out, expel, leave, pluck out, pull out, take out, thrust out, put forth, put out, send away, send forth, send out'. It is a forceful word that commands forceful action.

Jesus, grieved that the Temple in Jerusalem had become a place of commerce rather than a house of prayer, made a scourge of chords. Overturning the tables of the moneychangers, He drove them out (*ekballo*) of the temple, along with those selling oxen, sheep and doves (John 2:13–17). When Stephen was defending himself before the Jewish Council he so enraged the councillors that he was cast out (*ekballo*) of Jerusalem and stoned to death (Acts 7:57, 58). As Paul was being transported to Italy on an Alexandrian ship, the vessel and complement were caught in a violent storm that eventually destroyed the ship. On the second day some of the cargo was jettisoned, and on the third day the ship's tackle. As the fourteenth day approached, the ship was being driven into shallower waters near Malta, and the crew further lightened the vessel by throwing out (*ekballo*) the wheat into the sea (Acts 27:38).

Casting out the moneychangers from the temple, casting out Stephen from Jerusalem to his death, casting out the wheat from a foundering vessel, all constituted actions of determination and aggressiveness. And so it is in casting out demons from the lives of the people they have inhabited. This does not mean, however, that we treat the people being ministered to in a violent manner. Our aggressiveness is against the spirits, not the person they have afflicted. It is imperative that we differentiate between the person in need and the demonic powers at work in them. If you were being prayed for, how would you like people to minister to you?

Usually when I am setting people free I use my normal tone of voice. Sometimes I speak very quietly, so that others will not hear, in order not to embarrass the person. There are times when I speak loudly, but usually not for long. For years I used to wonder why I often felt to command loudly for a few moments or a short time. On a trip to Norway some years back, I heard the Lord say to me day after day as I ministered to people, 'The gift of faith is operating; the gift of faith is operating.' This was a revelation, as I had never considered a gift of faith operating in my life. It was then I realised why I would speak loudly at times.

As a teenager I did some boxing. When in the ring fighting an opponent, the aim was to win by landing more point-scoring blows on your opponent than he landed on you. To knock him out meant that you would win the match. A fighter was always looking for the moment to land such a decisive blow. I realised that as I was casting out demons, moments came when I felt a particular stirring of faith that made me want to speak strongly and often loudly. It was as if I had been placing blow upon blow on the enemy, and now was the moment of wielding the decisive knockout blow. Often, having spoken a strong word of command, I actually stop commanding for a while and just watch what God is doing to bring freedom into a life.

Some who observe demonstrations of God's power when words are spoken loudly, conclude that in order to set someone free one must 'shout'. This is not the case. We are not involved in forms or techniques, but endeavour to be led by the Holy Spirit. Also, we are all different personalities and God works through us in different ways. Do not be just a copy of how someone else ministers, but let the Lord work through you in a way that is natural to the type of person you are.

Manifestations

Three types of manifestations are experienced as demons are cast out of people.

1. Dramatic manifestations

As spirits leave, some do so with clear evidence of their departure, both to those being ministered to and those witnessing the deliverance. The spirits may cry out through the mouth of the person they have been inhabiting, often with vile utterances. The person my exhibit supernatural strength, requiring several people to hold them down. On occasion, some demons leave during vomiting. At times of dramatic demonic manfestation, some people being ministered to may not even be aware of what is happening.

Recently I ministered to a man who was struggling greatly in his life with demonic problems. Before becoming a Christian he had been involved in much sin, but now no longer wanted to live as he used to. Violence had been part of his former way of life, and despite much transformation he was still experiencing some conflict. He was soon to be married, but had regular nightmares in which he was murdering his fiancée. Although he loved her and would never want to harm her, he was scared of the possibility of doing something terrible.

I commanded spirits of murder and hatred to leave him in the name of Jesus. As I persisted, it seemed as if nothing was happening, although it most certainly was. After five minutes or so the man suddenly lurched forward onto the floor, as the demons being confronted manifested strongly. Four or five men had to hold him down during the next twenty or thirty minutes, as dramatic manifestations took place. After the battle was over and he had experienced a wonderful freedom, he asked what had happened. During the entire deliverance, once the demons had manifested dramatically he had been unconscious. He was aware of the freedom, but did not recall the process of receiving it.

It is important for those who may experience dramatic manifestations not to be alarmed, but to work with the Lord and with the people ministering to them, or, if alone, to work with the Lord in the process of deliverance. It is the spirits who are afraid. Be strong on the inside and take your authority in the name of Jesus over the spirits manifesting and command them to leave you. Sometimes the dramatic manifestations can be reduced in intensity by strongly resisting the spirits and insisting that they go. This is done not only by commanding them audibly to go, but by inward or inaudible commands that they will hear and obey. People seeking to limit all manifestations may actually hinder the deliverance, as some spirits will only go when a measure of manifestation is experienced.

The other extreme is that once a spirit begins to manifest, the person does not strongly resist, but instead gives place to fear and does not fight at all. This is sure to give the spirits the freedom to express themselves, with no deliverance taking place, so that both the person and those praying for them may become weary and discouraged. One must get on the attack!

2. Mild manifestations

As spirits leave, the person may experience mild manifestations. Many spirits leave with the breath; that is, they go out through the mouth and nostrils. Not all, but many spirits leave this way. The word 'spirit' in both the Hebrew and Greek languages (in which the Bible was written) also means 'wind' or 'breath'. This is why we read of unclean spirits crying out with a loud voice as they leave a person (Mark 1:26). Rising with the breath and going out through the mouth, they expressed themselves by using the vocal chords of the person they had been afflicting.

With mild manifestations, a person may sense the stirring of a spirit or spirits and feel them rise and leave through the mouth. This may be expressed in yawning, coughing, burping, etc. Other mild manifestations can be pressure or pain in an area of the body, and release from it as commands for the spirits to go are continued.

3. Imperceptible manifestations

It is absolutely imperative to realise that much deliverance takes place in people's lives without them feeling that anything is happening. We minister freedom by faith and we receive freedom by faith. This is why I refer to imperceptible manifestations.[1]

Some years ago I took a seminar in a Danish church which had been praying for people for deliverance for more than two years. After the seminar the pastor said to me, 'What a revelation; what a revelation!' He told me that he had seen numerous people set free, but had thought that if there were no manifestations evident, there was no deliverance. Now he knew that major deliverances could take place without any manifestations being seen or felt. Because many others need this same revelation, I repeat it again and again as I teach people how to come into freedom. Yes, there are dramatic and mild manifestations, but there are imperceptible manifestations as well. And of course, during a time of prayer some people may experience all three types of manifestation.

Not only did I have to learn about imperceptible manifestations from personal experience when setting myself free, but when the gift of discernings of spirits began to operate in my life, I could see or perceive spirits leaving people even though some of those being prayed for felt nothing was happening. I talk about this important gift of the Holy Spirit and how it operates in Chapter 12.

Where do spirits go?

As spirits are cast out of people in Jesus name, the question is often asked, 'Where do they go?' I have heard people telling them to go to hell, but Jesus did not give us authority to direct them to any location. He simply told us to cast them out. To know where they go we need to hear from Jesus the Son of God Himself.

> *'Now when the unclean spirit goes out of a man, it passes through waterless places, seeking rest, and does not find it. Then it says, "I will return to my house from which I came"; and when it comes, it finds it unoccupied, swept, and put in order. Then it goes, and takes along with it seven other spirits more wicked than itself, and they go in and live there; and the last state of that man becomes worse than the first. That is the way it will also be with this evil generation.'* (Matthew 12:43–45)

Spirits look on a human life as a house in which they live. When they are evicted, they are like unruly tenants who have been evicted by a landlord. They wander around looking for somewhere to rest, and if unable to find a place, will even return to their former abode hoping to gain entrance. If the 'house' is found to be unoccupied, the spirit will want to re-enter with other spirits even more wicked than itself. This is why it is so important for people seeking deliverance to be willing to follow Jesus and allow Him, by His Holy Spirit, to fill their lives with His presence. If I do not sense that someone wanting prayer for deliverance is prepared to follow Jesus wholeheartedly, I will not pray for them.

For a Christian walking rightly with God, there need be no fear of any spirit driven from their life regaining entrance. If, however, a person is walking carelessly and deliberately embracing sin, they need to be afraid. There is a healthy fear – the fear of the Lord – which keeps us from returning to sinful ways and protects us from demonic intrusion.

The armour of God

Wonderful as it is to be set free from demonic bondage, it is more wonderful to be kept from coming into it in the first place. Years ago in New Zealand, when my wife Shirley and I were involved in evangelistic ministry, we worked with teams from churches. Many in these teams had experienced radical changes in their lives through turning to Christ. When some of them gave testimony of being set free from alcohol addiction, crime, immorality and so on, Shirley said to me one day that she did not have a testimony. Why? Because she had never experienced the sinful ways of this world. Growing up in a godly home, one of eleven children serving the Lord to this very day, and having opened her heart to Jesus at four or five years of age, she felt disqualified from having something vital to testify about. My response was that her testimony was greater than the others, because she had been kept by God's power through the years as the result of choosing to follow Christ and walk in His ways.

If you have grown up in a godly home and have not walked in the sinful ways of the world, rejoice in your wonderful testimony! Surely it is better to be kept from bondage than to become bound and have to be set free? Never be ashamed of such a testimony. By choosing to walk in God's ways, much protection is experienced. In the book of Ephesians we are exhorted to put on the armour of God and thus be protected from the attacks of Satan:

> *'Finally, be strong in the Lord, and in the strength of His might. Put on the full armour of God, that you may be able to stand firm against the schemes of the devil. For our struggle is not against flesh and blood, but against the rulers, against the powers, against the world forces of this darkness, against the spiritual forces of wickedness in the heavenly places. Therefore, take up the full armour of God, that you may be able to resist in the evil day, and having done everything, to stand firm.'* (Ephesians 6:10–13)

The next five verses state the various parts of God's protective armour:

- the girdle of truth
- the breastplate of righteousness
- the shoes of the preparation of the gospel of peace
- the shield of faith
- the helmet of salvation
- the sword of the Spirit
- praying at all times in the Spirit

Putting on the armour

For years as a Christian I would wake in the morning and put on the armour for the new day by confessing Jesus Christ to be each

piece of the armour to me. Then it dawned on me that if I was
having to put on the armour every day, I must have taken it off. I
realised that I needed the armour on both day and night. From
that time on, I simply confessed that I was walking in the
protection of the Lord. Romans 12:12 exhorts us to lay aside
the deeds of darkness and put on the armour of light. Verse 14 tells
us to put on the Lord Jesus Christ and make no provision for the
lusts of the flesh. Important as it is to have a continual confession
on our lips of our identity in Christ and our protection in Him,
what is happening in our heart? If things are not right in our heart,
we will not know the keeping power of God, no matter what
confession may be on our lips. I once read the following descrip-
tion of the armour of God:

> 'The full armour of God is a set of life conditions that God
> wants to establish in our lives, that will enable God to work
> in us and hinder or prevent Satan from working in us.'

In Luke 11:21 we see reference to the armour of Satan, and it is
the opposite of the armour of God. We could therefore say:

> 'The full armour of Satan is a set of life conditions that Satan
> wants to establish in our lives, that will enable Satan to work
> in us and hinder or prevent God from working in us.'

Which kingdom are we living in? Which spiritual power do we
yield to day by day?

> *'Do not be deceived, God is not mocked; for whatsoever a man
> sows, this he will also reap. For the one who sows to his own flesh
> shall from the flesh reap corruption, but the one who sows to the
> Spirit shall from the Spirit reap eternal life.'*   (Galatians 6:7, 8)

Years ago I counselled a man who was greatly troubled. He
believed that he had AIDS, even though every medical test proved
otherwise. A strong fear gripped his life and no one could persuade
him that he was not infected. Personally, I believe he was under a
delusion, but most people who are deceived cannot recognise it.
How did this dilemma arise? A Christian businessman, he had
been away from home and staying in a motel opposite a striptease
joint. With time on his hands and knowing that no-one would
recognise him at this place of entertainment, he spent the evening
there and brought one of the strippers back to the motel and slept

with her. The next morning a fear came upon him that he had contracted the HIV virus because of this casual sexual encounter. From that time on, his life went downhill. When one doctor pronounced him free of AIDS he would go to another, and another, not believing their diagnosis. By the time he talked to me he said, 'I have lost everything – my wife, my children, my businesses. I only have one million dollars left!' I was unable to help him. He was in the hands of the tormentors (demons) and reaping the consequences of his wrong sowing. Had he been walking in the fear of the Lord, this situation would never have arisen. When the temptation first came to him to visit the striptease joint, he should have resisted it. He should have reaffirmed that he had chosen to walk in the paths of right-eousness and not of unrighteousness.

When we make a decision to do what is right and honouring to God, we can draw from God's strength and become an overcomer. But we have to make that decision. Remember the definition of God's protective armour: 'The full armour of God is a set of life conditions that God wants to establish in our lives, that will enable God to work in us and hinder or prevent Satan from working in us.' Do not give the devil a place. Maintain a confession of who Jesus is to you, but also keep your heart right with the Lord. What tragedies will be averted! What freedom will be maintained! What blessings will be experienced!

Sowing and reaping

The moment I surrendered my life to Jesus, 'eternity' was stamped on my heart. Before that time I had been engrossed in living only for the temporal. Now I became aware that it was important to be living in a righteous way, because there was a law of sowing and reaping working in every life which had repercussions both in time and eternity.

A small booklet came into my possession with some sermons by the late evangelist, Dwight Moody. His message on sowing and reaping had a great impact on me. He described life as a field bordered by the fence of time, and that each of us has a field into which we are sowing seeds day by day. As a consequence, we will all experience a reaping. He listed the following points, which I have often pondered over the years:

1.   When a man sows he expects to reap.
2.   A man reaps the same kind of seed as he sows.

3. Ignorance of the seed makes no difference.
4. A man reaps more than he sows.

We are all aware of the law of sowing and reaping in the natural realm, but have we considered how it applies to the spiritual realm? Knowing that we reap the same kind of seed as we sow, we do not plant potatoes and expect to reap carrots. We know that being ignorant of the seed we sow will not alter the kind of return we will get. Imagine asking a farmer, who is seeding his fields in the springtime, what kind of seed he is sowing. If he was to say he did not know, you would immediately think him very foolish. And yet this is how most people live. Daily they are sowing seeds into the field of their life, giving little or no thought as to what seeds are being sown or to the harvest they will inevitably reap. Incidentally, there can be crop failures in the natural realm but not in the spiritual realm. The final point carries the greatest impact: people reap more than they sow.

For a few years Shirley and I lived in one of the prime wheat-growing areas of Australia. Every summer I enjoyed helping some of my farmer friends harvest their crops. The amount of wheat harvested – and it was immense – resulted from a relatively small amount of seed sown. One day I actually counted the number of seeds on the heads of the stools of wheat produced by one little grain. There were over eight hundred new seeds from one seed sown. Applied to the spiritual realm, we can see this law bringing blessing to some and cursing to others.

As we sow seeds of obedience to God in the field of our life, as we sow seeds of love, kindness, forgiveness, honesty and so on, we are assured of a good return. If we sow seeds of rebellion, selfishness, anger, immorality, prejudice, dishonesty, etc., we are also assured of a return, but it will not be good. Multitudes are reaping the pain of careless sowing. The tragedy is that if we do not turn away from this wrong way of living, and turn to God and receive His forgiveness and His power to live rightly, we will continue to reap pain and eventually the eternal consequences of our sowing. When a person sows, they reap much more than they sow. Much, much more!

Are you daily choosing to follow Jesus? Are you embracing a lifestyle that will enable God to work in you and will hinder or prevent Satan from working in you? The choice is yours and mine. Sometimes I tell people that since becoming a Christian I have never backslidden, that is, gone back to the ways of the world. I also say that I have no intention of backsliding in the future. I say this not to boast, but to exhort others to be strong in their commitment to Christ. I know what I have been saved from, and I have experienced the delivering power of God. Why should I want to go back to the ways of darkness and bondage? Why should you?

Be strong in the Lord and in the strength of His might!

Chapter 9

Understanding Our Enemy

When Jesus commissioned His followers to cast out demons, He was not commanding them to deal with impersonal forces troubling people, but with living spirit beings that are just as real as we are. While we live and function in the seen world, demons live and function in the unseen world.

Just imagine two nations at war. What a tremendous advantage one army would have if somehow its troops had the ability to become invisible. This invisible army could cross borders, infiltrate the ranks of its foes with relative ease and strike without warning. Even when an attack took place, the army under attack would not know how to respond, unless it had some insight into what the invisible army was like and how it operated. Because our enemy is invisible, we too need this insight, so that when an attack comes we can counter-attack appropriately. More than that, with understanding we can go on the offensive, put the invisible foes to flight and destroy their stratagems.

I often say that when we know what we are dealing with, the enemy knows that we know, and that is when things happen. In other words, when we discern the work and tactics of this invisible enemy, we can make the appropriate spiritual response, rather than respond with merely natural – and therefore mainly ineffective – means. Spiritual warfare must be engaged in, fought and won, using spiritual weaponry.

> 'For our struggle is not against flesh and blood, but against the rulers, against the powers, against the world forces of this darkness, against the spiritual forces of wickedness in the heavenly places.'
> (Ephesians 6:12)

As the Bible so clearly reveals, our struggle is not primarily with fellow human beings, but with evil spirits working behind and through them. It is imperative, therefore, that we have understanding of how our enemy operates.

Personality of spirits

Evil spirits exhibit the characteristics associated with personality:

▶ *Self-awareness*

When Jesus confronted the ruling spirit in a man who was highly demonised, he asked the spirit its name. The spirit responded that its name was Legion (Mark 5:9). When He commanded a deaf and dumb spirit to leave a troubled boy, it did so only after throwing him into terrible convulsions (Mark 9:25, 26). Evil spirits have self-awareness, they know who they are and the tasks they have to carry out.

Paul was annoyed by the daily statements of a slave girl, who, although speaking the truth, was actually a vessel for utterances by a spirit of fortune-telling. When Paul's annoyance reached a peak, he commanded the spirit to leave the girl, and it did. This spirit knew who it was, and it had to obey the authority exercised by Paul in the name of Jesus. As a result, the girl could no longer function as a fortune-teller. The wrath of those profiting from the spirit was then directed against Paul and Silas, who were thrown into prison (Acts 16:16–24).

▶ *Knowledge*

Some Jewish exorcists who did not have a personal relationship with Jesus attempted to take authority over evil spirits. Consequently, they were not able to exercise authority in the name of Jesus. They could only say, *'I adjure you by Jesus whom Paul preaches'* (Acts 19:13). A spirit responded to these seven sons of Sceva, speaking through the lips of the man they sought to help, saying, *'I recognise Jesus, and I know about Paul, but who are you?'* (Acts 19:15). This spirit certainly had knowledge and was quick to say that it recognised who Jesus was.

When Jesus attended the synagogue in Capernaum, an evil spirit in a man was alarmed by His presence. Crying out through the man, it said, *'What do we have to do with You, Jesus of Nazareth? Have you come to destroy us? I know who You are – the Holy One of God!'* (Mark 1:24). Evil spirits have knowledge.

▶ *Speech*

In this account in Mark chapter 1, we read of an unclean spirit crying out, using the vocal chords of the person it inhabited. When evil spirits manifest they sometimes speak out in this way. The voice may sound the same as a human voice, or it may sound altogether different – leaving no doubt that it is not a human voice. In Mark 3:11 we read,

> *'And whenever the unclean spirits beheld Him, they would fall down before Him and cry out saying, "You are the Son of God!"'*

In times of public ministry, it is not uncommon for spirits to cry out as you approach someone to minister to them. The very anointing of the Holy Spirit triggers a demonic response in the individual that is both seen and heard.

Evil spirits also speak in the minds of people, but others do not hear them. Many people are troubled by inner voices. The words spoken can be downright diabolical and tormenting, or much subtler, even posing as the voice of God. If that is the case, a deceiving spirit is seeking to affect the person.

▶ *Will*

Will is the faculty of conscious and deliberate choice or action. Demons have chosen to rebel against God and to afflict people made in the image and likeness of God. They are without conscience, and deployed by Satan to cause people to struggle under heavy burdens, often of extreme intensity. Jesus said that He had come to give abundant life, whereas Satan was a thief who seeks to steal, kill and destroy.[1]

Jesus taught that when an unclean spirit goes out of a person it desires to return to the house it was evicted from, saying, *'I will return to my house from which I came'* (Matthew 12:44). Demons look on a human life as a 'house', and if driven out will often seek to re-enter. It is therefore important that Jesus fills the house by His Holy Spirit. Only as we are committed to following Jesus Christ and walking in obedience to Him, can we guarantee our house being kept free from demonic intrusion.

▶ *Emotion*

Just as we are emotional beings, so too are demons. Both in the scriptural accounts of confronting and driving out demons and in present-day encounters, evil spirits may express emotions such as fear when they are cast out. In Matthew 8:29 we read of the spirits in two demonised men expressing great fear: *'What do we have to do with You, Son of God? Have You come here to torment us before the time?'* The spirits knew they were to face eternal judgement and were afraid that their punishment would start sooner than anticipated. Often when casting out demons I remind them of the judgement to come, and tell them that the more they torment people in time, the greater will be their judgement in eternity.[2]

Some folk come to churches where there is lively praise and worship, good teaching from the Word of God, and opportunities for people to receive prayer for deliverance and healing. Yet they feel uneasy. This is often the result of evil spirits in them feeling very uncomfortable in such a setting, knowing that if the person they are binding stays too long, they may be driven out. The demons are uncomfortable and therefore the person indwelt by them feels uncomfortable – sensing the negative emotions felt by the demons. Often not knowing why they feel this way, a person may say that every time they go to such and such a church they feel uncomfortable, and may even stop going there.

Families of spirits

Spirits work together in groups or families. In other words, we are usually dealing with many spirits, not just one spirit, in an area of bondage. The Bible says of Mary Magdelene that Jesus cast seven demons out of her.[3] Personally, I do not believe that only seven demons were driven from her, but many more. There were seven areas of bondage, yes, but in each area of bondage there are usually multiple spirits to be dealt with.

In the Mark chapter 5 account of a demonised man coming to Jesus, the Scripture simply says that a man with an unclean spirit met Him. In the first seven verses of this account, every reference to the demonic is in the singular, and it appears that one very strong demon was tormenting this man. So strong was it, that even shackles and chains used to restrain the man had been broken. No-one was strong enough to subdue him. He would cry out and mutilate himself with stones, and lived among the tombs. Obviously the demon binding him was particularly strong. However, the account goes on to reveal that there were many spirits in him. I believe Jesus used this occasion to teach His disciples how demons operated, and how multiple demons may need casting out to set a person free.

For the record, talking of multiples, I believe that multiple personalities in a person are simply multiple demons in them. To treat these as parts of the human personality; to reconcile part with part; to get the parts not saved, saved; to merge the parts together and so on, is utter nonsense. This teaching and practice has no Scriptural basis, and those functioning in this kind of ministry have no biblical mandate. A spirit of deception is at work!

Even though this spirit cried out with a loud voice, *'What do I have to do with You, Jesus, Son of the Most High God? I implore You by God, do not torment me!'* and even though Jesus had said to this demon, *'Come out of the man, you unclean spirit!'* the account changes from the singular to the plural from verse 9: *'And He was asking him, "What is your name?" And he said to Him, "My name is legion; for we are many"'* (Mark 5:9). Why did Jesus ask this demon its name? Was it because He did not know it? No. Jesus knew the name of the demon and He knew that multiple demons inhabited this man, but by asking the demon its name at least two things happened.

First, the demon was forced to bow before the Son of the Most High God, and second, the disciples were taught that even though Jesus was commanding one spirit to come out of the man, He was actually addressing multitudes of spirits. Behind the ruling spirit in this life, or the strong man, there were many assistants! Jesus was filled without measure with the Holy Spirit and moved in the gift of discernings of spirits, so knew well what He was encountering, but the disciples did not. What an insight they were to receive! What an insight we need to receive. Spirits work together in groups or families.

There can be many spirits in a stronghold, all with the same name and the same function. If a stronghold of rejection binds a person, there is not one spirit of rejection to cast out, but many spirits of rejection. If a stronghold of fear binds someone, there is not one spirit of fear to be dealt with, but many spirits of fear.

Legions of spirits

In New Testament days a Roman legion was a military body of three thousand to six thousand foot soldiers, plus three hundred to seven hundred cavalry. Each legion of six thousand was divided into ten cohorts of three maniples each and each maniple into two centuries. In other words, there were sixty centuries or companies in every legion. Just as there was order, structure and chain of command in a Roman legion, Jesus was teaching His disciples something of the demonic structure that there can be in a human life. When Jesus sought to set the demoniac man free, He did not seek out a centurion but went right to the top – to the head of the legion. Once the leader had been dealt with, it would be so much easier to deal with the lesser ranking officers and common soldiers, so to speak.

Because spirits work together in groups, whenever I am casting out demons I may speak in the singular, 'Come out, you unclean spirit', but I always think in the plural, 'Come out, you unclean spirits'. No wonder this demoniac was in such a plight. There was not one spirit binding him, but a multitude. This poses a problem for those of us raised in the West, who find it difficult to grasp such spiritual realities. I mean, how many sardines will fit into a can? How many university students can squeeze into a telephone booth? How big is a demon anyway? We must open our hearts and minds to the Word of God and allow the Holy Spirit to grant us insight into the things that are spiritually discerned.

> 'Now we have received, not the spirit of the world, but the Spirit who is from God, that we might know the things freely given to us by God, which things we also speak, not in words taught by human wisdom, but in those taught by the Spirit, combining spiritual thoughts with spiritual words. But a natural man does not accept the things of the Spirit of God; for they are foolishness to him, and he cannot understand them, because they are spiritually appraised.' (1 Corinthians 2:12–4)

From personal experience, I know the reality of many spirits needing to be cast out of an area of bondage. Think of a mooring rope securing a vessel to a wharf: the bigger the vessel, the thicker the mooring lines. Some have thousands of very fine fibres woven together to make the ropes. Each strand is thin and can be easily broken. A few strands together can also be broken without much difficulty. However, put multiple strands together and it becomes impossible to break the strength of the combined fibres without a sharp knife. As in the natural realm, where some people are physically stronger than others, so in the spiritual realm. Some spirits have more strength or exert more authority than others, but generally speaking, spirits gain their strength through numbers. The stronger the bondage, the more spirits there are to be dealt with.

Learning to persevere

A person can receive deliverance from demons, say in the area of rejection, and notice a change has taken place, yet still be struggling with rejection, although perhaps not as much as before. For some this brings confusion, because they know they were delivered during a particular session of prayer and yet the need has resurfaced. Concerns arise that perhaps they allowed the spirits to re-enter. If so, how could this have happened? Perhaps the person sinned? But when did they sin, and so on.

What actually happened is this. A measure of deliverance from rejection did occur. Numerous strands of the rope were severed, but further strands need to be cut through. It is not that something went out and came back in. Something went out and stayed out, but more deliverance is needed; further strands must be cut for complete deliverance to be achieved. Of course, if a person was living carelessly and not diligently maintaining their relationship with God, spirits could have re-entered. Those walking in righteousness, however, should have no such fear. Some spirits have gone, but more need to be cast out. The person is not getting bound and free and bound and free, but freer and freer, until full freedom from rejection is reached.

How can a person know when full deliverance has been received? The answer is simple: they no longer have a problem with rejection as before. No more reactions of rejection trouble them. Sometimes a person can receive deliverance and yet not feel any different, and wonder why this is the case. Think of someone carrying a load of one hundred bricks on their back. If five bricks were taken off, they would probably not notice any difference in the weight. If another five bricks were taken off, again they might not be aware of a significant change. But as the process continues, five here and five there, the person will begin to notice a change taking place.

Sometimes a person suddenly becomes aware that a deliverance has taken place. A young woman asked for prayer after a Sunday morning service. She had struggled with depression for several years. When prayed for, she felt nothing happen. On the Monday, however, she suddenly realised that the depression had gone. Not only that, but pain from a whiplash injury that she had suffered for the same number of years had gone as well. She was excited, but wanted to test this healing before testifying publicly. When Wednesday night came, she shared with the congregation what the Lord had done for her on Sunday, and how she had not become aware of her freedom until Monday. Great deliverance can be experienced without a realisation of it at the time.

Conversing with spirits

In the account of the demoniac man in Mark 5, Jesus asked the demon its name, and I gave two reasons why I believe He did so. There are those who ask spirits their names and even hold conversations with spirits, seeking to draw information from them. Be aware that the testimony of demons is unreliable, because they lie and will seek to deceive if they possibly can. It is not that there will never be a time when you need to ask a demon its name, but you need discernment. If a demon responds by naming itself, is it telling the truth? Truly, discernment is required. Personally, I discourage asking evil spirits questions or holding conversations with them. I have seen people led into deception in this way. I would much rather ask the Lord Jesus for the information, because Jesus always tells the truth.

There is a gift of discernings of spirits and a gift of the word of knowledge, whereby we can hear from God, and need not rely on demonic testimony. God has not left the church without the means, through the Holy Spirit, to receive important knowledge and discernment that will break open lives to His delivering and healing power.

▶ Why the swine?

When the demons asked to be sent into the swine, Jesus gave them permission, knowing what would happen. The two thousand swine were so agitated by this intrusion that they rushed down a steep bank and were drowned in the sea.[4] Why, you ask, did Jesus allow this? I believe it was easier for the demons to leave when they had another house to go into. Certainly, it made it easier for the man with the 'legion' to experience deliverance. It is extremely traumatic for a person to receive such a major deliverance in a short period of time. Jesus was more concerned for the man than for the animals. The result of this marvellous deliverance was that the former demoniac became normal in every respect. He could think his own thoughts, clothe himself, hold a normal conversation and make rational choices. Only Jesus Christ could bring about such a transformation, and He continues to do the same today. What a wonderful Saviour He is![5]

How do evil spirits gain entrance?

The enemy has many opportunities to gain entrance into a person's life, and we will consider some of them. From the womb to the grave, Satan seeks to steal, kill and destroy. This does not mean that we have to be afraid of the enemy. Actually, Satan is afraid that a believer in Jesus Christ will recognise who they are in Christ, and use the authority Jesus has given them over the works of darkness. Also, I talk of entry points not to magnify the enemy, but to bring awareness of his tactics, so that we will be on the alert and can counter-attack where necessary. The enemy is afraid of us – we should not be afraid of him.

1. Generational sin

Ongoing sin at work in a life will give place to the activity of evil spirits. In fact, one of the functions of evil spirits is to lead people into sin. Unless this sin is dealt with as outlined in the Bible, the enemy continues to enjoy a lodging place in a person and to influence them negatively. Not only can our sin give spirits a place, but sin operating in former generations may have given spirits a place. Spirits can be passed down a generational line, finding a place even from the mother's womb. The Bible talks about the iniquities of the fathers being visited upon the children until the third and fourth generation. And it does not end there. Unless there is a turning to the true and living God through Jesus Christ his Son, this infiltration continues generation by generation.

When God gave Moses the Ten Commandments, the very first command was to not follow any other god apart from Himself. The second was not to fashion any idol representing another god, nor to worship it. If these laws were broken, there would be serious consequences:

> *'You shall not worship or serve them; for I the Lord your God am a jealous God, visiting the iniquity of the fathers on the children, on the third and fourth generation of those who hate Me, but showing lovingkindness to thousands, to those who love Me and keep My commandments.'*   (Exodus 20:5, 6)

It was around midnight and I was leaving a meeting. Two people were still in the building, an Indian lady and the youth pastor. The lady asked if I would pray for her. As I asked her name, I became aware that a curse was operating in her life. I rebuked a spirit of death, which immediately manifested and she fell to the floor while being delivered. As the word of knowledge flowed, I spoke out a breaking of every influence of Hinduism in her life. The deliverance was swift and powerful, and witnessed by the youth pastor. When the woman stood to her feet, she said that she was from a Hindu family, and the only Christian in her family. She was delighted with what the Lord had done for her.

The youth pastor then asked for prayer. When I asked his name, I became aware that he had been born out of wedlock, and as a result had come under a curse from the womb.[6] I took authority over spirits of rejection that had found a place while he was being formed in the womb, and he felt the spirits rising and leaving him. Again, the Lord worked swiftly and powerfully. When the prayer was over he expressed how wonderful he felt. Apparently, both he and his sister had been conceived out of wedlock and had been adopted shortly after birth. Only two weeks earlier, he said, they had been talking about the similar struggles they had experienced. He went on to say, 'I can't wait to see my sister to tell her what Jesus has done for me, because I believe He wants to do the same for her.'

Each of us has two birth parents, four grandparents, eight great-grandparents and sixteen great-great-grandparents, totalling thirty persons in all. What sort of entrance could have been given in the family line because of their sin? Are we struggling in any area because of bondage that has come down the generational line?

2. Personal sin

Just because we sin does not mean that we automatically open ourselves up to demonic bondage, although this does sometimes happen. For instance, the first time a person commits adultery, he or she might not only give place to adulterous spirits, or strengthen adulterous spirits already at work in their life, but could also could give place to spirits of guilt and shame. We must not be afraid in a wrong way of giving place to the enemy, but afraid in a right way. The fear of the Lord is a healthy fear that we all need more of. This fear keeps us from deliberately pursuing a life of sin, and therefore keeps us in a place of safety from enemy occupation.[7]

As a believer, when we are aware that we have sinned against the Lord, we are to immediately repent and ask God's forgiveness, and the blood of Jesus cleanses us from the defilement of sin and restores our relationship with God.[8] If we sin and deliberately keep on sinning, and are unwilling to deal with the sin and receive God's forgiveness, we are in danger of giving place to the activity of demons. The Scriptures warn us, as we have seen, not to give place to the devil through failing to deal with sin.[9]

3. Unforgiveness

Although unforgiveness comes under the category of sin, it is such a door opener for the demonic it is worth a separate mention. So many harbour unforgiveness and have given place to roots of bitterness.

> *'See to it that no one comes short of the grace of God; that no root of bitterness springing up causes trouble, and by it many be defiled.'*   (Hebrews 12:15)

Bitterness causes trouble both for the person harbouring it and for those they associate with. It gives place to the enemy, and can hinder freedom being received and physical healing being experienced.

A few years ago, a lady asked me for prayer for physical healing. For years she had struggled with many infirmities and pains. The previous week she had gone to my wife with the same request. Shirley had said she would pray for her when she was willing to forgive those whom she harboured unforgiveness towards. My answer was the same. It was imperative that she forgive those who had offended her. A week later she returned for prayer, having forgiven from her heart those she had been bitter towards. What she then said surprised me. She had begun to confess to the Lord her bitterness and to forgive those who had offended her, but there were so many people that it took seven hours of confession before everything was dealt with.

Seven hours! I do not need seven minutes or even seven seconds to deal with any unforgiveness. As soon as I sense any bitterness seeking to get into my life, I immediately deal with it. I refuse to harbour unforgiveness. It is too costly. Unforgiveness brings bondage and defilement. Needless to say, having dealt with the sin in her heart, the Lord Jesus touched her significantly.

4. Emotional crises

Is there anyone who has not experienced some form of emotional upheaval at one time or another? If a person has not yet, they certainly will in the future. However, the enemy seeks to use emotional crisis to gain entrance if he possibly can.

Life is full of crises from the womb until death. Crisis through being the object of an abortion that did not succeed. Coming into the world as a premature baby and being isolated from close contact with a mother for days, weeks or longer. Divorce tearing a family apart. Abuse of numerous kinds as a child growing up – physical, verbal, mental or sexual. Fear because of a father's drunkenness, outbursts of anger and violence. Teasing and rejection at school. Failing at school and never being able to succeed. A broken heart through being jilted in a relationship. Marrying and being rejected by a spouse for another. Sustaining a serious injury through an accident and all future plans having to be abandoned. The loss of someone very close through disease or accident. Being traumatised through civil war or unrest. Penniless because of gross injustice. A refugee with no place to call home. Poverty-stricken because of a natural disaster caused by wind, rain, drought or earthquake. The list goes on.

It is not that everyone comes into bondage through such crises, but certainly many do. Spirits of fear come in during times of fear. Spirits of bitterness come in during times of injustice. Spirits of depression and despair come in during times of loss, and so on.

5. Occult involvement

One of the most troubling phenomena of our generation, particularly in the West, is the increase of witchcraft in various forms and varieties. Through popular childrens' books, games, video games and movies, producers and promoters are out to make money by playing on the current fascination with witchcraft and the supernatural. Children are being taught to curse and control other people through such influences. Although people may think they are playing games, many are unknowingly opening themselves to demonic powers and bringing their lives into bondage. In the process, they grieve a loving God who made people to relate to Himself, in the realm of light, rather than relating to satanic powers who operate in darkness.

There is a great price to pay for entering the realm of working with evil spirits. Curses abound on those who do such things. True, Satan will see that some of those promoting such evil activity will become very rich, but what is temporal wealth in the light of accountability to God and the coming judgement? Jesus said,

> 'For what will a man be profited, if he gains the whole world and forfeits his soul? Or what will a man give in exchange for his soul?'
> (Matthew 16:26)

For any involved in occult activities, it is imperative that they change their mind about what they are doing, and renounce such practices and every spirit they have given place to through their involvement.

6. Pronouncements and vows

Words carry more influence and power than most of us realise. The Scripture says that death and life are in the power of the tongue. Words can be taken by God to impart encouragement and blessing, or they can be taken by evil spirits to bring discouragement and cursing.[10] Of course, many words are neutral, attracting neither of these anointings, nevertheless we need to be guarded in what we say, lest we curse rather than bless.

While living in Australia I remember vividly the lady next door cursing her son in a time of rage, shouting, 'I hate you, I hate you. I wish I could kill you!' How do you think those words may have affected her four-year-old son? Another lady we know desired to be reconciled to her father, who had rejected her throughout his life. When she visited him on his deathbed, hoping to hear words of love and acceptance, he continued to curse her and tell her that he hated her. Do you think that those words could have played a part in causing her to want to commit suicide after this failure in reconciliation? Others make inward vows that bind themselves from entering into the provisions and blessings of life:

- 'No one will ever hurt me again.'
- 'I will never get married.'
- 'I will never trust anyone again.'

And so on.

By making such vows, one is in danger of coming into bondage to an evil spirit that will seek to bring this vow to pass.

7. Ignorance

When a person is ignorant they can be taken advantage of. A group of us visited a European country for the first time. On arrival, we went to a restaurant and asked for the menu. We were told that there was no menu and we would have to eat what we were offered. Having finished our meal we paid the bill, not realising that we were paying three times what we should have. Once we become aware of meal prices in that country, we never ordered a meal again unless we could see it on a menu with the price alongside. We were easy prey for a local man who realised we were newcomers. Our ignorance caused us to be taken advantage of.

Demons will seek to rob us of freedom if we are not sure of what is normal or abnormal. We can be enduring a curse, rather than experiencing a blessing, if we do not know God's will on a matter. For instance, many Christians are labouring under the curse of sickness, believing it is God's will to endure such an affliction. If we believe this, we will not be seeking healing or be able to release faith in God for healing. In the Scriptures, we see that Jesus not only took our sins upon Himself at the cross and carried them away, He also took our sicknesses and diseases and carried them away. God's will is that we experience both forgiveness and healing.[11]

It is helpful to read Deuteronomy 28, which lists the blessings that follow those who obey God and the cursings that follow those who disobey Him. Many people are burdened by curses, believing it is God's will to be in such a state. Let us not be ignorant. Let us be an informed people through knowing the Word of God.

Recently a couple involved in church leadership asked me to pray for them for deliverance. I asked if there were areas where they knew that they needed to be set free. The husband had no difficulty in naming some, but his wife said she was not aware of any. I probed a little, hoping she would be able to express an area where she may have been struggling, but to no avail. She wanted prayer for deliverance, but was not consciously aware of any area of bondage. Fortunately, the Lord knows us so well and is concerned that we come into freedom. As we began to pray, strongholds of fear were exposed. This dear woman was extremely bound by fear and had struggled with fears all her life. She had known nothing but a life dominated by fear. Because this was 'normal', she did not know what it would be like to be otherwise. She could in all honesty say that she was not aware of any need. She was functioning on a level far below where God wanted her to be. Ignorance can give the enemy an opportunity to take advantage of us.

There are many more ways that give opportunity for evil spirits to gain entrance into a life, but we will move on to discover how we can become free from spirits of bondage. Before we do so, however, there is an important question to be answered.

Chapter 10

Can a Christian
Be Demon-possessed?

Can a Christian be demon-possessed? This is often asked, and the answer is of great importance. In this chapter we will look at the Scriptures that give clear insight on this issue. First, however, we should look at what the word 'possess' means. Its first meaning in Collins English Dictionary is 'to have as one's property, own'. Another meaning is 'to gain control over' or 'dominate'. The word 'possession' is listed as meaning 'anything that is owned or possessed; the state of being controlled or dominated by or as if by evil spirits'. Now let us turn to the Greek language from which our New Testament translations are derived. The word often translated as 'demon-possessed' is *daimonizomai*. According to Strong's Concordance and Vine's Expository Dictionary of New Testament Words, this word means 'to be exercised by a demon, to have a demon, to be vexed by a demon, to be possessed with a demon, to act under the control of a demon'.

When one thinks of possession one tends to think of ownership. So when the question is asked, 'Can a Christian be demon-possessed?' the answer would have to be No. That is, a Christian is not owned by the devil, but is owned by God. However, if the question is asked another way, 'Can a Christian have a demon or act under the control of a demon?' the answer would have to be Yes. The word 'possession' never occurs in Bible passages of evil spirits being cast out of individuals. Greek words for ownership or possession such as *katecho, ktaomai, huparcho, echo, peripoiesis, chorion, ktema* and *huparxus* are not in the original text. The idea of possession is the interpretation of the Greek term by Bible translators. The Latin Vulgate version of the Bible, prepared by St Jerome in the fourth century, translates *daimonizomai* with the simple expression, 'to have a demon'.

The Bible speaks of doctrines or teachings of demons:

> *'But the Spirit explicitly says that in the later times some will fall away from the faith, paying attention to deceitful spirits and doctrines of demons.'*   (1 Timothy 4:1)

One of the doctrines that demonic powers have successfully deceived many Christians into believing is that a Christian cannot be bound by an evil spirit. Western Christianity in particular has embraced this lie. As a result, many Christians struggle unnecessarily with inward conflicts that they find no answers for in their churches. The logic is that if a Christian cannot be bound by demons, a Christian does not need to experience deliverance from demons.

Is deliverance for the Christian or the non-Christian?

Deliverance is primarily for those who turn to Christ and choose to follow and serve Him. I know of no evangelist who goes around delivering people from demonic bondages and telling them that they do not need to follow Jesus, or that they can keep on living in sin once they have received freedom. Instead, the evangelist proclaims:

> 'Come to Jesus the Son of God. Jesus loves you and died on a cross for you. His death and rising from the dead have opened the way to the Father. Turn from your sin and surrender to the claims of Christ. There is forgiveness, deliverance and healing through Jesus Christ. Choose to follow Jesus now. Confess Him as your Lord. Let Him empower you by the Holy Spirit.'

It is as people respond to Christ that they can be prayed for to receive deliverance and healing.

Jesus clearly taught, as we have seen, that when an unclean spirit goes out of a person it will seek to return and bring some other spirits as well. This is why the 'house' needs to be occupied or filled with the presence of the Lord Jesus. If non-Christians receive prayer for deliverance and do not choose to allow Jesus to take control of their lives, there is no guarantee that they will retain any freedom received.

Saved while being delivered

Two recent experiences have confirmed to me the power of deliverance prayer for unbelievers whose hearts are seeking God. One Sunday in a church in Europe, I was to preach the gospel at a service specially designed to reach non-Christians. Before the service commenced, I inquired if there were many non-Christians in the meeting. A couple and their daughter were pointed out to me in the second row, and a few others. When it was time for prayer ministry after the preaching, this family responded. Through an interpreter, I was asked to pray for the daughter, who had asthma. I asked the wife if she was a Christian, and she said she was. She had opened her heart to Christ during the meeting when I had led people in a prayer of salvation.

The husband, however, told me he was not a believer. When I asked if he wanted to surrender his life to Christ, he said he did not want to do so. But he wanted prayer for the healing of an asthmatic condition. Lifting my heart to the Lord, I asked Him what to do. The man was not a Christian, apparently did not want to become a Christian, and yet was asking for healing. I felt led to go ahead and pray for him. When I took authority over spirits of infirmity, they manifested and he fell to the floor. After a few minutes, as he lay on his back amidst the manifestations, I heard him giving thanks to Jesus. I stopped praying and asked him if was now ready to give his life to Christ. He said he was. Right then and there, lying on his back at the front of the church, he asked God to forgive him and welcomed Jesus into his life. We then discovered something even his wife was not aware of. He had been secretly reading the Bible for about two years. He had been seeking God. His heart was open to the Lord.

Again, while speaking at a Youth With A Mission (YWAM) Discipleship Training School (DTS), I was told that one of the students from South Korea was not a Christian. Before the DTS began, she had been in touch with the school leaders to say that she was not a Christian, but was seeking God and requested admission to the school. The staff prayed and felt they were to allow her to come. On the Thursday, along with a woman staff member, we prayed with her at her request. Here she was, a non-Christian, asking for deliverance prayer. The Holy Spirit guided us for thirty minutes or so on how to pray. We came against spirits of unbelief, among others, that were blinding her mind and causing her to be unable to understand the gospel. Her background was Buddhist. All the time we were praying there were evident demonic manifestations as she was being set free. Suddenly she cried out, 'Now I can believe; now I can believe!' She then prayed to the Lord Jesus and had a significant life-changing encounter with Him She received the forgiveness of sins and the gift of eternal life.

We continued to pray and cast further spirits out of her life. Without warning, her body lurched back as particular spirits manifested. She grasped my left hand and squeezed it tightly – so tightly, in fact, that I was in pain because I had a wedding ring on one finger and my blood circulation was cut off. My fingers turned blue. Just as suddenly, a great release came in her life, resulting in the release of my hand, for which I was very thankful. She was filled with deep gratitude to God for what He was doing in her and with a great joy that only the Lord can bring. Although she was not a Christian when prayer commenced, she too came to Christ in the midst of receiving deliverance. God touched her because she was seeking to find Him and to know Him.

Spirit, soul and body

Before we look at the Scriptures which clearly indicate that a Christian can come under the influence of evil spirits, let us consider the makeup of a human being. Man has been created on a higher level than that of animals. Man has a spirit, whereas animals do not. Man has been created in the image and likeness of God (Genesis 1:26). The apostle Paul prayed,

> 'Now may the God of peace Himself sanctify you entirely; and may your spirit and soul and body be preserved complete, without blame at the coming of our Lord Jesus Christ.'
> (1 Thessalonians 5:23)

Man, through his spirit, has God-awareness; through his soul he has self-awareness; and through his body he has world-awareness.

▶ *Man's spirit*

It is through our spirit that we communicate with God. It is with our spirit that we worship God (John 4:24). It is into our spirit that Jesus comes to dwell when we confess Him as Lord. A spiritual birthing takes place when we say 'Yes' to Jesus.

> 'That which is born of the flesh is flesh, and that which is born of the Spirit is spirit.'
> (John 3:6)

It is in our spirit that we have the witness that we are a child of God:

> 'The one who believes in the Son of God has the witness in himself.'   (1 John 5:10)

> 'The Spirit Himself bears witness with our spirit that we are children of God.'   (Romans 8:16)

▶ *Man's soul*

The realm of the soul comprises our mind, emotions and will. Our mind: 'I think'. Our emotions: 'I feel'. Our will: 'I want'. Many of our struggles and battles take place here, particularly in the mind. The soul realm is subject to demonic infiltration. It is here that a Christian can 'have a demon' or 'act under the control of a demon', or we could use a transliteration of the word *daimonizomai* and say, be 'demonised'.

▶ *Man's body*

The body, through which we communicate to the world around us by means of our five senses, is the dwelling-place of both our soul and our spirit. Our body is the house we live in during our earthly sojourn. Once our bodily functions stop, we are released into the realm of eternity. The physical realm is another area where a Christian can 'have a demon' or 'act under the control of a demon' or be 'demonised'. Many struggle continually with one sickness or another. On the other hand, unbelievers can give entrance to evil spirits not only into the soul and body realms, but into their spirit as well, because they do not have the Holy Spirit indwelling their spirit, as the Christian does.

The Tabernacle of Moses

When God gave instruction to Moses to build a Tabernacle in which He would reside, it was to be made in three sections: the Outer Court, illuminated by the sunlight, the Holy Place, illuminated by the seven-branched candlestick, and the Most Holy Place, illuminated by the presence of God Himself. It was over the Most Holy Place that the Lord would presence himself in a pillar of cloud by day and a pillar of fire by night.[1] It was into the Most Holy Place that the High Priest alone would enter on the Day of Atonement and God would speak to him.[2] When God dwelt among His people Israel under the Old Covenant, it was in the Most Holy Place.

Just as the Tabernacle comprised three parts, so do our lives – spirit, soul and body. It is in the inner sanctuary of our spirit that God takes up His abode. As believers in Christ, our bodies are now temples of the Holy Spirit. Every true Christian has the Holy Spirit living in his or her spirit, or, as we usually say, in the heart. We know from experience, however, that we can have Jesus living in our heart and yet be struggling with an area of bondage or affliction in the soul realm (mind, emotions, will), or in our physical bodies. It is not that we are 'demon-possessed' – fully owned and controlled by Satan – but that there can be an area or areas in which we are in bondage, or under the influence of a demonic power, afflicted, demonised, or whatever term we choose to use.

Personally, I can confess to this reality. For years as a Christian and an evangelist, I struggled with afflictions in both the soul and physical realms. No-one could help me, or even understand my struggles. I was demonised and did not know it. All I knew was that I had major inward conflicts from which I could find no release. Fortunately, the time finally came when I received understanding about the source of these afflictions, and how to come into freedom.

Years ago Shirley and I were in a town to take a series of meetings on spiritual warfare and deliverance at the invitation of the Full Gospel Business Men's Fellowship International (FGBMFI). Ministers from a certain Pentecostal denomination were against these meetings lest some of their people be influenced by them. A special meeting was convened with the FGBMFI executive and a number of pastors from this denomination. The pastors' concern was our teaching that a Christian could be bound by demons, which of course they did not believe. As we talked, I said to the pastors that we really believed the same things but used different terms. I asked if they believed a Christian could be in bondage or afflicted. That was not a problem, because everyone knows a Christian can be bound by something, but to acknowledge it could be a demon was another matter.

Not long before this meeting, a certain well-known TV evangelist, who had exercised a powerful ministry for many years, had been exposed publicly for sexual misconduct. Unfortunately, this news had gone worldwide. The evangelist's problems went back into his childhood and he had apparently struggled with sexual problems for many years. Knowing that these men had probably once respected the evangelist and his ministry, I said that if this evangelist had not experienced deliverance from demonic bondages since his sin had been revealed, then he was in need of deliverance from evil spirits associated with sexual bondage.

The pastor who was senior among them, at least in age, asserted that the evangelist was not a Christian. He said this because he was unwilling to acknowledge the possibility that a Christian could be bound by evil spirits. Although I was sitting down, I stood up on the inside. Catching and holding his gaze, I spoke out that in his heart he knew that this man was a Christian. I knew I was speaking a word of truth. He hung his head and contended with me no further. The whole atmosphere then changed. One of the group opened up and requested help for a long-standing area of bondage in his life. We were back in the world of reality. Christians can be in bondage and need to be set free. By the time the meeting concluded all hostility had gone, in fact we were even laughing together. The next day one of the pastors phoned and asked if I would meet him at the local psychiatric hospital to join him in prayer for one of his church members. A woman who was a nurse had had a breakdown and needed help.

People everywhere struggle with areas of bondage in their lives, whether they are Christians or non-Christians. As Christians, we have a source of strength and power that those in the world do not have. Thank God that Jesus is in the business of setting people free today. For those who struggle to understand how a person can have the Holy Spirit and an evil spirit at the same time, I often ask, 'Can a person have the Holy Spirit in their life but also have sin in their life at the same time?' This, of course, is not difficult to accept. Every Christian knows from personal experience when they have sinned, perhaps even continued in sin, before they repented and were forgiven. Jesus does not leave our heart because of sin, although, of course, the indwelling Spirit of God is grieved if we persist in sin.

If Christians can have the 'darkness of sin' working in their life, then they can most certainly have the 'darkness of an evil spirit' working in their life as well. Sin attracts and gives place to demonic activity.

I have written two other books on deliverance, the first called *Christian Set Yourself Free*, the second, *Fear Free*. The first book was written after Shirley and I had visited a number of mission stations in Papua New Guinea. As we flew back to Australia I pondered on our time there. In every place, the missionaries themselves had asked us to pray for them for deliverance from demonic bondages.

These were key people with good ministries pioneering for the kingdom of God, and yet they were aware of needs in their own lives. This need among missionaries stirred me to put pen to paper to help others like them, and tell them how they could work with the Lord to come out of bondage into liberty.

We must not feel ashamed to acknowledge that we have problems in our lives and may need to be set free from areas of demonic affliction.

> *'The Son of God appeared for this purpose, that He might destroy the works of the devil.'*   (1 John 3:8)

What do the Scriptures say?

The following are some of the many passages that I believe clearly indicate, to those who have open hearts, that it is possible for a Christian to come under the influence or control of demonic powers. The good news, of course, is that Christians can be set free.

► *Matthew 6:9–13*

This prayer of Jesus, commonly known as the Lord's prayer, was to teach His disciples how to pray. The prayer concludes,

> 'And do not lead us into temptation, but deliver us from evil. For Thine is the kingdom, and the power, and the glory, forever. Amen.'

The word 'evil' in Greek is *poneros*, which is translated in various places in the King James Version of the Bible by the words, 'evil, wicked, wicked one, evil things, bad, lewd, harm, wicked person, wickedness, malicious and grievous'. In the Amplified Bible the verse reads simply, *'And lead (bring) us not into temptation, but deliver us from the evil one'*. Both 'evil' and 'the evil one' are correct renderings and either can be used to translate *poneros*. The New International Version, for instance, says, *'but deliver us from the evil one.'*

Jesus taught His disciples to pray to the Father to be delivered from the evil one. The evil one is the devil, being one of the words that Strong's Concordance gives as a translation of *poneros*. If it was not possible for a Christian to be bound by the evil one, why would Jesus teach His disciples to pray for deliverance from the evil one? Obviously a Christian can be bound by the evil one, and Jesus therefore taught His disciples to pray in this way.

▶ *Ephesians 4:26, 27*

> '*Be angry, and yet do not sin; do not let the sun go down on your anger, and do not give the devil an opportunity.*'

In the margin of my Bible the literal meanings of words are often given. The word 'opportunity' means 'a place', from the Greek *topos* from which we get such English words as topography. The King James Version uses the word 'place'. The context of this scripture is anger. There is an anger which is not sinful, but a line can be crossed from right anger into wrong anger, and is too often stepped over in some lives. We are exhorted to deal with difficulties the day they arise, even before the sun sets. If we do not deal with the wrong kind of anger, we can give place to the devil, that is, to evil spirits.

My youngest son, a teenager, often visits a friend's place not far away. Sometimes as he leaves I tell him to be home by a certain time and not to be late. Why? Obviously, because I know it is possible for a young person to be late. If it was impossible, I would not have to mention it. Likewise, if it were impossible for a Christian to give place to the devil, there would be no need for the Scriptures to tell us not to give place to the devil. Because a Christian can give place to the devil, the Scripture exhorts us not to do so.

During a summer camp I was ministering deliverance to a woman in the presence of her husband. At the time, I did not know that her husband, one of the leaders in the church, did not believe that a Christian could be demonised. He was a good man, but he had a problem with anger. His anger would often boil over and this greatly concerned him. Without thinking, I suddenly stopped praying for the wife, pointed to the man and addressed a spirit in him: 'You spirit of murder, come out of him in Jesus' name.' After a brief pause, a spirit of murder was flushed to the surface and he became 'another man' for the next few minutes. He arose and came for me like a wild animal, with his arms flailing and hands clawing the air.

Unbeknown to me, he had as a teenager taken up a firearm with the intent of killing his father. Only by others restraining him had this been prevented. This man was aware of what was happening as spirits of murder surfaced, but he was not in control of what was happening. That day he received deliverance from spirits of murder and anger. Never again did he struggle with the fact that a Christian could be bound by a demon. There is nothing like personally being set free by the power of God. As we reminisced years later, he told me that when the spirits of murder manifested they wanted to kill me. Before his very eyes I suddenly became invisible and he was aware of the spirits clawing the air before him, but there was no one there to harm! God is good.

In case such an incident should cause you alarm, let me say that I am not afraid of dealing with the demonic or of any manifestations that may occur. Neither should you be afraid, if you are a believer in Christ. The enemy is actually afraid of us. Jesus said,

> *'Behold, I have given you authority to tread upon serpents and scorpions, and over all the power of the enemy, and nothing shall injure you.'*   (Luke 10:19)

► **1 John 5:18–21**

> *'We know that no one who is born of God sins; but He who was born of God keeps him and the evil one* [poneros] *does not touch him. We know that we are of God, and the whole world lies in the power of the evil one* [poneros].'

The Amplified Bible reads:

> *'We know [absolutely] that any one born of God does not [deliberately and knowingly] practice committing sin, but the One Who was begotten of God carefully watches over and protects him – Christ's divine presence within him preserves him against the evil – and the wicked one does not lay hold (get a grip) on him or touch [him]. We know [positively] that we are of God, and the whole world [around us] is under the power of the evil one.'*

These verses are talking about a person who is not deliberately and knowingly committing sin, and therefore the evil one does not touch him. The Greek word translated 'touch' is *haptomai*, which means 'to attach oneself to' or 'to touch'. As we walk in the paths of righteousness, that is, in the ways that are right and pleasing to God, the evil one, the devil, is not able to attach himself to us. Conversely, if we deliberately and knowingly choose to walk in the paths of unrighteousness, that is, in the ways that are not right and are displeasing to God, we are in danger of 'giving place to the devil' or allowing a spirit to 'attach itself to us'.

Just because we may sin as Christians does not mean that we automatically open ourselves to an area of demonic bondage. If, we choose to continue in sin, there is a real danger of ourselves to demonic bondage.

► *2 Corinthians 10:3–5*

> *'For though we walk in the flesh, we do not war according to the flesh, for the weapons of our warfare are not of the flesh, but divinely powerful for the destruction of fortresses. We are destroying speculations and every lofty thing raised up against the knowledge of God, and we are taking every thought captive to the obedience of Christ.'*

Although we live in a physical body, we do not use material or earthly weapons in our overcoming of the powers of darkness. The Lord has given us spiritual weapons which are mighty through God to the destruction of fortresses. Where are many of these fortresses or strongholds located? In the mind, which is in the realm of man's soul, because speculations and thoughts surely have to do with the mind.

When we become aware of the activity of evil spirits, it is possible to credit the devil with every wrong thing that happens to us. Some people can go overboard and become unbalanced in the way they think and act. On the other hand, too little acknowledgment can be given to Satan, and he so often conceals his activity. Later, we will look at how we can know if a demon is the cause of a problem we may have.

Have you ever been forgetful? Who has not! Are you struggling with continued forgetfulness? Some years back I was praying for a Christian friend who had a major problem with forgetfulness, so much so that he decided to seek help. We can accept many things that God does not want us to accept. Many a time we need to stir ourselves to do something about a problem.

This man had a mobile business that required much driving around the city responding to calls. Again and again he would forget to turn off at the right street, and would realise this when he was far beyond it. Even driving home from work, he would often forget to turn off the freeway and as a result became very frustrated and wanted a solution to his problem. Recognizing that he needed deliverance from spirits of forgetfulness, I took authority over them in the name of Jesus Christ and commanded them to loose his mind. As we continued in spiritual warfare, I wished him to learn how he could take authority over the enemy as I was doing, so I asked him to continue taking authority for a while.

Now remember, he had come for prayer in one area only, that of forgetfulness. He paused for a few moments and then said, 'What area were we dealing with? I have forgotten.' He most certainly had a stronghold of forgetfulness in his mind and needed deliverance from these spirits. Just because we are prone to forget things, however, does not necessarily mean we need deliverance. But some who are reading this book do need deliverance from evil spirits of forgetfulness.

For years I struggled with distraction. All of us probably get distracted often, but for me this was a major problem. I would get so frustrated and distressed because of all the time I wasted and all the matters that would not be attended to. All because of distraction. Then I became aware of how evil spirits work and how they can influence the mind. Today I am free from the binding distraction that troubled me for years. Christians can be under the influence of demonic powers in the mind and need deliverance.

▶ Matthew 18:21–35

In this passage we read of the importance of forgiveness. Jesus told a parable of a slave who owed a king ten thousand talents or about US$10,000. Because the slave could not repay the debt, the king commanded that he and his wife and children be sold, along with all that he owned. The slave prostrated himself before his lord and begged for time to repay all that he owed, but the king did more than that. He freely released the slave of the entire debt. Some king!

This most fortunate slave had a fellow slave who owed him the equivalent of about a day's wages. Seeking him out, he seized him by the throat and demanded full repayment. Needing a little time, this second slave responded with the same words that the first slave had used before the king, but no mercy was shown. He was promptly thrown in prison until the debt was paid. When the king heard that the man he had forgiven so much was unwilling to forgive another so little, he was very angry. He summoned the unmerciful slave and reprimanded him, calling him wicked.

> *'And his lord, moved with anger, handed him over to the torturers until he should repay all that was owed him.'* (Matthew 18:34)

Who are the torturers or tormentors? Evil spirits.
The story does not end here. Jesus told this parable to teach us,

> *'So shall My heavenly Father also do to you, if each of you does not forgive his brother from your heart.'* (Matthew 18:35)

Jesus was talking to Peter, one of His disciples, as He told this parable. Any believer who deliberately holds on to unforgiveness in their heart and allows bitterness a place, will be handed over by the Father to the tormentors or evil spirits. Many a Christian and, might I say, many a non-Christian, is in the hands of the tormentors today. No amount of counsel or prayer from others will bring deliverance from such bondage until the person needing to forgive makes a decision to forgive from the heart.

It was Saturday night at a Christian University where a seminar on deliverance had been taking place. After the teaching of the Scriptures, we were about to move into a time of allowing the Lord to confirm His Word. Unbeknown to me, a young woman who lived nearby, slipped into the front row of the meeting just as I was encouraging people to look to the Lord Jesus to touch their lives and bring deliverance and healing. I later discovered that when she realized what was about to happen, she called on the Lord and said, 'Oh Lord, show me your power.' She had been a Christian only a few months.

As the ministry time commenced, demonic powers holding her in captivity manifested in a dramatic fashion that drew all attention to the front of the meeting. I took authority over the spirits and commanded them to leave her, and for a few minutes a battle ensued, but I could not set her free. Calling for some ministry team members, I asked them to take her out of the meeting and minister to her in private. The room where they took her was not far away, however, and over the next hour or so as God was touching people in the meeting, we could all hear the demonic manifestations coming from that room.

Shortly after she was taken out of the meeting, I just knew something about what needed to happen in the young woman's life, and spoke to the meeting about it as a teaching point. I said I was aware that she had unforgiveness in her heart and that she would not be set free until she was willing to forgive those who had offended her. Fortunately, those seeking to help her were actually confronting that very issue. As soon as I could, I joined the team and was asked to take over. This young woman had been deeply hurt by her father and her former boyfriend. The things she had suffered through her boyfriend were so evil that I have never told anyone, not wanting to put into the mind of another what a person can do when sin is allowed to reign. She had every natural reason to be filled with hate, and she was.

Knowing the importance of forgiveness from the heart, we continued to encourage her to do this, but every time she tried to speak it out she was overridden by the spirits of hatred within her that did not want to lose their place in her life. She would be tongue-tied. It took some time, but eventually she was able to speak out her willingness to forgive, and we were then able to address the spirits of hate that were so powerful in her life. A wonderful freedom came to her as we cast out the demons and she was filled with the Holy Spirit. At midnight, she was singing praises to God and enjoying a saturation of God's presence. Another Christian had forgiven from the heart and had been delivered from demonic bondage.

▶ *Acts 8:9–24*

Philip the evangelist was preaching the gospel in the city of Samaria, and multitudes were turning to Christ as they heard the Word and saw the miracles taking place. People were set free from demons and mighty physical healings were happening. In the city was a man called Simon, who was known to all because of the magic he practised. He had earned a great reputation on account of his magic arts, but when he saw what Jesus Christ was doing in the lives of people, he recognised a far greater dimension of power.

As many gave their hearts to Christ, he also responded:

> *'And Simon himself believed; and after being baptised, he continued on with Philip; and as he observed signs and great miracles taking place, he was constantly amazed.'* (Acts 8:13)

He believed, was baptised in water, and continued on – all signs that Simon had truly turned to Christ. No longer did he practice magic (verse 9).

When the apostles in Jerusalem heard what was happening in Samaria, they came to the city and began laying hands on the new believers, who became filled with the Holy Spirit. When Simon saw this dimension of power in operation, he desired to move in it also and offered the apostles money. Peter soundly rebuked him and said,

> *'Repent of this wickedness of yours, and pray the Lord that if possible, the intention of your heart may be forgiven you. For I see that you are in the gall of bitterness and in the bondage of iniquity.'* (Acts 8:22–23)

Greatly concerned, Simon cried out to the apostles to entreat the Lord for him (verse 24).

Without excusing Simon's sin, let us look for a moment at the situation. After years of being involved in occult powers, Simon had turned from the kingdom of darkness to the kingdom of God. He was a brand-new believer, but had lots of baggage from the past. He was accustomed to power and influence and had not yet learned the ways of God's kingdom, which are diametrically opposite to what he had been used to. Anyone coming from such a background would most certainly need deliverance to get established in their new-found faith in Christ. Simon was a Christian, but needed deliverance from demonic bondages.

Two years ago a man in his late twenties approached me in a Pentecostal church. He said that he moved in a spiritual gift, but was now questioning its source. Worried that he could bring a curse on his children if the gift was not from God, he was willing to forsake it, but needed to know whether the gift was from God or not. As he told me about his gift, I knew very quickly that it was not a gift of the Holy Spirit. It was of the psychic realm, and enabled him to know things that could only be known by revelation.

His grandmother was a leading psychic in that nation, a household name, and he had been assisting with some of her television programmes because she had not been well. As a result of his gift operating, he had received 30,000 letters requesting help. I encouraged him to renounce this psychic gift in the name of Jesus and to be set free from this generational power. My advice was that he should also make a public statement that he was no longer associated with the psychic realm. That he was a Christian I have no doubt. The Lord in His faithfulness was dealing with this man's heart about an area that had simply been a part of his family life as he grew up. There is a time when the Lord puts His finger on things in our lives and desires us to respond to the truth He reveals. This young man was a believer, but needed deliverance from a strong occult influence that was generational in nature.

► *1 Corinthians 12:7, 10, 25*

In this chapter we learn of the gifts or manifestations of the Holy Spirit. Nine gifts are mentioned, one of which is the 'discernings of spirits'[3]. We will look more closely at how this gift operates in Chapter 12. Suffice to say that these wonderful manifestations of the presence of Jesus are for the common good or blessing of the Body of Christ or the church, which is made up of all true followers of Jesus:

'But to each one is given the manifestation of the Spirit for the common good.'   (1 Corinthians 12:7)

Reading the entire chapter of Corinthians, we discover it talks of the human body being one body made up of many different members or parts. Likewise, the Body of Christ is made up of many members, together making one body or expression of the life of Christ. It is not that these manifestations are limited to the church, but in the context of this chapter it is talking about a body of Christian people and these gifts being for their common good. The 'discernings of spirits', then, like the other gifts, is given for the common benefit of believers in Christ.

One aspect of the functioning of this gift is to discern the presence or activity of a spirit or spirits in a life. Because the gift is for the common good of the Body of Christ, it is to discern whether or not an evil spirit is at work in the life of a Christian. If a Christian could not be bound by an evil spirit, there would be no need of the gift of discernings of spirits being given to the Body of Christ. But it is available. Why? Because it is possible for a Christian to be bound by evil spirits.

While conducting a seminar in a Pentecostal church that sought to equip its people in deliverance ministry, I found myself exhorting them in a way I had not thought of in advance. Pentecostal Christians believe in the gifts of the Holy Spirit and in their operation today. The tragedy is that many Pentecostals, and even Pentecostal denominations, deny that Christians can be bound by evil spirits.

I said, 'We are Pentecostals, amen?' Each time I made the response on behalf of the people. 'Yes, amen brother, amen.'

'And we believe in the ministry of the Holy Spirit, amen?'

'Oh yes, amen brother.'

'And we believe in the gifts of the Holy Spirit, amen?'

'Oh most certainly brother, amen.'

'And we believe in the gift of discernings of spirits, amen?'

'Amen brother, amen, amen.'

'Well, if the gift of discernings of spirits was operating in our Pentecostal churches,' I said, 'Pentecostal believers would not be saying that Christians cannot be bound by demons!'

The very declaration by Pentecostal leaders that a Christian cannot be bound by a demon, indicates that the gift of discernings of spirits is not operating in their midst – a gift they believe in. If it was operating, they would not and could not make such a statement. When that gift operates, one's spiritual eyes are opened to see into the unseen realm and see the reality of people, including believers, needing freedom from demonic bondage.

▶ *2 Corinthians 11:3, 4*

> *'But I am afraid, lest as the serpent deceived Eve by his craftiness, your minds should be led astray from the simplicity and purity of devotion to Christ. For if one comes and preaches another Jesus whom we have not preached, or you receive a different spirit which you have not received, or a different gospel which you have not accepted, you bear this beautifully.'*

Paul expresses his great concern that believers in Corinth could be deceived and led astray from the simplicity and purity of their devotion to Jesus Christ. Christians can be deceived! More than that, he was dismayed at their lack of discernment, so that they could readily listen to the preaching of another Jesus and therefore open themselves to a different spirit and, in reality, embrace a different gospel. Christians can 'receive a different spirit' other than the Holy Spirit when they respond to a different gospel and the preaching of another Jesus. Over nearly four decades of walking with the Lord, I have unfortunately witnessed believers whom I have known personally being seduced by these things. Another Jesus; a different spirit; a different gospel.

A seminar I know of is regularly attended by both Christians and non-Christians, at a substantial financial cost. It is led by a Christian and all the assisting team are Christians. During this seminar, the delegates are not allowed to be in touch with anyone on the outside, that is, no phone calls. No watches or clocks are permitted, so no-one knows what time of the day or night it is throughout the duration of the seminar. Meals are not at regular times. Uncouth language is encouraged, and the name of God or Jesus is not permitted. Each person has a soulmate other than their own spouse, if they are married. And the list of irregularities goes on.

A pastor who attended one of these seminars told me with enthusiasm of how, on the final night, lives were changed and people delivered from demonic bondages! Supernatural things were happening. But how could that be? If there was no preaching of the Word of God, no exalting of Jesus the Son of God, no proclaiming the work of the cross, no declaring His rising from the dead, no preaching of repentance, no calling people to surrender to the Lordship of Jesus Christ, how can people be delivered from demonic bondages? It is not possible!

The only explanation for the supernatural being evidenced is that another gospel was being proclaimed and a different spirit was at work and being received. It was not the Holy Spirit! What disappoints me the most is that some Christians, even leaders, are embracing this seminar and recommending it to other Christians. How can this be? Because a deceiving spirit is at work. Deceiving spirits seek to lead people astray and do lead some astray – even good people – so that they will receive another Jesus, a different spirit and another gospel.

Unbelief

Recently I pondered some statements made by the leader of a large denomination, about demonic activity in the life of a Christian. Basically, this leader denied that a believer could be demonised except in a few rare instances, and declared most problems to be merely psychological. The ignorance and unbelief in his statements greatly troubled me, as I thought of the many people under his headship needing freedom, but denied it because of the leadership's lack of understanding.

I then imagined a group of the top leaders of that denomination gathered in a special meeting to discuss whether or not a Christian could be physically blind. The reason for the discussion was a teaching going around the larger church, saying that a Christian could become blind and that Jesus was healing blind people today. Concerned that such a teaching would infiltrate their church, they agreed on a statement to be sent to all churches denying such a false teaching. It emphatically declared that it was impossible for a Christian to become physically blind, and consequently none of their people needed Jesus to heal them. But I could see that all the leaders left the meeting with the aid of a white cane. Every one of them was physically blind!

Jesus spoke of the scribes and Pharisees,

> *'But woe to you, scribes and Pharisees, hypocrites, because you shut off the kingdom of heaven from men; for you do not enter in yourselves, nor do you allow those who are entering to go in.'*
> (Matthew 23:13)

Four times after this statement He calls them blind guides and blind men. There are evil spirits of unbelief whose job is to keep people from understanding the truth of God's Word, and they exert much influence in many segments of Christendom today.

Barnabas and Saul were summoned by the proconsul of Cyprus, Sergius Paulus, to speak the word of God to him.

> *'But Elymas the magician (for thus his name is translated) was opposing them, seeking to turn the proconsul away from the faith.'*
> (Acts 13:8)

A spirit of unbelief opposes the Word of God, and seeks to keep people away from experiencing faith in God. Paul rebuked this *'son of the devil and enemy of all unrighteousness'*, proclaiming that he would be blind for a season, and immediately he was struck blind.

> *'Then the proconsul believed when he saw what had happened, being amazed at the teaching of the Lord.'*   (Acts 13:12)

While living in Australia, I had a very vivid dream in which the Lord showed me a future event, to forewarn me of opposition to come for teaching that a Christian could be bound by demons and therefore needed deliverance. In this dream I was in the midst of a group of Christian leaders, having to defend the very truths I am proclaiming in this book. The rejection I experienced was intense, and I left this gruelling meeting with my head bowed down in dejection. As I lifted my heart to God in the midst of my pain, I was suddenly caught up to a heavenly world, flying over it like 'Superman' and praising God with all that was within me. I had broken through into victory. Then I awoke.

That dream was to be fulfilled seven years later when Shirley and I were living in Canada. If the Lord had not forewarned me, and therefore prepared me for the opposition, I would very likely have left the ministry, as it was an extremely difficult time for both of us. The man who spearheaded the opposition to me was, strangely enough, a very good friend. Prior to the meeting that I had foreseen in my dream, I was before another group of leaders being reprimanded by him for my beliefs. His body trembled as he spoke. I will never forget what this dear man said to me: 'You are in deception to believe that a Christian can be bound by a demon. My whole being is crying out, "You are deceived!" Even to the roots of every single hair on my head, my whole being is crying out, "You are deceived."' Because of my love and respect for this man, a Christian leader, I did not rebuke him, but it was very evident to me that this was a manifestation of a spirit of unbelief. A man who so strongly opposed the truth that a Christian could be demonised, was himself demonised and did not know it. He was bound by spirits of unbelief.

As I make statements about some Christians or some segments of the church, they are not intended to be against people, but against the powers of darkness that influence people to reject the truth. I trust many of you will be stirred to reconsider what you have traditionally believed, if what you have believed is not true, and come out of unbelief into faith. There are many other scriptures we could look at which indicate that a Christian can be bound by demonic powers and therefore need deliverance, but we must move on.

Chapter 11

Recognising the Demonic

In order to be decisive in dealing with demonic powers binding human lives, a person must be confident that they are indeed dealing with the demonic. The question often asked is, How you can know with certainty whether the problem being addressed is really of a demonic origin, or perhaps simply of 'the flesh', that is, caused by or within the persons themselves because of undealt-with issues in their lives?

The Bible speaks of the works of the flesh.

> 'Now those who belong to Christ have crucified the flesh with its passions and desires.' (Galatians 5:24)

The flesh is to be crucified, not cast out. Again in Galatians 2:20:

> 'I have been crucified with Christ; and it is no longer I who live, but Christ lives in me; and the life that I now live in the flesh I live by faith of the Son of God, who loved me, and delivered Himself up for me.'

In this passage, the reference to the flesh speaks of living in a physical body, not of sinful actions. Demons, on the other hand, are not to be crucified, but cast out, as we saw clearly in the commission of Jesus. In other words, there is a way to deal with the flesh and there is a way to deal with the demonic. Many want the demonic to be dealt with, but are not dealing with – or not willing to deal with – issues of the flesh. Only as the flesh is dealt with can the demonic successfully be dealt with. A partial list of the sins of the flesh is given in Galatians 5:19–21:

> '*Now the deeds of the flesh are evident, which are: immorality, impurity, sensuality, idolatry, sorcery, enmities, strife, jealousy, outbursts of anger, disputes, dissensions, factions, envying, drunkenness, carousing, and things like these, of which I forewarn you just as I have forewarned you that those who practice such things shall not inherit the kingdom of God.*'

Obviously the list could be very much longer, for we read, '*and things like these*'. These deeds of the flesh could be summed up as:

- Actions that proceed out of a life not governed by God's Word and Spirit.
- Wilful violations of the standards of God.
- The natural consequence of a life out of union with God.
- Unbridled self-expression of a life in rebellion to God.
- A way of life indicating someone in need of salvation from the power of sin.

Notice also that a person living in the flesh is, in the end, excluded from the kingdom of God. Sin has consequences that are far-reaching and of eternal magnitude. For deliverance to be received and maintained, a person must yield to Jesus Christ, acknowledging Him to be Lord and Saviour. Having come into this personal relationship with God, the Christian is to live a life of obedience to God and to learn to be led by the Holy Spirit.

> '*But I say, walk by the Spirit, and you will not carry out the desire of the flesh.*'　　　　　　　　　　　　　　(Galatians 5:16)

Water baptism

Water baptism is a powerful affirmation of what has happened in the life of a person who surrenders to Christ. Jesus Himself did not commence His public ministry until He had been baptised in water and also baptised in the Holy Spirit. Jesus had no sin to repent of, as He was without sin, but knowing that we would have to confess and turn from sin, He set us an example in word and deed that being water baptised was an act of righteousness.[1] Every Christian needs to be baptised both in water and in the Holy Spirit. Water baptism is a public testimony that we have turned from sin and turned to God, whereas Holy Spirit baptism is the empowering of God to walk in this new way of life. We cannot live the Christian life in our own strength.[2]

The English word 'baptise' comes from the Greek *baptizo*, which in turn is derived from *bapto*, to dip. *Baptizo* means 'to make overwhelmed' (i.e. fully wet), according to Strong's Concordance of the Bible.

In Romans chapter 6 we read of Paul admonishing believers not to continue living in sin, but to consider themselves dead to sin, and to walk in newness of life through the outworking of resurrection life working within them:

> '*Do you not know that all of us who have been baptised into Christ Jesus have been baptised into His death? Therefore we have been buried with Him through baptism into death, in order that as Christ was raised from the dead through the glory of the Father, so we too might walk in newness of life. For if we have become united with Him in the likeness of His death, certainly we shall be also in the likeness of His resurrection.*'   (Romans 6:3–5)

We are to identify with the work of the cross. Not only was Jesus put to death on the cross, but our sinful fleshly nature was also put to death when He was crucified. Because of this we are to do three things.

Know, Consider, Present

1. **Know**

   '*Knowing this, that our old self was crucified with Him, that our body of sin might be done away with, that we should no longer be slaves to sin; for he who has died is free from sin.*'

   (Romans 6:6–7)

2. **Consider**

   '*Even so consider yourselves to be dead to sin, but alive to God in Christ Jesus.*'   (Romans 6:11)

3. **Present**

   '*...do not go on presenting the members of your body to sin as instruments of unrighteousness; but present yourselves to God as those alive from the dead, and your members as instruments of righteousness to God.*'   (Romans 6:13)

We must **know** what happened at the cross. When Jesus died, our sinful nature also died, and as a believer I am to **consider** myself dead to the dictates of my fleshly nature and alive to God through Jesus Christ. Daily, I must purpose to **present** my life to God, choosing to walk in newness of life rather than yielding to the desires of my old sinful nature.

Infant baptism

As a baby I was water baptised. To be honest, I was not immersed in water but had a few drops sprinkled on my head. When, as an adult, I became a Christian, many of my new Christian friends insisted that I be baptised, that is, fully immersed in water. I said that I had already been baptised and did not need to do it again. The more my friends pressed me to be water baptised, the more I dug my toes in. I had not studied the Bible and understood that water baptism was only for believers. Had I known that, I would have concluded that a baby was unable to exercise faith in God.

One Sunday I witnessed for the first time baptism by immersion, and immediately became aware that I too indeed needed to experience this. The people being baptised confessed Jesus Christ as Lord and Saviour, and that they had turned from their old way of life to walk in ways pleasing to God. On this confession, the pastor lowered each candidate into the water and fully immersed them, before lifting them up out of the water. What I witnessed spoke a thousand words. In identifying with Jesus and choosing to follow Him, those who were baptised had acknowledged that they were dead to the power of sin. Dead people are buried, and down they had gone into the water.

But Jesus promised a new life when we yield to Him, and from the waters of burial each candidate had been raised up out of death to celebrate resurrection life in Christ. An outward demonstration of baptism in water bore witness to an inward transformation of the heart. As soon as the service was over I approached the pastor and asked him to baptise me also. He was hesitant to do so without first instructing me in water baptism, so I found a church where I could be baptised the following Sunday. Having had a revelation on the meaning of water baptism, I wanted to be obedient to the Lord as soon as possible.

Following Jesus

A Christian is a follower of Jesus. A hymn writer penned it this way:

'I have decided to follow Jesus,
I have decided to follow Jesus,
I have decided to follow Jesus,
No turning back, no turning back.

The world behind me, the cross before me,
The world behind me, the cross before me,
The world behind me, the cross before me,
No turning back, no turning back.

Though none go with me, I still will follow,
Though none go with me, I still will follow,
Though none go with me, I still will follow.
No turning back, no turning back.

Will you decide now to follow Jesus?
Will you decide now to follow Jesus?
Will you decide now to follow Jesus?
No turning back, no turning back.'   (Source unknown)

- A Christian is a person who has turned from sin and yielded his or her life to Jesus Christ.

- A Christian is a person who is actively walking with Christ and choosing to live a life that is pleasing to God.

- A Christian is a person who, aware of having sinned, immediately asks God's forgiveness, so that the blood of Jesus can be applied to his or her life and fellowship with God can be restored and maintained (1 John 1:5–10).

- A Christian is a person who is regularly reading and meditating on the Word of God, so that the mind is being renewed and taught in the ways of righteousness (Romans 12:1–2; Psalm 1:1–3).

- A Christian is a person who is part of a body of believers who gather together to worship God and be taught from the Scriptures by means of ministry gifts the Lord has given to the church.

- A Christian is a person who testifies by word and by a righteous lifestyle that they are a follower of Jesus.

This list could go on, but I have purposely made these statements to indicate that being a Christian requires a life of determination, dedication and discipline to walk in the ways of God. The Christian life is not for the casual or half-hearted.

When Christians are diligent in maintaining a walk with God, yet find themselves struggling with inward conflicts that continue without resolution, they need to consider the possibility of some demonic influence at work. When believers feel bound on the inside and no amount of prayer, fasting, meditating on the Word of God, good counsel, etc., make any major or lasting difference to their plight, they need to consider the possibility of some demonic influence at work.

In the midst of my struggles, I was very disciplined in my seeking of God. I sought to diligently walk in the light and constantly filled my mind with the Word of God, memorising hundreds of scriptures. Important and helpful as these disciplines were, the release I sought was not forthcoming.

Discipline is important, but so is deliverance. Neither discipline alone nor deliverance alone is the answer. The blending of both is required. When a person is endeavouring to walk in the way I have described, but the problems persist, it is time to consider whether or not demonic powers are operating in a life. One of the advantages that evil spirits have over us is that they work in the unseen realm. Because we do not see them, we can easily say that they are not there when they actually are. The following are four ways in which we can recognise the activity of evil spirits.

1. Spirits have names that indicate their function

Every spirit has a name, which tells us the kind of influence it exerts. For instance, in Luke 13:10–17 we read of a woman who for eighteen long years had had a sickness caused by a spirit, and as a result was bent double and could not straighten up. Jesus released her from this infirmity with a word of declaration, then laid His hands on her and imparted healing power. She was able to stand upright, having been both delivered and healed. Her condition was caused by the work of a spirit of infirmity in her physical body, and her complete healing required the casting out of this spirit and an impartation of healing power. Both were necessary.

That raises the question as to whether every physical sickness is caused by the work of an evil spirit. In the case of this woman, the scripture specifically states that her sickness was caused by a spirit of infirmity. It thus infers that some sicknesses do not have a direct demonic root. However, there are undoubtedly spirits whose function is to cause physical sickness. If a person struggles for a long time with sickness, the question must be asked whether a spirit of sickness could be at work. Many people have never stopped to consider this possibility. We can be so naturally minded we do not consider what influence the spirit world could be having in the natural world.

For years I struggled daily with breathing difficulties, never entertaining the thought that the source of my affliction was demonic. What a surprise it was to suddenly become aware that what I had been burdened with for so long was caused by spirits of infirmity. My testimony is that I was healed when I was delivered from these spirits.

Realising that spirits have names indicating their function, we can ask ourselves the question again and again whether or not a spirit could be behind an area of need. In Timothy 1:7 we read that God has not given us a spirit of fear, but of love, power and of a sound mind. If a person is gripped and tormented by fears, could there be spirits of fear operating in their life? I simply ask this question because many of you have never thought this way before.

2. Behind every sin there are corresponding spirits

The list of sins that people give place to is extensive. Many are bound in areas of sin that have become a great distress to them. In the past, it may not have bothered them much to indulge in sinful ways, but now with the Lord at work in their life, they want to be free to please Him in every area, but find themselves powerless to do so. When a person who wants to live right cannot get free from the power of sin, a door of opportunity is given for guilt and condemnation to set in. Being the accuser of the brethren, Satan, through his evil spirits takes advantage to harass.[3]

There are spirits of guilt and condemnation that need to be recognised and dealt with in the name of Jesus. Guilt and condemnation can lead to discouragement and despair, and the spiral continues downward, as Satan is only in the business of destroying, not building up. Satan condemns us for our sin and says that we cannot be saved from it. There is no way out. God convicts us of our sin so that we can be saved from it. There is a way out.

One evening I ministered to a Christian worker who had struggled with homosexual desires for years. Though involved in missions and no longer a practising homosexual, he was still being greatly troubled by these spirits of lust. His sister was a lesbian. A time of ministry began and went on for many hours amid strong demonic manifestations. Jesus did a wonderful work in his life, so much so, that when he went to his room to sleep, he just lay upon his bed pondering the future. Thrilled with what the Lord had done, he was now filled with hope. A new kind of life lay before him. No longer would he have to wrestle with inward conflicts on a daily basis.

Six months later Shirley and I visited the same mission base. This man was living in another city, but heard that we were at the base and came to see us. He said that since he had received deliverance, he was completely free from homosexual desires and drives. To my surprise, he said that before he had received freedom, he was so overwhelmed with homosexual lusts that he was considering leaving missionary work to become a male prostitute. He was now living in the city with the highest rate of homosexual activity in his nation, yet he was wonderfully free and not at all attracted to men as before. Behind every sin are corresponding spirits. If you are bound in an area of sin and cannot get free, could there be a spirit or spirits behind the sin that need to be recognised and dealt with?

The need to forgive is such a common problem, where many struggle for a breakthrough. Some have been deeply hurt and have become very bitter as a result. Without realising it, many have opened themselves to spirits of bitterness, anger, hatred and the like. Even though they have forgiven those who have offended them, they still struggle with strong negative feelings about the person or persons they were bitter towards. This causes confusion and sows doubts as to whether or not they had sincerely forgiven from the heart. A person may well have forgiven from the heart, even though these bitter feelings still rise within. Why is this?

Because behind every sin are corresponding spirits. The sin has been dealt with, but not the spirits that were given access through the sin. It is therefore necessary to rebuke spirits in the area of the former sin. When the spirits are driven out, the full freedom is manifested. It is important to state that just because a person sins, it does not mean that he or she automatically gives place to a spirit that has to be bound. However, if a person deliberately keeps on sinning, there is the real danger of opening up to the powers of darkness and coming into bondage.

If we are walking right with God, we do not have to fear giving place to the evil one. If we are not walking right with God, we need to fear that we may give the enemy a place.

3. Negative emotions have corresponding spirits associated with them

We all experience both positive and negative feelings or emotions. Living in a fallen world, that is, a world out of harmony with God, and pursuing a way of life contrary to God's purposes and plans, we are all subject to emotional ups and downs. Is there anyone who has not felt disappointment, discouragement, sorrow, loneliness, anger, frustration, anxiety, worry and any of many negative emotions?

Of course we all have at one time or another. Just because we may be discouraged, does not mean we are bound by spirits of discouragement. If we are going through a time of grieving because of the loss of a loved one, this does not mean that we need deliverance from spirits of grief. However, in times of discouragement the enemy will seek to gain a foothold if he possibly can, and we may find we are dealing with more than just normal feelings. A spirit of discouragement can get a hold, making it harder to shake off the emotion of discouragement.

In times of sorrow, spirits of sorrow will seek to gain entrance, and once again we are dealing not just with normal feelings of sorrow, but with spirits of sorrow that will prevent us from completely getting over that which brought in the sorrow. Many people have deeply buried unhealed wounds. Many pursue a busy lifestyle that gives them little time to ponder the past and its pain.

Recently I was in Belarus and prayed with a lovely teenager who was continuing to grieve over the loss of her mother three years before. She had been only fourteen years of age at the time of her mother's death. The love she and her mother had felt for each other made the loss all the more grievous. Recognising that spirits of grief had taken advantage of this situation, I commanded them to leave her in the name of Jesus. For fifteen minutes I prayed with her, and a great burden was lifted. The next night when people were testifying of what Jesus had been doing in their lives, she was one of the first to rise boldly to her feet, and with a beaming smile say that the grief that would not go away had gone. She was radiant.

Many times in the future, I am sure she will look back and feel sorrow at having lost her mother at such an important time in her life. However, she will no longer be gripped with the sorrow she once felt. She has been set free from spirits of sorrow.

How many others are struggling with negative emotions such as sorrow, not realizing that beneath the pain are spirits of sorrow that they can be delivered from. On the cross, Jesus took our sorrows and carried them away so that we would not have to bear them.[4] If you are struggling with negative emotions and cannot break free from them, could there be spirits that have found a place that need to be recognised and driven out in Jesus name?

4. Through acknowledging areas of personal conflict

In the course of a year I minister to many people for deliverance from demonic bondages. Many who seek prayer have a written list of needs they are aware of. Sometimes the list is pages long, sometimes only a few lines. Those without a written list usually have a mental one. Before praying for a person, I usually ask them what areas they need to be set free in.

If a person is struggling with depression, they know about it. Likewise, if someone is bound by fear, lust, addictions, allergies, rejection, suicidal thoughts and so on, they know about it. By identifying these areas of need, the question should again be asked if there could be any demonic activity linked to the area of bondage. We need to do this because most people do not think this way at all. Again, this is not trying to blame the devil for every problem we have.

For many years a friend of mine struggled to give up cigarettes. He really loved Jesus and loved to minister to others, but longed to be set free to be more effective in his witness. No doubt he had asked God many times to set him free and no doubt many had prayed this for him. When in his area one day I phoned him to see how he was doing. He joyfully told me that he had not smoked a cigarette for some time. I was delighted, and wondered how he finally got free after such a long struggle. It happened this way. A friend had said to him that if he would not smoke for a full year he would give him $2,000. If within the year he did smoke, he would have to give his friend $2,000. With this incentive he had stopped smoking and had not taken it up again when the year ended. Not only did he gain $2,000, but he had saved $1,000 on cigarette purchases that he would have made over that year.

This story often comes to my mind, and I ask myself whether human willpower is being exercised fully in those who want to be set free. There are many, though, who are fully doing their part to overcome an addiction but cannot do so. This is where we can anticipate the help of Jesus to set us free. There are spirits of addiction, whose roots often go back in the generational line. What the person struggles with other family members may also have struggled with.

Are you struggling in some area of personal conflict and cannot break free? Could there be a spirit or spirits behind this area of bondage?

The four points outlined above will help identify many an area where deliverance is needed. In the next chapter we will look at abilities to discern the demonic through the ministry of the Holy Spirit. It is important though, to know that many spirits can be identified through the points just outlined. A person may never move in a revelatory gift of the Spirit, yet successfully identify many demonic bondages, and come into freedom by using the spiritual weapons God has given His people.

Chapter 12

The Gift of
Discernings of Spirits

The gift of discernings of spirits is of particular interest to me. The Greek word that is translated as 'discerning' or 'distinguishing' in many of our English Bible translations is actually in the plural. The correct translation is discernings or distinguishings of spirits.

Whenever I see a book on the gifts of the Holy Spirit, I automatically turn to the chapter on 'discernings of spirits' to see what the author has to say.

In my experience, I have never read in such a book how this gift operates. Usually the chapter is very good, with stories of deliverance, usually dramatic, but never telling how the gift works. A year ago I was waiting in a pastor's office in Finland, when I noticed a magazine with the words '**Discernings of Spirits**' highlighted on the front cover. Turning with eagerness to this article, I again read about deliverance encounters, all dramatic, but with no information on how the gift of discernings of spirits operated. In this chapter I will tell you how the gift operates, or at least how I experience it operating.

> 'Now there are varieties of gifts, but the same Spirit. And there are varieties of ministries and the same Lord. And there are varieties of effects, but the same God who works all things in all persons.'
> (1 Corinthians 12:4–6)

God is a God of variety. The same gift can operate through different people with different personalities in different ways, and yet the same or similar results are achieved. I have a number of friends who operate in the gift of discernings of spirits. In some ways we function similarly, in other ways quite differently. When I share what I experience, I want to be clear that this is how the Lord has taught me and uses me. In 1 Corinthians chapter 12 the gift of discernings of spirits is mentioned in the midst of nine gifts or manifestations of the Holy Spirit:

- word of wisdom
- word of knowledge
- faith
- gifts of healings
- workings or effectings of miracles
- prophecy
- discernings or distinguishings of spirits
- various kinds of tongues
- interpretation of tongues

These gifts are simply manifestations of God's presence, and we most certainly need His presence. To say these gifts have passed away, as some do, is to be living in ignorance and unbelief. It is to be like an ostrich with its head in the sand. The Lord is doing many amazing things around the world among His people where there is an openness and hunger for His presence, a longing to experience the reality and power of His kingdom, and where faith is strong. Might we add, and where great needs abound.

The word 'discern' means to recognise or perceive clearly. 'Recognise' means to know or identify. 'Perceive' means to become aware of something. Through the gift of discernings of spirits, therefore, we identify or become aware of the operation of evil spirits in a life through the ability of the Holy Spirit. There is a general discernment that every Christian should be experiencing and growing in. Just as a baby starts life on milk and then after a time begins to take solid food, so it is in the spiritual realm. As new-born Christians we begin to partake of the milk of God's Word, and as we grow spiritually we get into the solid food of the Word.

> 'But solid food is for the mature, who because of practice have their senses trained to discern good and evil.'   (Hebrews 6:14)

Our general discernment should be increasing all the time.

'I can do nothing on My own initiative'

Isaiah prophesied of the Saviour who was to come:

> *'And the Spirit of the Lord will rest on Him, the spirit of wisdom and understanding, the spirit of counsel and strength, the spirit of knowledge and the fear of the Lord. And He will delight in the fear of the Lord, and He will not judge by what His eyes see, nor make a decision by what His ears hear.'*   (Isaiah 11:2, 3)

Jesus moved in revelation knowledge. He was not limited to human insight.

▶ Seeing

> *'Truly, truly, I say to you, the Son can do nothing of Himself, unless it is something He sees the Father doing; for whatever the Father does, these things the Son also does in like manner.'*
> (John 5:19)

▶ Hearing

> *'I can do nothing on My own initiative. As I hear, I judge; and My judgement is just, because I do not seek My own will, but the will of Him who sent Me.'*   (John 5:30)

▶ Teaching

> *'When you lift up the Son of Man, then you will know that I am He, and I do nothing on My own initiative, but I speak these things as the Father taught Me.'*   (John 8:28)

▶ Commanding

> *'For I did not speak on My own initiative, but the Father Himself who sent Me has given Me commandment, what to say, and what to speak. And I know that His commandment is eternal life; therefore the things I speak, I speak just as the Father told Me.'*
> (John 12:49, 50)

▶ Abiding

> *'Do you not believe that I am in the Father, and the Father is in Me? The words that I say to you I do not speak on My own initiative, but the Father abiding in Me does His works.'*
> (John 14:10)

Jesus saw things from the Father; heard things from the Father; was taught things by the Father, commanded things by the Father and abided in the Father. He experienced a close relationship with the Father and was totally dependent upon Him, to such an extent, that He would say He could nothing on His own initiative. God wants us to enjoy a similar relationship of intimacy with and abiding in Himself where we also see and hear, and can be taught and told what to do. There is a level that God wants to lift us into that releases us from the limitations of purely human reason and response. We so often judge by what our eyes see and make decisions by what our ears hear.

It is not that, as Christians, we no longer need to think or reason or use our common sense. There is, however, a dimension we can enter into where we hear the Lord speaking to us. A dimension where we are led by the Holy Spirit and work together with Him, rather than formulating our plans and asking God to bless them.

A young woman came for prayer, and before she shared her need I noticed that her fingernails were extremely short. My immediate conclusion was that she had an area of anxiety or insecurity that manifested in fingernail biting. As she shared her need of physical healing from a rare illness that afflicted very few people in her country, she said that one of the symptoms associated with the illness was very short fingernails. She did not have a problem with fingernail biting at all! For the rest of my life, if I see someone with such short fingernails and conclude that they have a habit of biting them, I would probably be right. However, on this occasion I was wrong. I have many such stories to tell and I am sure you do as well. We can be such a mixture, at times really hearing from the Lord, and at times moving out of our own understanding.

Not only is it said of Jesus that He did nothing on His own initiative, but the Scriptures say the same regarding the Holy Spirit:

> 'But when He, the Spirit of truth, comes, He will guide you into all truth; for He will not speak on His own initiative, but whatever He hears, He will speak; and He will disclose to you what is to come.'
> (John 16:13)

May we, as believers in Jesus Christ, be lifted up more and more into to this realm of revelation knowledge, yet at the same time have our feet firmly on terra firma, so that we are not just heavenly minded and of no earthly use, as the saying goes.

Discernings of spirits

We tend to think that discernment is related only to discerning the demonic, but this gift is far wider in its application. Before we look at demonic discernment, let us look at other areas that come under 'discernings'.

1. Discerning the human spirit

To perceive or understand what is happening in the heart of an individual is of great assistance, particularly if we have a calling in which we are regularly relating to others. How easy it is for a person to be saying one thing with their mouth but another in their heart. That can be revealed through the gift of discernings of spirits.

Once when counselling a man I knew he was lying to me. So strong was this awareness in my heart that I confronted him about it. He denied that he was lying. Again I confronted him and again he denied it. A third time I confronted him. On this third confrontation, in an outburst of anger he admitted that he had been lying. I had pressed the point because I knew so strongly within myself that he was not telling the truth.

A man called Ananias and his wife Sapphira sold a piece of property and conspired to give only a portion of the proceeds to the apostles, while conveying the impression of giving the full amount. When Ananias brought the money to Peter, the apostle discerned this deceit and asked: *'Ananias, why has Satan filled your heart to lie to the Holy Spirit, and to keep back some of the price of the land?'* (Acts 5:3). This dishonesty was revealed through the discernment of the Holy Spirit.

Nathanael, through the encouragement of Philip, came to see who Jesus was. When Jesus saw him approaching he said, *'Behold, an Israelite indeed, in whom is no guile!'* (John 1:47). Guile speaks of clever or crafty behaviour, of duplicity or deceit. Jesus knew what was in his heart. Nathanael was a good man and Jesus discerned this from the beginning.

Paul and Barnabas were on the island of Cyprus. The proconsul, Sergius Paulus, summoned them in order to hear the word of God. Also present was a magician called Elymas, who was opposing them and seeking to turn the proconsul away from the faith.

> *'But Saul, who was also known as Paul, filled with the Holy Spirit, fixed his gaze upon him, and said, "You who are full of all deceit and fraud, you son of the devil, you enemy of all*

righteousness, will you not cease to make crooked the straight ways of the Lord?"'
                                                    (Acts 13:9, 10)

Paul discerned the evil heart of this man and pronounced a temporary curse on him, thereby showing that Jesus was more powerful than his master, Satan. Elymas was struck blind.[1] On this same journey they came to Lystra, where there was a man who had never walked, being lame from his mother's womb.

'This man was listening to Paul as he spoke, who, when he had fixed his gaze upon him, and had seen that he had faith to be made well, said with a loud voice, "Stand upright on your feet." And he leaped up and began to walk.'
                                                    (Acts 14:9, 10)

This seeing was more than natural vision, but a spiritual seeing or sensing through the ability of the Holy Spirit. Paul could discern what was happening in the man's heart.

On arriving to spend some time with a team of Christian workers, I met one of them, a middle-aged woman. When I saw her I became aware that if I was to pray for her there would be some difficulties. Because of this, I hoped she would not ask for prayer, but a few days later she did ask. You ask how I knew there would be problems? Well, there was just a knowing within me that this would be so. As I prayed for her, I had a real flow of understanding through the Holy Spirit, and she was in the course of being set free from bondages. Suddenly, in the midst of a flowing in prayer, I saw a wall go up between herself and me. It was like watching a brick wall being built in fast motion. On the screen of my mind I saw it all take place.

Instinctively, I also knew why she rejected my prayers and the freedom that God wanted to impart to her. Again you may ask how I knew why she cut me off. The knowledge was just there. As I was looking to Jesus to help me pray effectively, there was a deposit of understanding released within me through the indwelling Holy Spirit. I stopped praying and said that I was aware she had cut me off, and the reasons for it. She agreed with what I had to say. I then said there would be no purpose in my continuing to pray for her. I was firm, yet loving. Angrily she got up and stamped out of the room with the sort of response you might expect from a child. Leaving the house, she went for a long walk to get over her anger. I felt bad, but the couple with me encouraged me. When praying for her in the past she had responded to them in a similar manner. What I had sensed on meeting her had come to pass.

This couple also said that as I had prayed, I had touched problem areas in her life that she was unwilling to deal with, hence her response. I hoped she would not ask for further prayer later, but she did. In fact, when she returned from her walk, she asked for forgiveness for the way she had carried on. When another session of prayer took place she was open to receive from the Lord. There were no further difficulties.

I find that when this gift operates while I am praying with someone, there is a knowing as to whether the person is open or not, cooperating or not, has faith or not, and so on. This sensing or discernment is so helpful, as it enables one to speak words of encouragement or of exhortation as necessary.

2. Discerning the angelic spirit

Angels are spirits and their presence can be discerned. I am talking of God's angels, who are ministering spirits to those who will inherit salvation.[2] Personally, I have never seen an angel. A few Christians I know or know of really have seen an angel or angels. These encounters were the real thing, rescuing them from great danger and probable death. Shirley and I visited a third world country where angelic visitation was not infrequent, with angels of the Lord bringing messages from God to His people. It was so interesting to hear the missionaries tell of numerous angelic visitations. The very churches we visited were birthed by an outpouring of the Holy Spirit with signs and wonders and miracles. The supernatural was natural to these folk.

It is not uncommon to hear some Christians talking about seeing angels in such a matter-of-fact way that I frankly do not believe they are seeing them at all. A person can see things in their mind, and make all sorts of statements of seeing this or that, but in reality they are not seeing angels at all. Daniel saw an angel. Those with him did not, but sensed its presence and ran away in terror to hide themselves. Daniel fell to the ground as all his strength melted away, and his natural colour turned to a deathly pallor.[3] This was the real thing.

The Scriptures do say that God's angels can appear in a form we do not recognise and could even share a meal with us, because for that length of time they take on a human form.[4] Obviously, though, there are times when a person can discern or see an angel in their midst. Peter did. While he was in prison awaiting execution, the church prayed fervently for his rescue. As a result of this fervent prayer an angel was dispatched to rescue him. Waking him from sleep, the angel struck Peter's side and the chains fell off his hands. Following the angel, he passed the guards and came to the outer door of the prison, which opened by itself. All this time Peter was unsure whether he was seeing a vision or whether it was a real occurrence. Once outside the prison, however, he realised for certain that the Lord had sent an angel and he had been rescued.[5]

Last year I was privileged to assist in ministry a man who sees angels from time to time. He is aware of their presence when ministry is taking place, an awareness that few have. He is very sensitive to the unseen world, the ministry of the Holy Spirit and of angels. The spiritual gift of discernings of spirits is wider in scope than just discerning demonic powers.

3. Discerning the Holy Spirit

The very name of the Holy Spirit states that He is a spirit. His presence can be discerned and His will made known. In Acts 15 we read the account of a problem faced by the early church leaders. A number of Pharisees believed in Jesus Christ, yet insisted that those who did so should continue observing the Law of Moses. Gathering in Jerusalem, the apostles and elders discussed the problem at length and reached consensus through the help of the Holy Spirit. A letter was formulated to be sent to the churches. It read in part:

> 'For it seemed good to the Holy Spirit and to us to lay upon you no greater burden than these essentials: that you abstain from things sacrificed to idols and from blood and from things strangled and from fornication; if you keep yourselves free from such things, you will do well.'   (Acts 15:28, 29)

In Acts 16 we read of Paul and Barnabas passing through the Phrygian and Galatian region, having been forbidden by the Holy Spirit to speak the word in Asia. We are not told explicitly how the Holy Spirit spoke to them, but they did hear His voice and discern His will regarding direction.[6] Coming to Mysia, they planned to go to Bithynia, but again were not permitted to do so by the Holy Spirit. Again we are not told how God spoke, but He did, and they discerned what He wanted them to do.[7]

As a young evangelist, I was travelling with a team of evangelists holding meetings in trailer parks during the holiday season. We held only one meeting in each location, as we were visiting smaller camping grounds. This particular night we had our usual musical programme with testimonies and preaching, then returned to our base for the night with every intention of moving on the following day. That night I felt that God was speaking to me. It was just an inward sensing that we needed to return to the same location for a second night. Sharing this with the others, we prayed seeking God's will. Together we concluded that the Lord indeed was speaking to us to change our plans, so we did.

On the first evening our theme had been the love of God, and now it was the judgement of God. At the end of the presentation, I was privileged to speak to a teenager and introduce him to a personal relationship with Jesus Christ. He said that he had been in the meeting the previous night and the Lord had been speaking to him. During the night God spoke to him in a dream and told him that He wanted to come into his life. Even though good seeds from God's Word had been sown in his heart in the first meeting, and even though the Lord had spoken to him in the night, he still had not yielded his life to Christ. It required another gospel presentation and a challenge to follow Jesus to bring him into a right relationship with God.

I will never forget part of the prayer he prayed spontaneously from his heart as he confessed his sins to God and acknowledged Jesus as his Lord and Saviour. These very same words I have used on hundreds of occasions as I have encouraged others to pray and find God. They were simply, 'Lord Jesus, I welcome you into my heart.' This young man had a real encounter with God that night. It happened because, as a team, we discerned the Holy Spirit changing our plans and redirecting our steps. We can all discern the mind of the Holy Spirit.

4. Discerning evil spirits

A distraught father brought his son to Jesus to be set free from a spirit that made him mute. This spirit would seize him, dash him to the ground, cause him to foam at the mouth, grind his teeth and stiffen his body. Often it would seek to destroy the boy by throwing him into the fire or water. Jesus named a deaf and dumb spirit and commanded it to come out and never enter him again. The spirit cried out and threw him into terrible convulsions. As it left, the boy fell and looked as if he were dead, but Jesus took him by the hand and lifted him up. The presence of an evil spirit had been identified and cast out, never to trouble the lad again.[8]

In a synagogue where Jesus was teaching, was a woman who had suffered eighteen years from a sickness caused by a spirit. Her body was bent double and she was unable to straighten up. Jesus spoke a word of command that released her from a spirit of infirmity. He laid His hands on her she was immediately made erect again. A spirit of sickness had been identified and cast out, and a surge of healing power had restored the years of damage it had caused.[9]

Over a period of days Paul and Silas were bothered by a woman who had a spirit of fortune-telling. The spirit would cry out through her, saying that these men were servants of the Most High God who were proclaiming the way of salvation. Finally, Paul became greatly annoyed and turned and commanded the spirit to come out of her. It did, and she was no longer of any profit to her masters, who then had Paul and Silas arrested and put in prison. A spirit had been identified and driven out of the woman in the name of Jesus Christ.[10]

In the previous chapter we looked at four ways of recognising the presence of a spirit or spirits operating in a life:

- Spirits have names that indicate their function.
- Behind every sin there are corresponding spirits.
- Negative emotions have corresponding spirits associated with them.
- Acknowledging areas of personal conflict.

Again I wish to emphasise that many spirits can be identified and cast out without the operation of the gift of discernings of spirits.

Wisdom and knowledge

Working closely with the gift of discernings of spirits is the word of wisdom and the word of knowledge; two gifts of the Holy Spirit mentioned in 1 Corinthians 12. As they blend together, one can receive a word of knowledge followed by a word of wisdom and then discernings of spirits. These gifts are distinct, but discernible, in their operation.

- Words of wisdom are directive.
- Words of knowledge are informative.
- Discernings of spirits are informative.

We may have information, but how we use that information is extremely important. Without wisdom, sometimes the information can cause problems.

A young Christian man came forward reluctantly for prayer, encouraged by a friend. For a long time he had struggled with homosexual feelings and longed to be free. The reason he was reluctant to come forward in a public meeting was that he had been extremely embarrassed on two occasions in two previous meetings. Evangelists had pointed to him while preaching and said, 'Young man, you are a homosexual.' The information was correct, but the way of handling it was not. A wall went up between himself and preachers and he was not helped at all. That night, as he opened his heart and sought help, something wonderful happened. A time came during the ministry when the presence of God became so real that we embraced each other and wept profusely. We were immersed in the love of God and both expressed that we had never felt such love in our lives. It was awesome.

We must remember that God hates sin but loves the sinner. Jesus was the friend of sinners and had a heart full of compassion that they might be saved and delivered from their bondages. We too must love the sinner and allow God to work through us to reach them for Christ. As we minister with our understanding and with understanding that comes from God, we need to be moving in wisdom as well. I find that often it just flows. Without any effort, there is just a knowing of what to say and how to say it. So many times I marvel as this happens, because I know that I am moving in an ability that is from God and is certainly not of myself.

My wife Shirley often moves in a word of wisdom. I have witnessed this over many years both in church life and as a mother. Our daughter Carrie came to us at twenty-two months of age with much insecurity in her life, having been in a foster home from nine months of age. When Carrie was about four years old she was still struggling with insecurity. Shirley and I were going away for the weekend to speak to a gathering of parents on 'family', and to avoid distractions no children were to be present. We told our two children that they would be staying with friends whom we all knew well.

Carrie, however, insisted on coming with us. Since adopting her we had never left her for so much as a night, and this going away for a few days caused her to become insecure. As the weekend drew closer, we continued to say that she needed to stay with our friends, but she continued to say that she wanted to be with us. What were we to do? We had a ministry responsibility to fulfil, and yet we had a daughter who was really our prime responsibility. Shirley lifted her heart to the Lord to seek an answer to this problem. As she did so, an impression came to her that she believed had been given her by God. She called Carrie and said to her that if she wanted to come away with us for the weekend she could come, but if she wanted to stay with our friends she could stay with them. It was her decision.

Over the next few days we heard Carrie say again and again, 'I've got to make a decision. I've got to make a decision.' The very fact that she could come with us released the power of the insecurity. It no longer gripped her. A word of wisdom was the key. Carrie never did make her decision. As Shirley and I left for the weekend, we went as a family with our friends to an ice-cream shop. Amid the distraction of licking ice-creams, we went on our way leaving behind a happy daughter. She had a good weekend and so did we.

Receiving words of wisdom and knowledge

How do these gifts operate? As we lift our hearts to the Lord seeking His counsel, a thought comes to the mind; an impression comes to the heart; a picture is imprinted on the screen of our mind; you just know something you did not previously know. The Holy Spirit is speaking. It is important to stress that we do not become passive and empty our minds and wait for some impression to come. Our focus is the Lord Jesus Christ. We are looking to Him to speak to us through the Holy Spirit, and we are actively involved in the process of hearing God's voice. This impartation of wisdom and knowledge is so simple that we can often miss it. We must have a childlike faith.

> *'But if any of you lacks wisdom, let him ask of God, who gives to all men generously and without reproach, and it will be given him. But let him ask in faith without any doubting, for the one who doubts is like the surf of the sea driven and tossed by the wind. For let not that man expect that he will receive anything from the Lord, being a double-minded man, unstable in all his ways.'*
>
> (James 1:5–8)

When we see a person moving in a revelatory gift, particularly if there is a spectacular confirmation of the word spoken, we can be amazed and yet intimidated at the same time. We may be awed at the seeming spirituality of the person moving in the gift, but feel that God could never use us in that way. But the operation of a spiritual gift does not necessarily mean that the person is very spiritual. A gift is a gift: given at a moment of time to bless someone. The fruit of the Holy Spirit evidenced in a life indicates the moulding of that life to be like Jesus. We need both the gifts and fruit of the Holy Spirit, and God wants this to be the experience of every believer.[11]

How can I be sure it is God speaking to me?

Just because a thought comes to the mind, an impression comes to the heart, a picture is imprinted upon the screen of our mind, or there is a knowing of something, does not mean that the source of that understanding has come from God. Sometimes it may be God; sometimes it may be just from our own heart. Until you learn to clearly hear the voice of the Lord, I strongly urge you not to say, 'The Lord has told me this or that,' as you speak to someone. Too many people glibly use such phrases when God has not spoken to them at all! However, through experience a boldness of declaration can come, when you can boldly say that the Lord has told you something.

I once met a man who had been nineteen years confined to a wheelchair, paralysed from the waist down. He was very outgoing and the most joyful person I had ever met with such a handicap. What a wonderful testimony he was to the Lord Jesus. He had recently attended a conference on signs and wonders and had hoped that he would be healed. However, on three occasions people had approached him with 'words' from the Lord that were not from the Lord at all. These had brought him great discouragement. Words such as, 'The Lord has told me you fell from a tree.' Wrong! 'The Lord has told me you were in a motor vehicle accident.' Wrong!

Why do we have to ask God why a person is in a wheelchair. Can we not sensitively ask the person, 'How long have you been in a wheelchair? What happened to you?' Jesus asked a father who brought his son to Him to be set free, how long his son had been like that. Let us use our common sense and at the same time be open to receive words of revelation.[12]

As we begin to anticipate God speaking to us and an impression comes, say to the person you are seeking to help, 'I am sensing this or that. Does it mean anything to you?' The person may respond and say, 'Yes. How did you know?' Or, 'No, it does not mean anything to me.' If they do not bear witness to your words, you can easily withdraw them. If you had prefaced your words with, 'The Lord has told me,' it is difficult to retract such a statement. Does God make a mistake? There is a naturalness that we can experience moving in the power of the Holy Spirit that makes us approachable and enables people to receive from God through us.

Please do not turn on some religious voice and exhibit some religious holier-than-thou attitude. We are to walk in humility and not to put on religious airs.

As a new Christian I lived with some other young Christian men who were all involved in street evangelism. Into the house came a young man who had come to Christ through our witnessing. Frank had a problem with anger that continued even though he was now a believer. When he got angry it was very unpleasant in the house, and finally we had to say to him that if things did not change, he would have to find other accommodation. The time came when I was asked to be the spokesman to tell him to leave. Frank's response was that he did not want to leave, and he asked if I would pray for him to be set free from the anger. Having no experience whatever in praying for people, I lifted my heart to God and prayed a prayer that I now have uttered so many times I have memorised it – 'Help!'

Into my mind came three words that to me had no relevance at all to the situation. I pushed them aside. Not knowing how to start praying, I continued to ask God for help. Again these seemly unrelated words were before me. Again I dismissed them. As I silently kept asking God for help and these words kept coming back, I finally asked Frank if these words meant anything to him: 'The swimming hole.' To my surprise Frank yelled out, 'Yes!' And then the full story unfolded.

Around the age of ten he was with some of his friends at the swimming hole when he was ducked and held under too long. He nearly drowned. After being taken to the river bank, his friends continued to swim, not realising how serious things had been. As Frank watched the boy who ducked him enjoying himself, while he was trying to get over the ordeal, an anger rose within him towards the boy. Since that moment he had had a problem with an uncontrollable anger that would often rise up, an anger he desperately wanted to be free of. A word of knowledge had pinpointed the entrance of the anger and enabled the issue of forgiveness to be addressed. The voice of the Lord came and I nearly missed it, as I tried to understand with my mind words of revelation that seemed to have no connection to the problem in front of us.

It was to be years before I ever experienced another word of knowledge. Why? Because no one told me how this gift operated, and how I could tune in to hear the voice of the Lord. As we tread cautiously, asking the person being ministered to if a word on our heart has any relevance to them, and we find again and again people answering in the affirmative, our confidence grows that we are indeed hearing from God. There can be times when God does speak to us, yet when we ask a person about it they say No. We could think that we had not heard from God when actually we had. There are times when, from experience, I know that God is giving me words about a person and yet they do not bear witness to them or acknowledge them.

Sometimes a person will speak to me long after a time of ministry, saying that there were some areas I addressed when I prayed that they did not understand. Time had passed and now they could see clearly why. This is where, through experience, we can minister boldly, because we know with certainty that the Lord is speaking to us and working through us.

A group of leaders desired prayer, so one by one I prayed for them. Coming to one man, I sensed three areas of need in his life that God wanted to minister to. Before praying I mentioned them, but he denied them. Because I knew that the Lord was speaking to me, I again mentioned these three areas. He again denied they were problems for him. I spoke sensitively, not wanting to embarrass him in any way. Without his agreement I felt that I could not pray according to the revelation I had received, so I just prayed a general prayer over him. As soon as the ministry time was over he asked to speak to me privately. He acknowledged each of the areas I had raised and wanted prayer. For some reason he could not let others know he had these particular needs. If I was not experienced, I could have thought that I was wrong, that God had not spoken to me, because the words were seemingly not accurate, when God had indeed spoken.

Keep in mind that we cannot push ourselves on people or seek to override their wills. If you truly have a word from God and share it, and the person does not want ministry, just leave things where they are. Some people need to become more open, some need to exhibit more humility and some need to get more desperate before you can really help them.

Ministering in confidence

When you know what you are dealing with, the enemy knows that you know, and that is when things happen. In other words, when you know you are dealing with demonic powers binding a life, you can go after them with authority and great boldness because you know what you are dealing with. As you exercise authority in faith – things happen!

The first time I moved in the gift of discernings of spirits I was in a ministry situation, praying in faith, when I saw what was taking place on the inside of the person. As I was speaking to demonic powers, believing that the words of authority I exercised in Jesus's name were driving out the spirits I was naming, I suddenly saw the spirits, their reactions, and their departure from the person. Because I actually saw the demons, I knew instinctively that the gift of discernings of spirits was beginning to operate. For a number of weeks, as I was involved in prayer ministry, I continued to see the demons I was coming against and would see their reactions to the commands to go in Jesus's name and see them being driven out. Before then, I would pray in faith knowing that deliverance was taking place, but now I could see it.

This 'seeing' was not as one sees with natural sight, but a seeing with spiritual sight. Also, I would see before me the name of the spirit or spirits that God was dealing with. All of this was projected on my mind, and I would simply speak out what I was 'seeing'. I knew the revelation was from God because of the results: people were being wonderfully set free. Some were set free amid dramatic manifestations, others with mild manifestations, others with imperceptible manifestations. If people felt nothing happening as deliverance was taking place, I would encourage them because I could see it happening. The operation of this gift enabled me to pray at length for people who experienced imperceptible manifestations, because I was guided not by outward manifestations but by what the Holy Spirit was showing me.

The Lord Jesus has not left His church without the ability, through the Holy Spirit, to uncover, name and drive out wicked spirits of bondage. Thank God for the gifts or manifestations of the Holy Spirit!

As the weeks went by, discernment continued to operate, but I no longer saw the clear forms of demons. Instead, I would see areas of darkness, some intense, some not so intense, with the names of the spirits written before me. As I commanded the spirits to go I saw portions of the darkness lifting and breaking up as areas were dealt with. The results were the same. Demons coming out with various kinds of manifestations. There was also a knowing of how one area of bondage was linked to another. A knowing of whether the person had faith or not, and a sensing of the heart of the individual I was ministering to. I began to recognise when the word of knowledge would switch to a word of wisdom, and then on to discernment, and so forth. As I have said, these gifts of revelation flow beautifully together.

With the passing of the years I have found discernment coming in other ways as well. Call it just a knowing. If you were with a group of very hungry people and suddenly everyone, apart from yourself, began to sniff and exclaim, 'Pizza! Pizza!' you might wonder what was happening. If you had never heard of pizza, never tasted pizza, never smelt pizza, you would not at first have a clue what was happening. On being told that pizza was a food they all enjoyed, you might well ask, 'How do you know it is pizza?' The reply would be, 'Because we can smell pizza.' Pizza has its own aroma, as does freshly baked bread. The sense of smell had operated in each of the pizza lovers, hence the excitement. That keen sense of assurance came because all had eaten pizza many times and enjoyed the smell of it.

Just as there is a natural sensing we can experience, there is also a spiritual sensing. Suddenly you just know something. How do you know? Well, you just know. A spiritual sensing picked up something. It may be knowledge that has been imparted to you. It may be sensing particular spirits binding a person. It may be just a knowing how to proceed, or what to say with a wisdom that has been imparted. There are times when dealing with a person that I can just tell them about themselves. People then say, 'You read my mail,' or something to that effect. You just know something and the wonderful thing is that you were not striving for that under-standing. A spiritual gift had simply operated.

Ministering in rest

When you know that you can 'do nothing on your own initiative', I mean when you really know this, it releases you from striving. When you know that you are not wise enough, not knowledge-able enough, not discerning enough, then you are able to look to Jesus for His help. I find that one of the main keys to moving in the power of the Holy Spirit is to be in a place of rest in your heart. You are not trying to produce anything through your own abilities.

Before I ever experienced any revelation flowing, I was in a place of striving. I tried so hard to hear the voice of God, and when I received nothing I would be frustrated and discouraged, because I so wanted to see people helped by God's power. Perhaps that is how you feel yourself. I would encourage you to keep on desiring the manifestations of the Holy Spirit, as we are exhorted to do in the Scriptures.[13] Also, in the midst of that desiring, be open to that impression, that quickening, I have described. There comes a time when God does speak, and it must be acted on in faith. That leads me to three words.

Revelation, declaration, confirmation

▶ *Revelation*

Revelation is a revealing or disclosing; especially a striking disclosure of something not previously known or realised. The Holy Spirit reveals something. What do we do with it?

▶ *Declaration*

In the context of praying for others, once a word of revelation has been imparted, it is to be spoken out. We declare it.

▶ *Confirmation*

As we speak out the word God has given, that word is confirmed or made alive by the Holy Spirit and accomplishes what God intended. God confirms His word, not necessarily our word! To confirm means to 'establish, make certain, ratify'. After Jesus had risen from the dead we read of the disciples,

> *'And they went out and preached everywhere, while the Lord worked with them, and confirmed the word by the signs that followed.'*   (Mark 16:20)

Of course, when God speaks, there is a releasing of faith that makes it easy to speak out or declare what He has spoken. This is part of moving in rest.[14]

Sometimes God speaks a word to you that is not to be spoken out in the presence of others, but to be taken before Him in prayer. There is still a confirmation to come, which may happen quickly, or much time may pass before the evidence is revealed to the senses, confirming or completing what God said.

During a ministry time in a meeting a young woman asked if I would pray for her. She told me that there had been a barrier between herself and God for eight years that she wanted removed, so she could again experience God's presence as in the past. Others had prayed for her but the barrier remained. Not knowing what to say, I lifted my heart to the Lord and said, 'Help, Lord.' Immediately a word of knowledge came in the form of a question, and I asked, 'Have you ever had an abortion?' She was visibly shocked and said, 'Yes, but my husband told me not to tell you. In fact, I have had two abortions.' That question had revealed the source of the barrier. Eight years earlier, she had been involved sexually with the man she was to marry and had conceived. An abortion followed. Another conception led to a another abortion. No-one could be told because her boyfriend was the son of a pastor!

Because it was nearly midnight, I met her and another Christian woman two nights later. What a wonderful encounter she experienced with Jesus. The barriers of guilt and shame as well as other bondages were removed from her life, and the closeness of fellowship with God was restored. Revelation, declaration, confirmation!

A woman remained for prayer at the close of a meeting. Only the pastor and his wife were there apart from myself. I asked this woman what she wanted the Lord to do for her and she replied, 'The Lord will show you.' I did not want to hear such a response. I often ask people if there is something they want to share or some need they want to make known. But instinctively I knew that this woman could not open up to me and that I was not to pressure her. How did I know? 'Pizza!' A spiritual sensing was operating. I lifted my heart to the Lord and prayed my usual prayer, 'Help.'

All I knew about this woman was her first name. I started to pray in faith, believing that God would help me. I was like an aircraft on a runway beginning to take off. As I kept praying with my understanding, I felt the lift-off and I was flying, in the sense that I was being upheld, inspired and guided by the Holy Spirit to pray effectively. After a few minutes of praying for her I just knew something. How did I know. Well, I just knew. 'Pizza!' I stopped praying and said, 'You have unforgiveness in your heart towards your father, don't you? You have been raped, haven't you, and you have never forgiven the man who raped you?' I declared. She acknowledged what I had said was true, and I exhorted her to forgive both of these men. She said she could not. I opened the Scriptures and spoke of the need of forgiving from the heart. After some minutes she came to a place where she could from her heart forgive them.

With this matter dealt with, I continued to pray. As I did so, it was like watching a radar screen with images upon it. I saw various spirits, such as spirits of hatred, hatred of men, fear of men and the fear of being murdered. The names were written across the spirits. Taking authority over them in Jesus name I saw them leave her as I persisted in praying, or should I say, saying. There is a time to pray, but a time to say (to command). Altogether I prayed one hour for this woman, and much of the time she was crying. At the end, she gave each of us a strong, heartfelt hug and went on her way rejoicing. The pastor and his wife were thrilled. She was part of their congregation and they knew her well. Previously, they told me, they had tried to speak into the areas addressed in prayer but she would not allow them to help her. She had been very closed. The fact that she had stayed after the meeting and asked for prayer was a miracle in itself, they said. Every area I had been led to pray into was 'right on', they told me, even to the fear of being murdered. Apparently the man who raped her was serving a prison sentence, although not for rape. He had raped her so brutally that he was doing time for attempted murder. No wonder she had a fear of being murdered!

From knowing only her name, I was led to address major issues of need in her life. Our Heavenly Father really loves us and desires that we might be made whole. He knows everything about us. Through the gifts of the Holy Spirit, we can work together with Him to bring the power of His salvation into human experience.

Receiving the gift of discernings of spirits

How does one receive the gift of discernings of spirits? I am regularly asked, as I travel, to lay hands on someone and impart the gift of discernings of spirits. This puts me on the spot. Who am I to impart a gift from God? Some people just want things served up on a platter. I do not doubt the sincerity of many who ask, but some want things the easy way.

First, we need to be seeking after God Himself and not just His gifts. The ministry we exercise flows first and foremost out of our relationship with Him. Hearing His voice has to do with developing a relationship with God.

> *'If then you have been raised up with Christ, keep seeking the things above, where Christ is, seated at the right hand of God.'*
> (Colossians 1:1)

Second, we need to be earnestly desiring the giftings of the Holy Spirit.

> *'Pursue love, yet desire earnestly spiritual gifts...'*
> (1 Corinthians 14:1)

The source of these gifts is God Himself, not man. If we are not seeking God first, we certainly should not be seeking man. After listing the gifts of the Holy Spirit in 1 Corinthians 12, the scripture goes on to say,

> *'But one and the same Spirit works all these things, distributing to each one individually just as He wills.'*
>
> (1 Corinthians 12:11)

There are two ways in which a gift of the Holy Spirit is imparted. The first is directly from God, without any human participation, while the second is from God with human participation. On the day of Pentecost, when the Holy Spirit came upon the gathered disciples, they were all filled with the Holy Spirit and began to speak in other tongues, declaring God's mighty deeds in languages they had never learned. God had directly endued them with this power.[15] When the disciples at Ephesus were filled with the Holy Spirit they also spoke in tongues, as well as prophesied, after Paul had laid his hands on them. God indeed was the source of the life and giftings that flowed, but Paul was the vehicle God used to release this new dimension of power through the laying-on of his hands.[16]

The gifts of the word of knowledge, word of wisdom and discernings of spirits can likewise be imparted directly from God, or there can be an impartation through the laying-on of hands by one believer to another. In my own experience, these revelatory gifts began to function quite independent of any human participation. However, there are times when a spiritual gift is imparted through the laying-on of hands and the speaking of words of commission.

When I was ministering to a pastor one day, he expressed his great longing to move in the gift of discernings of spirits. For many years he had desired to be a vessel through which captives could be set free. While we were praying, I felt that the Lord wanted to impart that gift and that I was to lay hands on him and release it. The next night, while ministering to people after the preaching of the Word, I noticed a couple at the back of the meeting. The woman was a friend from childhood and I assumed the man with her was her husband, whom I had never met. It became obvious that they were waiting to talk to me, but so many were seeking ministry I could not get to them. Meantime I noticed the pastor talking and praying with them. When we did meet, I too prayed for the husband. The couple then expressed amazement, saying that the pastor had prayed for deliverance in exactly the same areas and exactly the same order. I called my pastor friend over and, reminding him of the prayer the previous day. I said that there had been an impartation and that the Lord was now encouraging him, so he would realise that the gift of discernings of spirits was now operating in his life.

When am I to function in a gifting?

When the gift of discernings of spirits began to operate in my life, I found that I often knew things about people. It was not that I was looking to know, yet often I did know. I was aware of particular spirits binding people while we talked in ordinary conversations. This troubled me. What was I to do? Should I tell them what I was sensing? Should I offer to pray for them? If I did not pray, was I grieving the Holy Spirit? Surely if God was showing me something, I needed to act upon that revelation?

At that time that my friend Ken Wright came to visit, a man who moved strongly in words of knowledge and prophetic ministry. He had had years of experience in hearing the voice of the Lord, and what he shared lifted a heavy burden from me. He talked about a garden. Imagine a couple who had a beautiful garden. The wife cared mostly for this garden, because she had a passion for plants and flowers. She knew the names of every plant and waited in anticipation for the budding and blooming of the flowers. Although the husband liked having a nice garden, he knew few if any of the plants' names, and was not at all sensitive to them.

One morning that all changed. As he walked out of his front door, he suddenly noticed a lovely flower. He drew near and smelled its fragrance and called for his wife to come. Looking here and there in the garden, he was aware of the varieties of flowers, their colours and scents. They had been there all the time, but he had neither noticed nor appreciated them. Now his eyes were opened to see things he had not seen before.

My friend likened this to my experience. There were things in peoples' lives that had been there that I had not seen before, but now all this had changed. Suddenly I was noticing things, sensing things. A whole new world of awareness had opened up because a gift had been imparted by the Holy Spirit. He told me I did not have to rush here and there and say things to people because I knew certain things about them. A discernment was beginning to operate, but I was not to feel obligated to act on all that I was sensing. There would be times, however, when I would have the opportunity to minister to different individuals.

Motivation for moving in Holy Spirit giftings

It is important that we consider why we want to move in the gifts of the Holy Spirit. Correct motives are essential if we are to serve the Lord with a pure heart. Why do you want to operate in a gift of the Holy Spirit? You may say that you want to see Jesus uplifted and that is very good. Also that you want to see people really helped and that is also very good. But if the question is pressed, some would have to say that they want to be seen to be important and to have a great ministry. Such motivation is completely wrong.

It is essential that our purpose in experiencing God's power is that Jesus Christ may be honoured and praised, and that people are truly touched and blessed by an encounter with Him. If you are seeking the gifts in order to impress others how spiritual or important you are, then stop seeking.

Jesus sent out seventy disciples to preach about God's kingdom. They returned with great joy because the demons were subject to them, but His response was sobering:

> *'Do not rejoice in this, that the spirits are subject to you, but rejoice that your names are recorded in heaven.'* (Luke 10:20)

Linking this to other statements in Matthew's gospel, we are further sobered to consider the great responsibility we have of representing Jesus Christ on this earth and being accountable for how we have ministered in His name.

Jesus warned that each of us is walking on one of two roads in life: the broad road that leads to destruction and the narrow road that leads to life. He then warned of false ministers who appear to be sheep, but in their hearts are wolves. Speaking of good trees that bear good fruit and bad trees that bear bad fruit, He went on to say these fearful words:

> *'Not everyone who says to Me, "Lord, Lord," will enter the kingdom of heaven; but He who does the will of My Father who is in heaven. Many will say to Me on that day, "Lord, Lord, did we not prophesy in Your name, and in Your name cast out demons, and in Your name perform many miracles?" And then I will declare to them, "I never knew you; depart from Me you who practice lawlessness."'* (Matthew 7:21–23)

These statements were addressed to people who were charismatic in their Christian experience. Actually, every believer should be filled with the Holy Spirit and experiencing the manifestations of the Spirit. Somehow I feel it is going to be a little awkward for some believers on the day of accountability to answer why they chose to reject the empowering of the Holy Spirit.

For the first few years of my Christian life I did not understand these words, but now I do. I have been around long enough to have seen, as well as known, some Christian leaders who have functioned powerfully in spiritual giftings from God, but were later revealed to have been living in sin, often for many years. All the while, however, a spiritual gift or giftings were visibly at work in their lives. The answer lies in Romans 11:29 where we read, *'the gifts and calling of God are irrevocable.'* 'Irrevocable' means incapable of being recalled, repealed or annulled. When God entrusts someone with a spiritual gift, it is not a conditional loan dependent on their good behaviour, to be withdrawn on any inappropriate behaviour. A gift is a gift. This is why a person is sometimes charged with some serious moral downfall, yet all the time the immorality was going on they moved in spiritual giftings. God did not withdraw that gift or gifts because of sin. If it was a conditional loan, then it would have been withdrawn, but it was not withdrawn because God gave a gift.

Just because we see someone moving in spiritual authority and giftings does not always mean that they are right with God in their heart. An individual may have started right and served for many years with right motivation, but something happened to bring a fall. How we need to guard our hearts from the intrusion of sin! How important to have close relationships with other believers who can speak to us if they sense any irregularities.

Degrees of anointing

If I was to measure on a scale of one to ten the degrees of anointing I have experienced; one being the lower end of the scale while ten being the strongest, I would be misguided; I have learned from experience that I cannot always measure degrees of anointing by feelings. Daily I purpose to walk right with the Lord, yet sometimes the anointing feels like a one or two on the scale, while at other times it is a nine or ten. Why this intensity of anointing changes or appears to change is not fully known to me, but because it is not always as strong as I would like, it makes me rely on the Lord constantly.

If I always 'felt' a strong level of anointing, perhaps I would feel sufficient in myself and not need the Lord so much. He has ways of reminding us just how dependent we are on Him. Having said this, some of the greatest movements of the Holy Spirit I have witnessed have taken place, not only on the high level of sensing His presence, but when the anointing seems very weak. It is so true that we walk by faith and not by sight.[17]

Chapter 13

Weapons of War

While we are aware of war in the natural realm, one of the purposes of this book is to make us aware of war in the spiritual realm. As we have seen, what happens in the unseen world directly affects what happens in the seen world. The converse is also true, that what happens in the seen world directly affects the unseen world.

As Christians, we are called to war. Our God is a God of war. So often the Bible talks of the Lord of hosts, that is, the Lord of the angelic forces that battle the forces of Satan. True and lasting peace will never be negotiated in Washington or any other national capital. Only as nations submit to the King of kings and Lord of lords, Jesus Christ the Son of God, will true peace come to this earth. Only as battles are fought and won in the invisible world will there be lasting peace in the visible world. An excellent book on spiritual warfare I would recommend for an in-depth study of warfare in the Bible is *God at War* by Gregory A. Boyd (InterVarsity Press). It is not for the casual reader, but the serious student of the Word of God.

As we overcome demonic powers that bind our lives or the lives of others, we do so only with the use of spiritual weapons. Weapons are required in any war and the army with the superior weaponry usually wins. Our weapons are the most powerful of all and, unlike conventional weapons, never need updating.

> *'For though we walk in the flesh, we do not war according to the flesh, for the weapons of our warfare are not of the flesh, but divinely powerful for the destruction of fortresses. We are destroying speculations and every lofty thing raised up against the knowledge of God, and we are taking every thought captive to the obedience of Christ.'* (2 Corinthians 10:3–5)

Let us now consider some of the weapons of spiritual warfare. Although we live in a physical body, we do not rely on natural weapons but on those that are spiritual to overcome the spiritual forces of wickedness. The launching-pad for these weapons is the mouth. It all has to do with what we say.

The name of Jesus Christ

There is no other name so powerful as the name of Jesus. Jesus is the eternal Son of God.

> *'In the beginning was the Word, and the Word was with God, and the Word was God. He was in the beginning with God. All things came into being by Him, and apart from Him nothing came into being that has come into being.'* (John 1:1–3)

> *'And the Word became flesh, and dwelt among us, and we beheld His glory, glory as of the only begotten from the Father, full of grace and truth.'* (John 1:14)

> *'For by Him all things were created, both in the heavens and on the earth, visible and invisible, whether thrones or dominions or rulers or authorities – all things have been created by Him and for Him.'* (Colossians 1:16)

He who had the first word will also have the last word.[1] Jesus is God, and yet so many denigrate His name. The Creator became the Saviour, but He can only save those who call upon His name.[2] Everyone will one day see Jesus Christ as He really is. For some it will be a glorious meeting, for others a terrifying encounter.[3] Every true believer has the right, indeed the mandate, to exercise authority in the name of Jesus. As we come against evil spirits, we do so in the name of Jesus Christ. Jesus has bestowed on us the right to use His name. When we use this all-powerful name we are standing in the place of Jesus. We are representing His kingdom. We are releasing His power. It is an amazing privilege we have as Christians.

By working to destroy Jesus through betrayal and crucifixion, Satan was, unknowingly at the time, setting himself up to experience his most humiliating defeat, a defeat witnessed in the unseen domain, and a defeat from which he will never recover. What Satan thought to be his greatest triumph turned out to be his greatest blunder.[4] The prophecy God spoke after the fall of Adam and Eve had found its fulfilment:

> *'And I will put enmity between you and the woman, and between your seed and her seed; He shall bruise* [crush] *you on the head, and you shall bruise* [crush] *Him on the heel.'*   (Genesis 3:15)

Because the Son was willing to take upon Himself a human form, and identify with man's sinfulness by dying on a cross, the Father has highly exalted His Son.

> *'Therefore also God highly exalted Him, and bestowed on Him the name which is above every name, that at the name of Jesus every knee should bow, of those who are in heaven, and on earth, and under the earth, and that every tongue should confess that Jesus Christ is Lord, to the glory of God the Father.'*

> (Philippians 2:8–11)

Commissioning His disciples to preach the gospel after He had risen from the dead, Jesus said that in His name they would cast out demons, speak with new tongues, experience protection in times of peril and heal the sick. All of these would be accomplished in and through His name.[5] When Paul cast a spirit of divination out of a woman, he did so in the power of Jesus name:

> *'... Paul was greatly annoyed, and turned and said to the spirit, "I command you in the name of Jesus Christ to come out of her!" And it came out at that very moment.'*   (Acts 16:18)

Are you using this mighty weapon?

The Word of God

When God speaks a word, it is sent to accomplish what He wants to happen. It is full of power. The Scriptures speak of the rain and snow coming from heaven to water the earth and make it bear and sprout, providing seed to the sower and bread for the eater.[6] Just as the rain and snow come down from above and produces great fruitfulness, God says of what He speaks:

> *'So shall My word be which goes forth from My mouth; it shall not return to Me empty, without accomplishing what I desire, and without succeeding in the matter for which I sent it.'*

> (Isaiah 55:11)

The Word of God is full of power to make things happen!

> *'For the word of God is living and active and sharper than any two-edged sword, and piercing as far as the division of soul and spirit, of both joints and marrow, and able to judge the thoughts and intentions of the heart.'* (Hebrews 4:12)

Not only are we to speak in the name of Jesus as we come against demonic strongholds, but we are to speak words that have their source in God. Just as Jesus did not speak on His own initiative but words that the Father told Him to utter, we too, are to speak God's words.[7] Whether we speak words from the Scriptures or words that the Holy Spirit directs us to say at a particular moment, we are speaking words that are living and active, words that bring deliverance and healing. Words spoken through the inspiration of the Holy Spirit are words quickened by the Holy Spirit.

> *'And when the evening had come, they brought to Him many who were demon-possessed; and He cast out the spirits with a word, and healed all who were ill.'* (Matthew 8:16)

Just as Jesus released deliverance and healing through words that He spoke, we are to do likewise. One of the protective pieces of the armour of God is the Word of God.

> *'And take the helmet of salvation, and the sword of the Spirit, which is the word of God.'* (Ephesians 6:17)

The Word of God is called the sword of the Holy Spirit. A sword is a hand weapon, having a long strong blade with a sharp point for thrusting, and one or two sharp edges for thrusting and striking. It is used in close encounters. The Word of God in our mouth is as a sword against the enemy. The prophet Isaiah said,

> *'He has made my mouth like a sharp sword.'* (Isaiah 49:2)

The apostle John in his revelation described how he saw Jesus. He spoke of the face of Jesus shining like the sun, of His head and hair like the whiteness of snow, His eyes like a flame of fire, His feet like burnished bronze and His voice like the sound of many waters.[8] He also stated,

> *'... out of His mouth came a sharp two-edged sword.'* (Revelation 1:16)

When Jesus was tempted by the devil He used this sword. He countered the words of Satan with the Word of God. *'It is written,'* He declared, and quoted the precise scriptures to meet each attack.[9] We are to know the Word of God so that we also can speak the Word to counter the attacks of the evil one. God's Word in our mouth is as a sharp sword.

Are you using this mighty weapon?

The blood of Jesus

The late Lewis Jones wrote the melody and words of the well-known hymn, 'There is Power in the Blood':

> Would you be free from the burden of sin?
> There's power in the blood, power in the blood,
> Would you o'er evil a victory win?
> There's wonderful power in the blood.
>
> Would you be free from your passion and pride?
> There's power in the blood, power in the blood,
> Come for a cleansing to Calvary's tide
> There's wonderful power in the blood.
>
> Would you be whiter, much whiter than snow?
> There's power in the blood, power in the blood,
> Sin-stains are lost in its life-giving flow
> There's wonderful power in the blood.
>
> Would you do service for Jesus your King?
> There's power in the blood, power in the blood,
> Would you live daily His praises to sing?
> There's wonderful power in the blood.
>
> [Chorus]:
> There is power, power, wonder-working power
>   in the blood of the Lamb;
> There is power, power, wonder-working power
>   in the precious blood of the Lamb.

How true are these words! No substance in the universe has the power to change the lives of sinful human beings like the precious blood of Jesus. Only the blood of Jesus can forgive and cleanse from the ravages of sin. Only the blood of Jesus can release the bonds of wickedness that enslave those who are captive to the evil one. In the book of Revelation, we read of believers overcoming Satan:

> *'And they overcame him because of the blood of the Lamb and because of the word of their testimony, and they did not love their life even to death.'* (Revelation 12:11)

What does this mean? It means that we are to say what the Word of God says about the blood of Jesus. It means that we must hold our lives lightly and be willing to lay them down for the sake of the gospel if required. If we confess Jesus as Lord, we can boldly declare such statements as:

- 'I am in a covenant relationship with God through the blood of Jesus Christ' (Mark 14:24).
- 'I have confidence to come into the presence of God by the blood of Jesus Christ' (Hebrews 9:14).
- 'I am cleansed from all sin by the blood of Jesus Christ' (1 John 1:7).
- 'I have peace with God through the blood of Jesus Christ' (Colossians 1:20).
- 'I am justified by the blood of Jesus Christ' (Romans 5:8, 9).
- 'I am sanctified by the blood of Jesus Christ' (Hebrews 13:12).
- 'I am purchased by the blood of Jesus Christ' (Acts 20:28).
- 'I am redeemed by the blood of Jesus Christ' (Ephesians 1:7).
- 'I have a cleansed conscience through the blood of Jesus Christ' (Hebrews 9:14).
- 'I am an overcomer through the blood of Jesus Christ' (Revelation 12:11).

The confession of the power of the blood of Jesus is a most powerful weapon to use to break the bondages of evil spirits and to resist their attacks.

Are you using this mighty weapon?

Praise

Praise means to 'extol in words or in song; to magnify; to glorify'. No-one is so great and so deserving of this approbation than God the Father and His Son Jesus Christ. The Scriptures exhort us to praise God, and so we should, for He who is both Creator and Redeemer is surely worthy of all praise.

> *'Praise the Lord!*
> *Praise God in His sanctuary;*
> *Praise Him in His mighty expanse.*
> *Praise Him for His mighty deeds;*
> *Praise Him according to His excellent greatness.*
> *Praise Him with the trumpet sound;*
> *Praise Him with harp and lyre.*
> *Praise Him with timbrel and dancing;*
> *Praise Him with stringed instruments and pipe.*
> *Praise Him with loud cymbals;*
> *Praise Him with resounding cymbals.*
> *Let everything that has breath praise the Lord.*
> *Praise the Lord!'*
>   (Psalm 150)

Thanksgiving, praise and worship are all linked; thanksgiving leads to praise, praise lead to worship. The heart of Lucifer, who desired the place of supremacy that was rightfully God's, is revealed in Isaiah 14:13, 14:

> *'But you said in your heart, "I will ascend to heaven; I will raise my throne above the stars of God, and I will sit on the mount of assembly in the recesses of the north. I will ascend above the heights of the clouds; I will make myself like the Most High."'*

Lucifer wanted to sit in this exalted place and to receive the glory that goes with it and the adoration of creation. When Satan tempted Jesus, and took Him to a high mountain and showed Him all the kingdoms of the world and their glory, he said, *'All these things will I give you, if you fall down and worship me'* (Matthew 4:9). Satan wants to be extolled; he craves position, power and praise.

As the One worthy of all praise, Almighty God is released to work in power when He is magnified, and magnified in the midst of battle. This is so clearly seen in the account of king Jehoshaphat and the people of Judah, when a combined army of Moabites, Ammonites and Meunites began to advance against them.[10] Jehoshaphat earnestly sought the face of the Lord and proclaimed a fast throughout Judah. Unless God intervened on their behalf, defeat and destruction was certain. People came from all over Judah to seek the Lord in Jerusalem. The king proclaimed the greatness of their God and pleaded for His help.

In the midst of their praying, the Spirit of the Lord came upon Jahaziel, who spoke a word of direction from God as to what they were to do to release His judgement on their enemies. The people of Judah were not to be afraid, but to go out before the approaching army the next day. They were not to fight, but simply to stand still and see God at work on their behalf. Believing what the Lord had spoken, the king and the people fell down and worshipped Him, while many of the Levites stood and praised the Lord with a very loud voice.[11] The next day the people rose early and went out to the wilderness of Tekoa, with singers going before them exhorting the people to give thanks to the Lord. What an unusual way to win a war; yet win they did.

> *'And when they began singing and praising, the Lord sent ambushes against the sons of Ammon, Moab, and Mount Seir, who had come against Judah; so they were routed. For the sons of Ammon and Moab rose up against the inhabitants of Mount Seir destroying them completely, and when they had finished with the inhabitants of Seir, they helped to destroy one another.'*
>
> (2 Chronicles 20:22–23)

By the people obeying God's word and praising Him for the victory, multitudes of Judah's enemies, intent on murder and destruction, were themselves destroyed. So great was the spoil strewn over the countryside that it took three days to collect it. Not only was an army defeated, but much wealth was gathered unto the people of God. After praising God in the valley Beracah on the fourth day, Jehoshaphat and the people returned to Jerusalem with much joy amid the sound of harps, lyres and trumpets. Praise had played a major part in the overcoming of their enemies.

Are you using this mighty weapon?

Speaking in tongues

After rising from the dead, Jesus appeared to His disciples over a period of forty days before ascending into heaven. His last words to them were to wait in Jerusalem for an empowering of the Holy Spirit that would enable them to be His witnesses in the nation and to the remotest parts of the earth.[12] Ten days later it happened.

> *'And when the day of Pentecost had come, they were all together in one place. And suddenly there came from heaven a noise like a*

violent, rushing wind, and it filled the whole house where they were sitting. And there appeared to them tongues as of fire distributing themselves, and they rested on each one of them. And they were all filled with the Holy Spirit and began to speak with other tongues, as the Spirit was giving them utterance.' (Acts 2:1–4)

Living in Jerusalem were devout Jews from many nations, who were amazed to hear these followers of Jesus speaking in their own languages. What were they saying? *'...we hear them in our own tongues speaking of the mighty deeds of God'* (Acts 2:11). While wondering what this all meant, Peter stood up and preached to the thousands who had gathered to see this phenomenon. With decisive boldness, he spoke from the Scriptures that this indeed was the fulfilment of what the prophet Joel had predicted.[13] As he spoke of Jesus, His death and resurrection from the dead, and His exaltation as Lord and Christ, some three thousand people turned from their sins and became followers of Jesus.[14]

When the disciples were empowered by the Holy Spirit, they received a gift to speak in languages they had not learned. This ability was a sign of the working of the Holy Spirit in their lives.[15] Charles Wesley wrote the well-known hymn that expresses the believer's yearning to adequately express the praise due to God:

'O for a thousand tongues to sing
My great Redeemer's praise,
The glories of my God and King,
The triumphs of His grace.'

Wonderful and important as it is to express praise to the Lord in our mother tongue, so often there is an inability to fully express what is in our hearts. By speaking in tongues when praising God, this sense of limitation is removed. There is a three-fold purpose for speaking in tongues.

1.   Ministering to God

'For one who speaks in a tongue does not speak to men, but to God; for no one understands, but in his spirit he speaks mysteries.' (1 Corinthians 14:2)

2.   Ministering to oneself

'One who speaks in a tongue edifies himself' (1 Corinthians 14:4)

As we speak in tongues we are edifying or building up ourselves in our faith.

3. **Ministering to others**

> *'With all prayer and petition pray at all times in the Spirit, and with this in view, be on the alert with all perseverance and petition for all the saints.'* (Ephesians 6:18)

One of the types of praying and praying in the Spirit is to pray in tongues.[16]

The Bible speaks of *'various kinds of tongues.'*[17] There is a speaking in tongues that is purely devotional, that is, between an individual and God; and there is a speaking in tongues to bring a message to a person or persons, usually accompanied by the interpretation. Personally, I fully believe that every believer who desires to be filled with the Holy Spirit can speak in tongues. It is such a wonderful gift of God to assist us in our relationship with Him and in our ministry to others. If you are a Christian and do not speak in tongues, you should start seeking to do so.

When this gift is used to bring a word to someone it is usually accompanied by the interpretation, but we can also speak a word in the person's own language, as on the Day of Pentecost. After more than sixteen years of praying for people, during or after the time of ministry I have sometimes discovered that when I spoke in tongues I was actually speaking in the individual's mother tongue or in a language that they understood. Although I know only English with my understanding, I have spoken in such languages as Italian, Swahili, Maori, Russian, Japanese and Finnish. At such times I am usually naming and commanding demons to leave people, or else prophesying or bringing words of encouragement – all the while speaking in tongues.

Two years ago I was praying for a couple who had been leaders of several churches in the Democratic Republic of Congo. Because of the turmoil there, they had had to flee to save their lives. However, most of their adult children were still in Africa and they carried a great burden for their welfare. During the time of ministry I felt the Holy Spirit prompt me to pray for their children. Before praying, I lifted my heart to the Lord and desired to pray in their mother tongue or a language they understood. I then began to pray in a language I had never heard myself speak before. I felt very inspired, and the language sounded very African to me. After praying in tongues, I began to pray in English and was amazed at the flow of authority I experienced. I was asking big requests of the

Lord, things I would not have thought of asking myself. Then I began praying in tongues again and it sounded very African. As I again prayed in English, I was not only asking big things from God, but prophesying of things that were to unfold regarding God's provision for the family.

A third time I prayed in this African-sounding tongue and again in English. The whole time I prayed for the children, I was in a flow of great authority and liberty. When the ministry was over, no mention was made that I had spoken in a language they understood. The next afternoon this couple asked if they could have a few minutes with me before I returned to Canada. They expressed gratitude for the prayers for their children, and explained that there were five tribes in the area they came from – Bembo, Bazimba, Lega, Bango Bango and Kisongo. The African-sounding tongue I had spoken in was, I discovered, actually Kisongo. Each time I had spoken in Kisongo, I then had spoken in English exactly what I had spoken in Kisongo. No wonder they were encouraged as the Lord spoke in a language they were so familiar with, about concerns that were so important to them. As I pondered what had taken place I realised that not only had the gift of tongues been in operation, but the gift of interpretation of tongues as well.[18]

Four months ago in a meeting in Sweden I was praying for a woman whom I thought was Swedish. I was casting demons out of her speaking both in English and in tongues. You may ask how I know that I am casting out demons as I speak in tongues and the answer is simple: I feel very militant. I just know I am engaged in spiritual warfare and I see the fruit of what I am doing in demons being driven out of lives. This woman experienced a major release from spirits of anger and rejection that had bound her for years. The next day she approached me and said she was from Finland, and that as I had prayed for her there was a time when I began to speak in Finnish, commanding the demons to leave.

Only a year before, when in Finland, I had had a similar experience when praying for a Finnish man. What a wonderful weapon is speaking in tongues. No wonder the enemy hates this gift.

Are you using this mighty weapon?

Empowering of the Holy Spirit

As our mouths are used to launch these powerful weapons, we must be aware that formulating words alone is insufficient. It is only as the Holy Spirit inspires us, energises us, guides and empowers us that our words made alive and potent. In other words, we are not talking of using formulas to confront the enemy, but working together with the Lord as we engage in battle and being totally dependent on Him.

There are 'religious' people who have all the right talk, but their words lack power and do little or nothing to shatter strongholds. As I explain below, faith is very important, and the words we speak are to be words of faith. For now, we need to realise our dependency upon the Holy Spirit as we overcome the enemy. Speaking of Jesus, the Scripture says,

> '...God anointed Him with the Holy Spirit and with power, and how He went about doing good, and healing all who were oppressed by the devil; for God was with Him.'   (Acts 10:38)

We too need the anointing, enabling and empowering of the Holy Spirit.

Jesus cast a dumb spirit out of a man who was then free to speak. Some who witnessed this miracle marvelled, while others criticised the Lord, demanding a sign from heaven. Knowing their thoughts, Jesus confronted them and made it very clear that they had witnessed a sign from heaven:

> 'But if I cast out demons by the finger of God, then the kingdom of God has come upon you.'   (Luke 11:20)

These unbelievers knew that the Old Testament spoke of the finger of God. It was the finger of God that produced the signs and wonders in Egypt. When the magicians were unable to produce the lice, as Moses had, they exclaimed to Pharaoh that this was the finger of God at work.[19] When Moses was on top of Mount Sinai, God gave him two stone tablets engraved with the Ten Commandments. They were written by the finger of God.[20]

Jesus was declaring that the same power that was responsible for the miracles in Egypt and the writing of the Law on tablets of stone, was working with Him in setting free those bound by evil spirits. The Matthew account of this incident simply says,

> 'But if I cast out demons by the Spirit of God, then the kingdom of God has come upon you.'   (Matthew 12:28)

Who is the finger of God? None other than the Holy Spirit of God.[21]

If Jesus the Son of God needed to be filled with the Holy Spirit to perform signs and wonders, how much more do we need this equipping of the Holy Spirit. To be baptised or filled with the Holy Spirit is not an optional extra for the Christian, but an absolute necessity. Being filled with the Holy Spirit should not just be an experience that took place in our past, but a daily reality. There may have been a moment in the past when we asked Jesus to fill us with His Spirit, and He did so, but are we filled with the Holy Spirit today? Ephesians 5:18 says,

> *'And do not get drunk with wine, for that is dissipation, but be filled with the Holy Spirit.'*

In the Amplified text, *'be ever filled and stimulated with the Holy Spirit.'* We need to continually be filled with the Holy Spirit.

Receiving the infilling of the Holy Spirit

You may be a Christian, but have never been filled with the Holy Spirit and wonder how this can take place. Jesus is the One who baptises or fills a believer with the Holy Spirit.[22] If your heart is right with God and you are desiring to be filled with the Holy Spirit, then simply pray and ask Jesus to fill you. Receiving an empowering of the Spirit is by faith. For some it will be a dynamic encounter, for others not so. As you ask Jesus to fill you, begin to thank Him that He is imparting a new measure of the Spirit's power into your life. Begin to thank Him in your own language for what is taking place, whether you feel anything happening or not through your senses.

Do not be in a hurry as you wait on the Lord. Keep thanking Him for the impartation of power. As you thank Him, be open to speak out any syllables of a new language that are on your lips or that you feel stirring within you. You cannot speak in a known language and an unknown language at the same time. Begin to speak out the new sounds and syllables by faith. Those syllables will become words and those words will become sentences of praise to God.[23] If you do not begin to speak in tongues initially, do not be disappointed, but keep desiring to do so. It may be as you awake in the morning you will find a new language stirring within you. Speak it out. You could be washing the dishes and the language is suddenly there. Speak it out. It may be in a corporate worship service that you will find the gift of tongues released. Sing it out.

When I first arrived in Canada, I was asked to visit a newcomer to the area where I was living. It took me some time to find the house, and when I did I hesitated to knock. Inside I could hear a man weeping profusely. Finally I knocked and an older man answered. He invited me in and told me of a burden he was carrying for one of his children. As we talked, I discovered he had been a Pentecostal Christian for fifty years but had never spoken in tongues. Many had prayed for him but he had never received the gift of tongues. This had caused much disappointment. Asking if he would like me to pray for him to be filled with the Holy Spirit, he responded positively. As we began to pray, he became tense and was straining to receive from the Lord. I told him to stop straining and relax. Again we prayed and again he became very tense. This went on for twenty minutes. I kept telling him to stop striving. To relax. To receive by faith an infilling. Finally, he stopped his straining. It had taken him fifty years to get to such a place! In this place of rest and faith, Jesus filled him with His Spirit and the man began to praise the Lord in a language he had never learned. He was thrilled!

It is by faith we ask for an infilling and it is by faith we receive.

Chapter 14

Laying-on of Hands

As Jesus was delivering and healing, He often stretched out His hands and laid them on those He was ministering to. When He did so, an impartation of divine power took place.

> 'And while the sun was setting, all who had any sick with various diseases brought them to Him; and laying His hands on every one of them, He was healing them. And demons also were coming out of many, crying out and saying, "You are the Son of God!" And rebuking them, He would not allow them to speak, because they knew Him to be the Christ.'
> (Luke 4:40, 41)

Not only did Jesus lay hands on people; He commissioned His followers to do likewise.[1] As we do this at the appropriate time and in the appropriate manner, we are to anticipate a divine impartation of power as well.

Today, the laying-on of hands is not uncommon. Numerous groups, from New Age practitioners to some in the medical profession, practise laying-on of hands. However, we are not talking of what is practised in either the occult or secular realms, but the biblical practice of laying-on of hands. There is a major difference. Christians should never allow anyone to lay hands on them unless the person is a fellow believer or believers and it is done within the biblical context. Laying-on of hands is not just a physical exercise but a spiritual one, and to submit to a non-biblical practice of it is to subject oneself to demonic influence and possible demonic impartation.[2]

What does the Bible say?

What then does the Bible say about the laying-on of hands? The following clear definition and the three purposes for the laying-on of hands that follow have been ably penned by Derek Prince in his Foundation Series book.

▶ *Definition*

The laying-on of hands is an action in which one person lays his hands on another person with a definite spiritual purpose in mind.[3]

▶ *Purposes*

1. To transmit a spiritual blessing or authority to the one on whom hands are laid.[4]

2. To acknowledge publicly some spiritual blessing or authority already received from God by the one on whom hands are laid.[5]

3. To commit to God for a special ministry or task the person on whom hands are laid.[6]

Sometimes all three purposes are fulfilled when hands are laid on a person. The words 'imparting-acknowledging-commissioning' encompass the biblical 'laying-on of hands'. There are several early accounts of this.

Jacob and Joseph's sons

In Genesis chapter 48 we read of Jacob blessing his grandchildren Manasseh and Ephraim, the sons of Joseph. Jacob intended to transmit a blessing to each of them and laying hands on them was an important aspect of this. Joseph steered his children toward Jacob so that Jacob's right hand would be placed on Manasseh, his elder son, and his left hand on Ephraim, his younger son. Normally the first-born would receive the greater blessing, but Jacob purposely crossed his hands and placed his right hand on Ephraim's head and his left hand on Manasseh's. This action displeased Joseph, but Jacob had intentionally placed his right hand on his younger grandson in order to impart the greater blessing. Jacob explained to Joseph that Ephraim would become greater than his elder brother. The Lord knew the heart of each of Joseph's sons and the purposes He had for them, and had directed Jacob's actions.

We see from this account that the laying-on of hands was practised by the early patriarchs. Often, when hands are laid on a person, prayers and pronouncements are made over them. In chapter 49 we read of Jacob making pronouncements over his twelve sons. These were prophetic utterances pregnant with power and destiny.

Moses and Joshua

In the book of Numbers we read:

> *'So the Lord said to Moses, "Take Joshua the son of Nun, a man in whom is the Spirit, and lay your hand on him; and have him stand before Eleazar the priest and before all the congregation; and commission him in their sight. And you shall put some of your authority on him, in order that all the congregation of the sons of Israel may obey him." And Moses did just as the Lord commanded him; and he took Joshua and set him before Eleazar the priest, and before all the congregation. Then he laid his hands on him and commissioned him, just as the Lord had spoken through Moses.'*
> (Numbers 27:18–20, 22–24)

We see later the result of this imparting-acknowledging-commissioning.

> *'Now Joshua the son of Nun was filled with the spirit of wisdom, for Moses had laid his hands on him; and the sons of Israel listened to him and did as the Lord had commanded Moses.'*
> (Deuteronomy 34:9)

In each of these instances, something powerful happened through the laying-on of hands. They were no mere empty actions, but significant occasions in which God imparted something to each person.

Sometimes in church life we see merely the form of laying-on of hands. This is not what God intends. He wants us to experience life, not mere religious forms devoid of power.

Five New Testament purposes for the laying-on of hands

While we could look at numerous examples of the laying-on of hands under the Old Covenant, we will now turn to the New Covenant (Testament), which applies to us today. It gives five purposes for the laying-on of hands.

1. Appointing deacons

In the fledgling church in Jerusalem the apostles wished to be free from having to minister to the daily needs of people, such as the widows, and to be set aside for the ministry of prayer and the Word of God. At the apostles' suggestion, the church chose seven men full of the Holy Spirit and wisdom to be in charge of these practical ministrations.

> '*And these they brought before the apostles; and after praying, they laid hands on them.'* (Acts 6:6)

From these deacons who were set aside and commissioned through the laying-on of hands, powerful ministries emerged. Stephen became a great preacher who was martyred for his faith, while Philip became an evangelist with mighty signs and wonders accompanying his preaching.[7] Although not specifically recorded in the New Testament, the laying-on of hands was probably used when elders were ordained in the churches by the apostles.[8]

2. Sending out of apostles

The word 'apostle' means literally 'one sent forth'. In the church at Antioch five prophets and teachers are named: Barnabas, Simeon, Lucius, Manaen and Saul.

> '*And while they were ministering to the Lord and fasting, the Holy Spirit said, "Set apart for Me Barnabas and Saul for the work to which I have called them." Then, when they had fasted and prayed and laid their hands on them, they sent them away.'*
> (Acts 13:1–3)

Obviously an impartation took place, because the call of God on Barnabas and Saul was acknowledged and they were commissioned for a particular task. As a result of their missionary journey, many Gentiles turned to Christ and wonderful miracles attested to the resurrection of Jesus from the dead.[9]

3. Impartation of spiritual gifts

Writing to the church at Rome, Paul expressed a desire of his heart.

> '*For I long to see you in order that I may impart to you some spiritual gift to you, that you may be established.'* (Romans 1:11)

Although not specifically mentioned, the laying-on of hands was probably involved in the imparting of such gifts. When Paul exhorted Timothy to be an example to other believers, he added,

> *'Do not neglect the spiritual gift within you, which was bestowed upon you through prophetic utterance with the laying on of hands by the presbytery.'*   (1 Timothy 4:14)

Here we read of a spiritual gift imparted through the laying-on of hands by a group of Christian leaders. Notice that a prophetic utterance accompanied this impartation – a word was spoken and a spiritual gift released. In a later letter Paul again exhorts Timothy:

> *'...I remind you to kindle afresh the gift of God which is in you through the laying on of my hands.'*   (2 Timothy 1:6)

4. Baptism in the Holy Spirit

The New Testament records five accounts of people being baptised or filled with the Holy Spirit, three of which involve laying-on of hands. On the Day of Pentecost and in the house of Cornelius, the Holy Spirit fell on those who were gathered and filled them all. There was no laying-on of hands.[10] However, when Philip the evangelist preached the gospel in Samaria, followed by miracles of deliverance and healing, the new believers had been baptised in water but were not yet empowered by the Holy Spirit:

> *'Now when the apostles in Jerusalem heard that Samaria had received the word of God, they sent them Peter and John, who came down and prayed for them, that they might receive the Holy Spirit. For He had not yet fallen upon any of them; they had simply been baptised in the name of the Lord Jesus. Then they began laying their hands on them, and they were receiving the Holy Spirit.'*
> (Acts 8:14–17)

Through the laying-on of hands, then, the empowering of the Holy Spirit often takes place.

5. Physical healing

One of the signs to follow the preaching of the gospel is the healing of the sick:

> *'...they will lay hands on the sick, and they will recover,'*
> (Mark 16:18)

Jesus laid down the pattern of how He wanted His disciples to minister to people. The healing of Peter's mother-in-law is mentioned in three of the four gospels, and each account gives information that the others do not.

Luke's account:

'And He arose and left the synagogue, and entered Simon's home. Now Simon's mother-in-law was suffering from a high fever, and they made request of Him on her behalf. And standing over her, He rebuked the fever, and it left her; and she immediately arose and waited on them.' (Luke 4:38, 39)

Matthew's account:

'And when Jesus had come to Peter's home, He saw his mother-in-law lying sick in bed with a fever. And He touched her hand, and the fever left her; and she arose, and waited on them.'
(Matthew 8:14, 15)

Mark's account:

'Now Simon's mother-in-law was lying sick with a fever; and immediately they spoke to Him about her. And He came to her and raised her up, taking her by the hand, and the fever left her, and she waited on Him.' (Mark 1:30, 31)

In the first account, the emphasis is on rebuking the fever – the command of faith. In the second, on Jesus touching her – the touch of faith. In the third, on Jesus lifting her up – the action of faith. Put these accounts together and we see the full picture of what happened more or less simultaneously. Jesus came to Simon's mother-in-law and saw her plight. He rebuked the fever, cast out the spirit of infirmity; took her by the hand to impart healing power and then lifted her up, giving her the opportunity to respond to His word and touch, and rise up from sickness into freedom and health. All three ingredients were necessary for the healing to be received and maintained. The command of faith: the touch of faith: the action of faith.

Sometimes we seek to lay hands on someone to minister physical healing, but we have failed to cast out a spirit or spirits of infirmity at the source of the problem. Deliverance from evil spirits and physical healing are often very closely linked. To be involved in healing ministry is to be involved in deliverance ministry, and vice versa.

Guidelines for the laying-on of hands

1. Walking right with God

It should not be necessary to make such a statement, but it has to be made. To be representing God and His kingdom, a person needs to be walking in a right relationship with God. If they are not doing this, then they should not lay hands on anyone. As I have said, the laying-on of hands is not just a physical exercise, it is primarily a spiritual exercise. There is always the possibility of a wrong impartation should someone be walking in darkness and not in the light.

2. Under authority to be exercising authority

To be exercising authority in the kingdom of God it is important not only to be rightly related to God and subject to His authority, but also to be rightly related to other believers, in a local church setting or fellowship, and be subject to authority within that body of believers. This is not an issue of some people controlling others, but of all having submissive hearts one to another. It should be emphasised that submission is not unquestioning obedience.[11]

3. Knowing how to keep protecting oneself

Because the laying-on of hands is primarily a spiritual exercise, people practising it need to know how to protect themselves from any wrong impartation emanating from the person on whom hands are laid. By claiming protection through the blood of Jesus they need have no concern about this.

4. Ministry is in faith

All ministry is by faith, and so it is when hands are laid on someone. One does not have to feel that anything is happening to know that it is indeed happening.[12]

5. It is the laying-on of hands, not the leaning-on of hands

Some people are not sensitive to this. Take the weight of your hand or hands on yourself and do not lean on a person you are praying for. Neither should you push someone over when you pray. Encourage the person to receive from God while they are standing on their feet. If the Holy Spirit touches them in such a way that they fall down, so be it, but do not push them over to impress others that God is working through you.

6. Be sensitive as to where you lay your hands

There are places where it is not appropriate for someone to place their hands. Men should be particularly sensitive as to how they minister to women. Women also need to be sensitive how they minister to men. Men, give no appearance of evil as you minister to the opposite sex. It is good if a woman can minister to a woman and a man to a man. If a man is praying for a woman and laying hands on her, it is good if a woman is also assisting in the ministry, particularly if the prayer is taking place in a private setting.

7. Pray with your eyes open

As mentioned above, if you pray with your eyes open you will often see with your senses a little of what the Lord is doing. To have your eyes closed is to be shutting out this awareness.

8. Be sensitive to the person you are praying for

Pray for others as you would like them to pray for yourself. Some find it hard to receive from others, so be aware of this. Some need to receive a gentle approach to ministry and will close off if you come on too strongly. Respect the person you are praying for.

9. Be sensitive to the leading of the Holy Spirit

It is not what we are doing, but what God is doing, that brings life to the one we are praying for. Seek to be led by the Lord as to how you pray and what you are to say as you minister.

10. Always walk in humility

When we really know how dependent we are on the Lord to minister life to others, walking in pride will not be an issue. When God uses us, it is so important that we give all the praise to Him and encourage the one receiving to do the same.

Questions asked about laying-on of hands

The following are some questions commonly asked about the ministry of laying-on of hands:

1. *'I am a new Christian. Can I lay hands on someone and pray for them?'*

    Yes, as long as you are walking by the guidelines just mentioned.

2. *'I am not completely free myself but love to pray for others to be set free. Could I impart a wrong spirit to the person I am praying for?'*

    If you are walking right with God and have a genuine love for the person you are praying for, there need be no fear of imparting a wrong spirit to someone else. God does not wait until we are completely free before He uses us. The issue is to do with our hearts. Have a right motivation and go for it.

3. *'I never feel anything when I lay hands upon someone. I know some that do. Is there something wrong with me?'*

    No, there is nothing wrong with you. We are called to walk by faith, and when we pray for others it is always by faith, not feelings.

4. *'How many people should pray for just one person for deliverance? I have seen many gather around a person and begin to pray and it seems a little overpowering to me.'*

    A good question. It depends on the type of prayer ministry. For instance, if you were farewelling someone from your church who was going on a mission trip, it would be natural to have many gather around and stretch out their hands. If you were praying deliverance for someone, however, it would usually be advisable to have one to three people doing this. I am not saying that you should not have more, but a smaller team makes it more personal. If others wished to assist, they could be interceding in another room.

5. *'Is it always necessary to lay hands on someone when you are ministering deliverance to them?'*

    No, it is not necessary. However, I personally like to do so because I know that an impartation takes place through the laying-on of hands.

6. *'If I am to pray for someone, should I ask them if it is okay for me to lay hands on them?'*

    Sometimes you will sense that you should ask this question, particularly if the person is of the opposite sex. On occasion, the response will be that they would rather you not do so. Respect their wishes.

7. *'Can any Christian lay hands on others and pray for them, or is it only people in leadership who can do this?'*

    According to the commission of Jesus in Mark chapter 16, all believers can lay hands on those who are sick and minister healing. It is not just for Christian leaders. If you have a burden to minister to others, talk to your pastor and let him know your desire. If your church has a ministry team, perhaps you could become part of that team and then have both the opportunity and the authority within your local church setting to minister freely.

Personal journey

I was raised in a church setting where nobody laid hands upon anyone, so when I became a Christian I was unfamiliar with this practice, which I observed in other churches or Christian gatherings. The moment I came to Christ my life was radically changed in many ways, yet I had tremendous inner conflicts that I found no answers for, nor relief from, until a number of years had passed. During this time I did not lay hands on other people and pray for them, even though I was an evangelist. I had no thought that I might be bound by evil spirits, just that I needed to be set free from some inner problems.

Out of the integrity of my heart I chose not to lay hands on others, just in case something of my problems could be transferred to them. Looking back, I can see that the Lord restrained me because I needed so much deliverance myself. When God brought great release in my life, I then felt I could freely lay hands on others. As minister of pastoral care in an inner-city church, I began to pray for others to be set free, and laid hands on all who asked for ministry. Over the first few weeks of this, nearly everyone I prayed for told me, either during the ministry time or afterwards, that fire came through my hands.[13] Not feeling the fire and yet hearing these comments day after day, made me very aware that God was doing something powerful, even though I did not sense it. As a result, much confidence came to me that when I laid hands on others something was happening, even though I did not feel it.

Over the years I have continued to lay hands on nearly everyone I have prayed for to receive deliverance. From time to time, I still have someone say that heat or fire came through my hands when I prayed. Often I have a spiritual sensing of an impartation taking place, but not a physical awareness or feeling. Ministering in faith, I simply lay hands on others and believe that God is doing something good for them. I could not count the numbers I have ministered to with the laying-on of hands, and I am never afraid to place my hands on anyone. The Lord has taught me how to keep myself. As I begin a prayer time I lift my heart to Him and pray quietly, so others do not hear. I simply thank God for fresh anointing as I minister and for protection through the blood of Jesus.

Chapter 15

The Power of Faith

It is possible to be well-versed in the nature and work of evil spirits, as well as in the weapons of war God has given His people to set captives free. However, the weapons must be used to be effective, and they are to be used in faith. The Christian walk is a faith walk:

> 'And without faith it is impossible to please Him, for he who comes to God must believe that He is, and that He is a rewarder of those who seek Him.' (Hebrew 11:6)

> 'For we walk by faith, not by sight.' (2 Corinthians 5:7)

If we walk by faith, we do not walk by sight. If we walk by sight, we do not walk by faith. When Moses fled Pharoah's household after attempting to defend an fellow Israelite from harsh treatment, the Scripture says:

> 'By faith he left Egypt, not fearing the wrath of the king, for he endured, as seeing Him who is unseen.' (Hebrews 11:27)

Despite the difficulties he was going through, Moses kept his eyes on the Lord, seeing Him who is unseen, and was strengthened by so doing. He walked by faith, not by sight!

A distraught father brought his demonised son to Jesus. The disciples had been unable to release the boy, and when Jesus knew that, He said,

> 'O unbelieving and perverted generation, how long shall I be with you? How long shall I put up with you? Bring him here to me.'
> (Matthew 17:17)

Can you sense the exasperation in these words? Jesus continually walked by faith and not by sight. He was endeavouring to teach His disciples to do the same, and suffered another disappointment. He knew the power of faith! Jesus then rebuked the demon troubling the boy and it left him immediately. The disciples asked why they had been unable to cast it out. Jesus replied:

> 'Because of the littleness of your faith; for truly I say to you, if you have faith as a mustard seed, you shall say to this mountain, "Move from here to there," and it shall move; and nothing shall be impossible to you.'　　　　　　　　　　　　　　(Matthew 17:20)

Young's Literal Translation of the Bible simply says, 'through your want of faith.' Jesus also added, 'But this kind does not go out except by prayer and fasting' (Matthew 17:21). We see here that two important factors were required for the deliverance to succeed: faith and fasting! The disciples were lacking in both.

What is faith?

> 'Now faith is the assurance of things hoped for, the conviction of things not seen.'　　　　　　　　　　　　　　(Hebrews 11:1)

The King James Version says,

> 'Now faith is the substance of things hoped for, the evidence of things not seen.'

Faith is the substance or assurance of things hoped for. It is so real it is called a substance. A dictionary definition of 'substance' is 'a material of a particular kind or constitution'. Faith is something of a particular kind or constitution that comes from God, which is tangible and can fill our lives. When received and released into action, it produces great results.

One of the first deacons appointed in the church in Jerusalem was Stephen, of whom the Bible says that he was full of faith and of the Holy Spirit.[1] It is possible to be filled with faith, just as it is possible to be filled with the Holy Spirit. Faith is not ethereal, but real. Jesus said that mustard-seed-sized faith would move mountains! He never literally moved elevations of the earth's surface as He walked the land of Israel, but He certainly moved other kinds of mountains, such as those of sin, sickness, affliction and death. He was a mountain-mover and He wants us to be as well.

There can be strongholds of affliction in our lives – call them mountains of affliction – that seem as immovable as Mount Everest. Yet they can be moved. How? By faith! Jesus pointed to the lack of faith and fasting as the key to why the boy was not set free. He went on to say,

> '...*if you have faith as a mustard seed, you shall say to this mountain, "Move from here to there," and it shall move; and nothing shall be impossible to you.'*   (Matthew 17:20)

Mountains of the kind Jesus was referring to are moved by speaking to them! There is a time to pray, but there is a time to say – that is, a time to take authority over them; a time to command their removal. In Luke 17:6 Jesus said,

> *'If you had faith like a mustard seed, you would say to this mulberry tree, "Be uprooted and be planted in the sea," and it would obey you.'*

In my margin it says, *'would have obeyed you.'*

When we speak to a mountain of affliction in faith, something happens. Not that it might happen, or possibly could happen, but it does happen. Words spoken rebuking mountains must be spoken in faith. Without faith in operation, nothing will happen. Without faith, the words spoken may be technically correct, but devoid of power. It is only the word of faith that is quickened by the Holy Spirit.[2]

Again we read of faith being the key to removing mountains in 1 Corinthians 13:2:

> '...*and if I have all faith, so as to remove mountains, but do not have love, I am nothing.'*

As well as emphasising the importance of faith, we see how imperative it is for love to be the basis of all that we do. The last verse of this chapter says,

> *'But now abide faith, hope, love, these three; but the greatest of these is love.'*   (1 Corinthians 13:13)

Faith, hope and love are closely linked and work so beautifully together.

'But since we are of the day, let us be sober, having put on the breastplate of faith and love, and as a helmet, the hope of salvation.' (1 Thessalonians 5:8)

Faith and love together form a breastplate that protects the heart, while hope is a helmet that protects the mind. We all need faith and love in the heart and hope in the mind.

How does faith come?

'So faith comes from hearing, and hearing by the word of Christ.' (Romans 10:17)

The previous verses speak of the need of people being sent out to preach the good news of Jesus Christ. As God's word is heard with understanding, faith is released in the hearts of the hearers. Faith comes through hearing the word of God.

How does hope come?

'Now faith is the assurance [substance] *of things hoped for, the conviction* [evidence] *of things not seen.'* (Hebrews 11:1)

Faith in the heart produces hope in the mind. Said simply, faith produces hope! As the word of God imparts faith into the heart of the hearer, hope is released into their mind. That hope will not disappoint, as it is based on genuine faith in the heart. Hope in the mind, without a basis of faith in the heart, will often bring disappointment. There is no guarantee of this hope being fulfilled. Faith is in the realm of the heart. Hope is in the realm of the mind. Many people hope for things that may or may not come to pass. Both faith and hope have to do with the unseen. However, while faith has to do with the present, hope has to do with the future.[3]

Faith is now! Hope is future!

Faith in action

Friends of ours live in a small country community. The town comprises one main street with a handful of shops, including two grocery stores. Some years back, one of the grocery stores tried to attract more business by offering $1,000 worth of mechanical tools to the winner of a draw linked to purchases. On paying for groceries, the purchasers could write their names and telephone numbers on the back of the receipts and place them in a special box. On a set day, a draw would take place and the winner presented with the tools.

Many in the community purchased groceries and put their receipts in the box. All hoped to win the tools. However, the hope in the mind of one person had a basis of faith in the heart. When our friend Sharon put her receipt in the box, the Lord spoke to her that she would indeed win the draw. Faith comes by hearing the word of God. As soon as she heard the Lord's voice, faith came into her heart and hope into her mind. The hope in her mind, which was to do with the unseen and the future, had a basis of faith in her heart. Because she is very bold, she told many of her Christian friends that she knew she would win the draw because the Lord had spoken to her. And win she did! The hope in her mind had had a firm foundation of faith in the heart.

We need both faith in the heart and hope in the mind. It is also important to understand that mountains are removed by faith, not hope. And it is the word of faith that we speak, not the word of hope, that destroys mountains of affliction.

From hope to faith

For years I hoped to be set free, but no freedom came. No matter how hopeful I would be, my hopes were always disappointed. Looking back, I realise that hope alone is insufficient to release the delivering power of God into action. God responds to faith – not hope! To tell you of my journey from hope to faith I must continue my testimony begun in Chapter 7.

'Graham, I believe you need deliverance from evil spirits.' These were the words of the state and national director of the evangelistic organization I was serving in. As I had shared the long-standing struggles I had endured, he had made this startling statement. Noel Gibson then asked if I would be willing for him and his wife Phyl to pray for me for deliverance. I said I would think about it. Having been disappointed so many times in the past when I had opened my heart to others and sought help, I did not wish to be disappointed again.

When I agreed to be prayed for, a time was arranged for Noel and his wife to come over. Joined by my wife Shirley, the first session of prayer began. Noel asked if I would be willing to submit to the counsel he and Phyl would give, and I readily consented. Since becoming a Christian I had chosen the way of submission, and wanted to be open and teachable to all that God would say to me through others. Little did I know how I would be tested on this. Noel began to come against evil spirits that he believed were behind my breathing difficulties and commanded them to leave me. Almost immediately, there was a reaction within that surprised me. Something began to stir in my stomach region and I felt I was being torn inside. A spirit rose up and cried out through my mouth as I was thrown to the floor. So began the first of many sessions where my friends tried to set me free. After some hours I was exhausted, but no freer. Another time of ministry was scheduled, then another and another. Over some months, many hours were spent in trying to get me set free. Always there were dramatic manifestations, and always the sessions ended with no freedom being experienced.

From that first session I was plunged into the darkest period of my life. God seemed so far away and Satan so near. God seemed so powerless and Satan so powerful. I despaired of ever being set free. A number of times I was close to death because of the unusual things that were happening. I continued in my evangelistic duties throughout, but all hell had broken loose on the inside.

There came a day when I believed I heard God speak to me. He told me that if I would go to a certain mountainous location and fast and pray for one week, then I would be set free. When I told my counsellors this, they said they believed Satan had spoken to me and if I went to this location I might commit suicide. Numerous suicides took place there because the high cliffs beckoned troubled people to opt out of this world. I was convinced God had spoken to me and could not receive their counsel. It was important that I did what God told me, and not man. Noel then reminded me of the commitment I had made to submit to their counsel. Was I still willing to maintain a submissive heart and submit to their directives?

This caused me to struggle. I had to obey God, and yet I had committed myself to obey the counsel of my leaders. Finally, I told them that I believed I was one hundred per cent right when I said that God had spoken to me, and they were one hundred per cent wrong when they said God had spoken to them; but I would obey them as unto the Lord. On this response, they laid hands on me and commanded spirits of deception to leave. As they prayed, I actually felt a measure of freedom come into my mind, and then realised that they had been right all along and I had been wrong. A spirit of deception had led me astray, but now I was free from its influence. Had I gone to that mountainous place, there was a strong possibility my life might have ended, given the state I was in.

Seeking the help of others

Experienced as they were, my counsellors were greatly perplexed. Never had they encountered a case like mine. It was time to seek the help of others. A respected missionary from South Vietnam was asked to assist. After listening to my problems, he said that it was not possible for a Christian to be bound by evil spirits, and that I was under a curse because I had not been obeying the Lord fully. This man told me to read Deuteronomy 28, which spoke of the blessings that would come on God's people if they would obey Him, and the cursings that would come if they disobeyed Him. Once I obeyed the Lord, I would no longer have these problems, he said.

What devastating counsel! Since becoming a Christian, I had made it my goal to know and obey the Lord. Sincere as this man was, his counsel was not at all helpful. On the contrary, it was detrimental. Without an understanding of the spirit world and how demons can afflict people, he could offer me no assistance.

Another man was asked to help. He had been pastor of a large Pentecostal church. Listening to my story and quest, he also informed me that Christians could not be bound by demons. He had nothing to offer. Looking back, I am grateful that these men were willing to offer their services, but what a sad state some sections of the Christian church are in when senior leaders are blind to basic spiritual realities. How many multitudes of tormented believers have sought the help of leaders, to be told that the problems they were struggling with were not demonic in nature when they most certainly were. I have met many in this plight.

To my dismay, it was arranged for me to see a psychiatrist in the city. Because of the fear of insanity that tormented me, this was the last person I wanted to go to. However, as we were all so desperate to find solutions, I willingly continued to be guided by my counsellors. The psychiatrist listed eight treatments he could offer me and asked me to choose which I preferred. I found this strange. Of the eight, I remember only three: the taking of LSD, electric shock treatment and hypnotherapy. None was appealing. I could not make a decision in the state I was in, and asked the psychiatrist to do so. He chose hypnotherapy. After a few visits he told me he could not help. A further prescription for sedatives was given, and I went on my way no better than before. Where could we turn? Why was there no breakthrough? Why did God not heed our earnest cry for help?

Then a Baptist evangelist was asked to help, but the three sessions with him on the team were like all previous sessions. Great battles, many manifestations, but no breakthroughs, or so it seemed to me. During the third session, the team stopped praying and conferred together. The conclusion was that I had been set free from the spirits of infirmity they had commanded to leave, and that the time of ministry was over. I had felt no deliverance take place and was just as bound as ever, so I thought. As we drove across the city, my counsellors told me that there would be no more prayer as they were unable to help me any more.

The last vestige of hope left me. It seemed that there was no way to break free from the demonic bondages so evidently holding me in captivity. What was I to do? Where could I turn? Was there anyone who could help me come into freedom?

A major breakthrough

Two mornings later I awoke breathing freely. Something had happened during the last prayer time, as my counsellors had said, but because I had been so congested it took two days before all was clear and I could appreciate what the Lord had done. To say I was encouraged would be an understatement. After years of seeking the Lord for hours every day in prayer, at last a breakthrough had taken place.

Shortly after this, Shirley and I were asked to relocate within the state and take over leadership of one of the branches of the work we were in. This we did, knowing that our director and his wife would not be praying for me again. We were now on our own in regard to breaking through into greater freedom. A major break-through had taken place in the physical realm, but we all knew that breakthroughs were also needed in the soul realm as well – in the area of mind, emotions and will.

My patterns of seeking God earnestly continued, but I did not find the freedom I so longed for. I had no idea how to break into it. Despite the many good things that could be said about serving in this new post, I continued to struggle daily with inner conflicts. On one occasion, as Shirley and I were travelling to a town to fulfil ten days of evangelistic commitments, I began to feel very ill. Shirley took over the driving while I was curled up in great distress. It became necessary to return home and phone to say that I was ill and the meetings would have to be postponed. For three days I lay in bed in a heavy depression, unable to rise up. Such were the constant struggles I faced.

The time eventually came when I felt the Lord tell me to resign from the evangelistic association and wait upon Him until He told me what to do next. Little did I realise that eighteen months were to pass before that directive would come. Ahead lay a most difficult period. Unknowingly, I was to go into a death experience, before partaking of resurrection life.

'What is all the heart?'

Of the eighteen months that were to lie ahead, the first twelve were to be the most difficult. Free from the evangelistic duties that had occupied my time, I was now able to seek the Lord day and night. Walking the country roads, I called on the Lord to set me free from bondages. I did not know how to seek Him more earnestly than I was doing, or had done over the years.

'What is all the heart?' I would say to the Lord. If I had to relive the years that had passed and had the opportunity to seek God again, there would be few changes I would make. Since becoming a Christian, I had been very earnest in seeking the Lord and in serving Him. In that first year I fasted three months, as I did everything I knew how to be in a place where God could bless me. After twelve months I said to Shirley that I felt like a dead man, so dead, in fact, that I felt I was under the ground – buried – and yet I was walking on top of the ground. I had died to this world and had died to God's call to be an evangelist. I felt I would never preach again unless God did a miracle.

In this state of brokenness a miracle indeed took place, and it happened while I was sleeping. God spoke to me in a dream. It was not an ordinary dream, but a spiritual dream that stays with me to this day, so powerfully did it impact me. The Lord showed me three future events before they took place. At that time I wondered if I had a future, if I ever would be free; but through the dream God made it clear that many wonderful things lay ahead. It was like being in a cinema watching events unfold on the screen, yet at the same time I was fully involved in what was happening. There were three scenes, and after each scene I was suddenly caught up to a heavenly realm where I was flying over an incredibly beautiful country below, shouting praises to God with all my heart and strength.

In scene one, I saw and experienced a wonderful deliverance. As the sequence unfolded, I saw the demonic powers binding me and their ferocity, but all the while I was getting freer and freer. As I witnessed this, I became aware that my deliverance was going to be progressive; it was not going to happen all at once. Up to that time I had been anticipating a miracle touch from heaven, when all my bondages would be dissolved in moments. Now I realised freedom would be received through a process. Time was to pass. With this revelation, a settling came into my heart and I no longer strained for an instant release from all bondage. Then I was caught up to the heavenly dimension.

Scene two was quite different. I saw the adoption of two children take place. This sequence was covered in a light mist, so although I was aware that we were to adopt two children, the Lord was not giving me all the details. When I was suddenly caught up to the heavenly dimension and flying over it as before, I was aware of a small girl with me. She spoke two words – words that broke a wall I had had around my heart about having children: 'Hullo daddy!' For a moment I felt what it was like to have a father's heart, and it was a good feeling. Again, I shouted praises to God with all that was within me.

There were two reasons why I did not want to have children. One was that I was concerned that the inner turmoil I struggled with could be something my children would struggle with as well. If they had these problems, I would not know how to help them. The second reason was that whenever I heard a baby cry, a power rose up inside me and I would want to kill that baby. It made me afraid of what I might do to a child of my own. I needed deliverance from a spirit of murder, but did not understand that at the time. I am glad to say that, through the process of deliverance that was to follow, this problem was eliminated.

Scene three was different again. I witnessed being before a gathering of ministers who were opposed to the message of deliverance I am sharing in this book. It was a very difficult experience. Both scenes one and two had been so positive, but this was negative. In the dream, I left the church in which the meeting had been held with my head down, because of the distress of my heart. So much rejection had come my way. By an act of my will I lifted my eyes toward the heavens, and was suddenly caught up for a third time to a heavenly dimension. So glorious was this experience that I was praising God with all that was within me. There was an awareness that I would come through this trial in victory.

Then I awoke. Shirley was fast asleep alongside me and I could not understand this, as I had been making so much noise praising God. Waking her, I shared the incredible things that I had witnessed. There was to be a future for us. Freedom, yes; a family, yes; and some opposition as well. It is so amazing, that as time has passed, what God foretold and forewarned me of has come to pass exactly as I witnessed it in the dream. God, being God, knows the end from the beginning![4]

However, wonderful and encouraging as the dream had been, I was still just as bound as before and did not know how to get free. Continuing to seek God in prayer, I wondered how the dream was to be outworked. By this time I was drained of strength. I knelt by my bed one day and told the Lord I no longer had the ability to keep seeking Him as I had been doing. I was at the end of my resources. Many times in the past I thought I had come to this place, but always managed to keep going. This time it was different, as I really was depleted of the energy needed to keep on keeping on.

'I want you to rise up in resurrection life'

While on my knees I heard the voice of the Lord. It was not audible, but it might as well have been, so loudly did He speak within me: 'I want you to rise up in resurrection life!' My reaction was one of surprise, not so much that God had spoken, but what He had spoken. For years I had called upon the Lord to help me. I had been expecting Him to do something, when all the while He was expecting me to do something! Letting out an exasperated cry I said, 'But how, Lord?' Into my heart came two words, again loud and clear: 'By faith!'

A key was being placed into my hands that was to unlock many doors, not only in my own life but in the lives of others. When God speaks a word, faith comes by hearing that word, and an impartation of faith was placed in me. I could feel it. I was strengthened by it. A keen sense of direction was now mine. An excitement filled my life. Over the next few days I read every scripture I could find to do with faith, both in the Old and New Testaments. Shirley and I had lived by faith for years, relying on God for our daily provision. We knew how to trust God in this area. He had provided for us during all the months of waiting on Him, but how to rise up in resurrection life out of demonic bondage, by faith, we had no idea. Then the day came when the understanding was imparted.

Asking and receiving

While reading the story of Jesus cursing the fig tree in Mark's Gospel, a verse was quickened to me by the Holy Spirit. I saw something I had never seen before:

'...all things for which you pray and aşk, believe that you have received them, and they shall be granted you.' (Mark 11:23)

For years I had asked, asked, asked, yet never received from God what I had asked for. The Lord was showing me that I needed to receive, by faith, that which I asked of Him. There is a prayer of faith where we ask and keep on asking, but for my situation the Lord was quickening the particular type of prayer mentioned in this passage.[5] My imagination became alive. I saw, as it were, in the heavenly realm, every blessing that Jesus had purchased for us through His death and rising from the dead.[6] I saw an account in the heavenly realm that was mine. With the understanding that came through this promise in the scripture, I asked the Father in Jesus's name for deliverance from the bondage I was in.

Having asked the Lord for freedom, I then received, by faith, what I had just asked Him for. As I asked and received, it was as if I saw that provision taken from God's vast storehouse and placed into my personal account. Something happened in the unseen realm, but something also happened in my heart. A victory came on the inside that I had never experienced before. A new measure of faith had been imparted to me, for when God's word is heard and received, it brings faith. Now I would be fighting the enemy, not for the victory, but from a position of victory. Something significant had taken place. I was beginning to rise up in resurrection life, by faith.[7]

Jesus said that when we prayed and asked, we were to believe that we had received the provision and it would be granted us. 'Grant' means to 'bestow, confer, transfer'. Even though this provision was not yet being experienced in my life in the earthly realm, I had received it by faith, and God's promise was that it would be granted me. Now I needed to stop asking God for His provision and start thanking Him for its manifestation in my life. This took a little adjusting in the way I prayed. Having asked God for freedom for so many years, it was rather different to be thanking Him for it instead. As I kept thanking Him day after day, it felt as if nothing was happening. Nevertheless, I knew something was happening, not because of feelings, but because of God's word. If I received by faith that which I had asked Him for, then it would be granted me.

A few weeks had gone by when we were visited by a Christian worker whom we had not met for a long time. As he was about to leave he offered to pray for us. He received a word of knowledge concerning an event that had happened to me as a child and prayed into that situation. As he did so, I felt something happening inside. It was nothing dramatic, but I felt a small amount of freedom come. It was so small it was almost indiscernible, yet I felt it. This was very encouraging, as it was the first such feeling I had experienced since receiving deliverance by faith. Our friend went on his way with no awareness of how important his short prayer had been.

Continuing to thank God for the manifestation of freedom, I noticed further freedom coming. The process was slow, yet gradual. There were no manifestations of demons during this time as before, but changes were taking place. Without any feelings to guide me, simply God's word, I was indeed rising up in resurrection life by faith. An excitement was growing. After years of praying, the answers were being manifested at last.

Speaking to the mountain

Because I had been so helped through the account in Mark's gospel of Jesus cursing the fig tree, I read this passage every day. Then one day a further two verses were quickened to me, as verse 24 had been before. The day after Jesus had cursed the fig tree, He and His disciples passed it again. Peter exclaimed with amazement that the fig tree had withered from the roots up. Jesus responded,

> *'Have faith in God. Truly I say to you, whoever says to this mountain, "Be taken up and be cast into the sea," and does not doubt in his heart, but believes that what he says is going to happen, it shall be granted him.'*   (Mark 11:22, 23)

More understanding unfolded about how I was to work with the Lord to come into freedom. I had an awareness that God was saying that He and I knew we were dealing with demonic strongholds in my life, and that I was to take up my spiritual weapons and begin to use them against these strongholds. It was right that I should be thanking Him daily for the manifestation of freedom, but I was to be intelligently involved in taking the process a step further. I needed to speak to these mountains. To take authority over them in Jesus's name. As I did so, I was to believe that what I said was causing something to happen. Not that something could happen, or possibly might happen, but that something was happening!

I saw that 'faith is now'. This revelation made it clearer than ever how I could rise up in resurrection life by faith. Now I began to spend time every day coming against different areas of bondage that were holding me in captivity. Just as an archer aims for the bull's eye on the target and then releases the arrow, so I aimed right at an area of bondage and released the weapons of spiritual warfare.

'I come against all discouragement in Jesus name. Enemy, you have no place in my life. You are defeated. The blood of Jesus has redeemed me. Leave me now. I expel you. I drive you out. You have no place in me. My body is a temple for the Holy Spirit. Thank you Lord, that You are working with me and setting me free. I praise You for Your great deliverance.'

With such declarations as these, I started 'speaking to the mountains'. As I did so, I believed that what I was saying was happening. How did I know that deliverance was taking place? Because of what Jesus had said. If I was to speak to a mountain, not doubting in my heart, but believing that what I was saying was happening, something indeed was happening. I was breaking into freedom. I was rising up in resurrection life – by faith!

As the days became weeks, I continued in warfare. There were no demonic manifestations to guide me that the enemy was being stirred and defeated, but I knew he was. The Word of God alone was directing me to be an overcomer. It was purely by faith that I was prevailing. To my joy, I noticed changes taking place far more quickly than when I had just been thanking the Lord for freedom. My mind was becoming lighter, as depression and discouragement were leaving me. My whole being was being impacted by God's delivering presence. It was not because I was sitting before a counsellor, or standing at an altar call, or asking God to help me. I was speaking to the mountains. I was casting out the demons just as Jesus commissioned us to.

The first book I wrote on deliverance is called *Christian Set Yourself Free*. This title was chosen because of this understanding that we can release God's power and command freedom. Jesus Christ is the Deliverer, of course, but we are to work together with Him to bring freedom to ourselves and to others. It is not that we do it all, or that Jesus does it all, but that we work together with the Lord. Jesus told us to cast out demons, to heal the sick, to cleanse the lepers, to raise the dead. As we do our part, the Lord is with us to do His part.[8]

Pick-and-shovel faith

When the Lord was imparting understanding to me through the dream, the exhortation to rise up in resurrection life, the need to ask and receive, the importance of speaking to the mountains, I was not feeling strong in myself. God came to me in the midst of a wilderness time, when I was going through a death experience and had come to the end of my resources.

Everything I needed to rise up and press on was imparted to me from God. So it was, that when I saw the need to speak to the mountains in my life, I was not filled with a large deposit of faith. There was a small measure of faith, however. Each time God had spoken to me, faith was imparted. I say this to encourage you. You may feel you do not have much faith, but use the measure of faith you have and it will grow. As I began to speak to the mountains, I did not have 'atomic bomb' faith – just one command and the mountains were all obliterated! Nor did I have 'dynamite' faith – a few commands and major landslides taking place! But I did have 'pick-and-shovel' faith – and so do you.

Every believer has a measure of faith. Small as it may be, start using your measure and it will increase. When I took authority over the mountains, I used my pick-and-shovel faith. Daily I picked away. I believed that what I was saying was happening. I could believe that something was happening, even though it was very small.[9] Over the years my faith level has grown, and it is still growing. It is exciting to experience times of 'dynamite' faith being released as I pray for others. Even more exciting is to experience 'atomic bomb' faith, when the Lord does powerful things in moments. We all have to start with what we have. Use your pick-and-shovel' faith and watch it grow.

Set free to serve

Initially, as this process of deliverance was taking place, I struggled for a time with thoughts that I was being selfish, because I was focusing on myself and not others. It soon became evident that these thoughts were from the enemy, who sought to discourage me and stop me from engaging in warfare. I did not want to be self-centred, but to be set free to be able to help others, so I rejected the thoughts.

Persevering in engaging the enemy and breaking free from his holds, I was becoming freer and freer. One day I said to Shirley that I could not wait to get back into service for the Lord. Shortly after this a door of opportunity opened wide, and we relocated and became part of a vital inner-city church. After a while we were both invited on staff. Shirley became the leader of the music ministry and I became minister of pastoral care. As a pastor, I had ample opportunity to pray for people in the same way God had taught me to pray for myself. So began a deliverance ministry that continues to this day.

My greatest delight, though, is not that the Lord uses me to set others free, but to see others trained to do the work of the ministry; others becoming involved in bringing freedom to those who are bound; others experiencing the joy of working together with the Lord.

'Just say the word'

Because the understanding of faith is so crucial, let me refer you to one further passage of Scripture that clearly shows faith in operation. A centurion came to Jesus requesting help for his servant, who was in much torment and distress. Jesus told the centurion He would come and heal his servant.

> *'But the centurion answered and said, "Lord, I am not worthy for you to come under my roof, but just say the word, and my servant will be healed."'* (Matthew 8:8)

The centurion went on to say something that made Jesus marvel and declare that He had not found so much faith in anyone in Israel. And this man was a Gentile! What did he say?

> *'For I, too, am a man under authority, with soldiers under me; and I say to this one, "Go!" and he goes, and to another, "Come!" and he comes, and to my slave, "Do this!" and he does it.'* (Matthew 8:9)

As the result of this faith, Jesus said to the centurion,

> *'"Go your way; let it be done to you as you have believed." And the servant was healed that very hour.'* (Matthew 8:13)

Recognizing that Jesus not only exercised great authority but was under authority to the Father, the centurion expressed that he too was under authority. Higher ranking officials were over him, all the way up to Caesar himself. Under his authority, however, were one hundred soldiers as well as numerous slaves and servants. As a man under authority and exercising authority, whenever he spoke a word of command something always happened. Always! As believers in Jesus Christ we are under His authority and commissioned to exercise authority over unclean spirits. Whenever we speak a word of command as we come against enemy bondages, something always happens!

Faith is now!

Chapter 16

Persevering and Prevailing

As a teenager I briefly considered a career in the New Zealand Army. In every high school there was a Cadet Corps and I was the regimental sergeant major in my school. On several occasions I spent time in military camps of the regular army, but decided that army life was not for me. Why? Because of the rigorous training regime in the camps. I was sure that there was an easier way of life. In my youthfulness, I imagined the rest of life being long treks, showering en masse, and being disciplined by forced marches for getting into mischief. Instead, I joined the Mercantile Marine.

When someone joins the military there is an initial period of training, even rigorous training, in order to prepare a person for combat. Warfare requires trained personnel who can be thrust into battle and who will not fold under pressure. One of the requirements of being a good soldier is to be able to persevere in the most difficult situations. 'Persevere' means 'steady persistence in adhering to a course of action, a belief, or a purpose'. It speaks of steadfastness. 'Prevail' means 'to be greater in strength or influence'.

As Christian soldiers, we are to prevail over our spiritual enemies through persevering in the midst of conflicts. God's Word exhorts us to *'take up the full armour of God, that you may be able to resist in the evil day, and having done everything, to stand firm'* (Ephesians 6:13). An evil day speaks of a season of intense conflict, and in such a conflict, perseverance is required in order to prevail. Every time I see a certain cartoon I chuckle. It shows a frog being swallowed by a pelican, but the frog's arms are outside the beak and its hands are firmly grasping the bird's neck trying to throttle it. The caption reads: 'Never Give Up.' As Christians we are involved in warfare, yes; but the victory has already been won by Jesus Christ.[1] Satan and his hosts know that they have been defeated, but hang on in defiance not wanting to concede defeat.

We need to know that we are on the winning side and have been given authority by Jesus to overcome every work of the evil one. However intense the battle, we should never give up!

> *'Behold, I have given you authority to tread upon serpents and scorpions, and over all the power of the enemy, and nothing shall injure you.'* (Luke 10:19)

There are some, unfortunately, who are unwilling to engage in spiritual warfare and have adopted a passive attitude. Taking every blow the enemy wishes to strike them, they are like doormats, allowing the enemy to walk all over them. On the contrary, we are to be walking all over the enemy. What else does treading upon serpents and scorpions mean? Some reading this book need to make a decision to rise up out of passivity and begin to engage in warfare. To stop being intimidated by the enemy; to engage in combat; to prevail over him through the power of the Holy Spirit. Are you willing to turn from passivity to become a warrior for Christ?

In the book of Revelation are seven letters written to the seven churches in Asia Minor. These letters contain commendations, exhortations, rebukes and promises from the Lord Jesus Christ. Each concludes with an exhortation to be an overcomer and states the reward for those who do overcome.

To the church in Ephesus:

> *'To him who overcomes, I will grant to eat of the tree of life, which is in the Paradise of God.'* (Revelation 2:7)

To the church in Smyrna:

> *'He who overcomes shall not be hurt by the second death.'* (Revelation 2:11)

To the church in Pergamum:

> *'To him who overcomes, to him will I give some of the hidden manna, and I will give him a white stone, and a new name written on the stone which no one knows but he who receives it.'* (Revelation 2:17)

To the church in Thyatira:

> *'He who overcomes, and he who keeps My deeds unto the end, to him I will give authority over the nations; and he shall rule them*

with a rod of iron, as the vessels of the potter are broken to pieces, as I also have received authority from My Father; and I will give him the morning star.'   (Revelation 2:26–28)

To the church in Sardis:

'He who overcomes shall thus be clothed in white garments; and I will not erase his name from the book of life, and I will confess his name before My Father, and before His angels.' (Revelation 3:5)

To the church in Philadelphia:

'He who overcomes, I will make him a pillar in the temple of My God, and he will not go out from it anymore; and I will write upon him the name of My God, and the name of the city of My God, the new Jerusalem, which comes down out of heaven from My God, and My new name.'   (Revelation 3:12)

To the church in Laodicea:

'He who overcomes, I will grant to him to sit down with Me on My throne, as I also overcame and sat down with My Father on His throne.'   (Revelation 3:22)

It is clear, as we read these letters, that the Lord wants us all to become overcomers. Every one of us faces, and will face, challenges that call us to be conquerors through Christ. We can face the challenges and persevere through to victory, or we can withdraw from the challenges and miss out on the rewards. The choice is ours.

Paul's perseverance

For a fine example of one who persevered amid afflictions many of us know little or nothing about, look at the life of Paul the apostle. Formerly called Saul, he was in his pre-Christian days an avid hater of Jesus and His church. As such, he was feared by the Christian community. While on his way to Damascus to seize Christians to take back to Jerusalem for trial, he had an encounter with the risen Christ that changed his life forever. In the midst of a blinding light from heaven, Jesus revealed Himself to Saul and spoke to him. Saul then knew that the One who had been crucified had indeed risen from the dead. He yielded his life fully to Jesus from that moment.

Such was the brilliance of the light that had shone around Saul that he became blind and was led into Damascus by the hand.[2]

In Damascus was a believer called Ananias, whom the Lord spoke to in a vision, telling him to go to the street called Straight and inquire at the house of Judas for a man from Tarsus called Saul. The Lord told Ananias that Saul had had a vision in which he saw Ananias lay hands on him so he could regain his sight.[3] Ananias said to the Lord that he had heard about Saul and the harm he was wreaking on the Christians in Jerusalem. Jesus reassured him that Saul was now a believer:

> *'Go, for he is a chosen instrument of Mine, to bear My name before the Gentiles and kings and the sons of Israel; for I will show him how much he must suffer for My name's sake.'*
>
> (Acts 9:15, 16)

Paul indeed was to suffer for being a frontline soldier of Christ, but what a triumphant life he lived! With authority he could exhort Timothy to,

> *'Fight the good fight of faith; take hold of the eternal life to which you were called, and you have made the good confession in the presence of many witnesses.'*   (1 Timothy 6:12)

In his second letter to Timothy, written from prison in Rome, Paul looked back over a courageous life. He could say,

> *'I have fought the good fight, I have finished the course, I have kept the faith; in the future there is laid up for me the crown of righteousness, which the Lord, the righteous Judge, will award to me on that day; and not only to me, but also all who have loved His appearing.'*   (2 Timothy 4:7, 8)

Paul fought a good fight! Paul anticipated a great heavenly reward.

Get on the attack!

If we are to be overcomers we must learn to go on the attack against the enemy. To remain passive is to give the initiative to Satan and lose the battle by default. Even being defensive is inadequate, that is, fighting only when we are attacked. Defence at best only prevents defeat, but it will never win a war. The enemy's position is vulnerable – but only to attack! We are to dictate the terms of the battle; we are to engage in aggressive warfare; we are to persevere and prevail. David had mighty men who gathered with him: first the three, then the thirty, then many other men of calibre. Men who knew how to engage their natural enemies and persevere in combat until they prevailed over them.

Josheb-basshebeth, Eleazar and Shammah

'These are the names of the mighty men whom David had: Josheb-basshebeth a Tahchemonite, chief of the captains, he was called Adino the Eznite, because of eight hundred slain by him at one time; and after him was Eleazar the son of Dodo the Ahohite, one of the three mighty men with David when they defied the Philistines who were gathered there to battle and the men of Israel had withdrawn. He arose and struck the Philistines until his hand was weary and clung to the sword, and the Lord brought about a great victory that day; and the people returned after him only to strip the slain.' (2 Samuel 23:8–10)

'Now after him was Shammah the son of Agee a Hararite. And the Philistines were gathered into a troop, where there was a plot of lentils, and the people fled from the Philistines. But he took his stand in the midst of the plot, defended it and struck the Philistines; and the Lord brought about a great victory.' (2 Samuel 23:11, 12)

Abishai, chief of the thirty

'And Abishai, the brother of Joab, the son of Zeruiah, was chief of the thirty. And he swung his spear against three hundred and killed them, and had a name as well as the three. He was most honored of the thirty, therefore he became their commander; however, he did not attain to the three.' (2 Samuel 23:18, 19)

Benaiah, son of Jehoiada

'Then Benaiah the son of Jehoiada, the son of a valiant man of Kabzeel, who had done mighty deeds, killed the two sons of Ariel of Moab. He also went down and killed a lion in the middle of a pit on a snowy day. And he killed an Egyptian, an impressive man. Now the Egyptian had a spear in his hand, but he went down to him with a club and snatched the spear from the Egyptian's hand, and killed him with his own spear. These things Benaiah the son

of Jehoiada did, and had a name as well as the three mighty men.
He was honoured among the thirty, but he did not attain unto the
three. And David appointed him over his guard.'

(2 Samuel 23:20–23)

Mighty warriors indeed!

Prevailing over Amalek

After a miraculous deliverance from four hundred and thirty years
of Egyptian bondage, the Israelites soon encountered an attack
from the Amalekites at Rephidim. While Joshua and chosen men
fought valiantly against Amalek and his people, Moses stationed
himself on a hill overlooking the battleground and stretched forth
his hand, holding the staff that the Lord had given to him. When
Moses interceded with the staff of authority extended toward
Joshua and his men, the Israelites prevailed in the battle. When
Moses became weary and his hand heavy, so that he could not
hold out the staff, the Amalekites prevailed. Then Aaron and
Hur supported his hands, one on one side and one on the other,
until sunset. Israel prevailed over Amalek through persevering in
battle; each man in his place; each man fulfilling his particular
duty.[4]

Prevailing over the Amorites

Once the Israelites had crossed the Jordan and begun to take the
land of Caanan, the fear of God came on the inhabitants. This
prompted the Gibeonites to send a delegation to Joshua, pretend-
ing that they had come a long journey from a far-off land and
wanted to be in covenant with Israel. Without seeking the counsel
of the Lord, Joshua and the leaders made a covenant with them.
Three days later the Israelites discovered that the Gibeonites were
actually their neighbours. This caused complaining among the
people of Israel against their leaders, but a covenant is a covenant,
and the Israelites could not attack the Gibeonites.[5]

When Adoni-zedek, the king of Jerusalem, heard that the
Israelites had captured Ai, destroyed Jericho, and that the Gibeonites had made a covenant with Israel, he called on four other kings
to join him in attacking the Gibeonites. This prompted the
Gibeonites to send a message to Joshua calling for help. Because
of the newly made covenant, Joshua and the Israelites responded
immediately:

'So Joshua went up from Gilgal, he and all the people of war with him and all the valiant warriors. And the Lord said to Joshua, "Do not fear them, for I have given them into your hands; not one of them shall stand before you." So Joshua came upon them suddenly by marching all night from Gilgal. And the Lord confounded them before all Israel, and He slew them with a great slaughter at Gibeon, and pursued them by the way of the ascent of Beth-horon, and struck them as far as Azekah and Makkedah. And it came about as they fled from before Israel, while they were at the descent of Beth-horon, that the Lord threw large stones from heaven on them as far as Azekah, and they died; there were more who died from the hailstones than those whom the sons of Israel killed with the sword. Then Joshua spoke to the Lord in the day when the Lord delivered up the Amorites before the sons of Israel and he said in the sight of Israel, "O sun, stand still at Gibeon, and O moon, in the valley of Aijalon." So the sun stood still, and the moon stopped, until the nation avenged themselves of their enemies. Is it not written in the book of Jashar? And the sun stopped in the middle of the sky, and did not hasten to go down for about a whole day. And there was no day like that before it or after it, when the Lord listened to the voice of a man; for the Lord fought for Israel. Then Joshua and all Israel returned to the camp to Gilgal.'

(Joshua 10:7–15)

This entire story has been quoted so that we can ponder how intensely the Israelites persevered in battle. When the call for help came, they quickly went on the offensive. Fearlessly they set out to engage in battle. Already the men of war had been up all day and it was time for rest. Instead, they marched all night in order to dictate the terms of the battle. What a way to start a fight! Obviously, supernatural strength was needed to persevere and prevail over their enemies. As Israel worked together with the Lord, a victory followed unlike any other before or since. The Lord caused large hailstones to fall down from the sky, bringing great destruction to the Amorites. If that was not supernatural enough, Joshua was inspired to speak to the sun and the moon and command them to stop in the heavens. For almost twenty-four hours they ceased moving, granting more time to the conquering Israelites. Never had there been a day like this day. Then the Israelites returned to Gilgal.

How many hours had the men been awake? How many hours had they engaged in battle? Talk about persevering and prevailing. Supernatural signs. Supernatural power. Supernatural victory.

Time in taking the land

From this victory, further battles followed, until all thirty-one kings west of the Jordan had been defeated.[6] Between five and six years passed from the beginning of the offensive until the land was taken. That required a commitment to warfare and a persevering in warfare until what had been begun had been completed.

> *'So Joshua took the whole land, according to all that the Lord had spoken to Moses, and Joshua gave it for an inheritance to Israel according to their divisions by their tribes. Thus the land had rest from war.'*   (Joshua 11:2)

Rest from war! What a wonderful place to be in! However, there were still pockets in the land where the enemy had not yet been overcome. These enclaves proved to be thorns in the side of future generations. They also gave the Lord the opportunity to test new generations of Israelites and see if they would be willing to engage in warfare.[7] Where the enemy has established a foothold in our personal lives, many bondages are fortunately broken with a minimum of warfare, while other bondages are so firmly established that much warfare is needed. This is why we must be committed to persevere in order to prevail over our enemies. If we will commit ourselves to work together with the Lord to take the land of our life for His kingdom, the Lord will most certainly be committed to strengthen us supernaturally so we can persevere and prevail.

Rest and refreshment

In the midst of talking of the intensity of the warfare, let me take another perspective for a moment. Because my journey from bondage into liberty required much perseverance, and because of my ministry as an evangelist, in which I am continually releasing people out of bondages, I am very conscious of warfare. However, the Lord wants us to enjoy times of change – seasons of rest and refreshment.

In my yard I have an aviary where I keep birds, a hobby from my youth. During the summer I enjoy boating and fishing. Every autumn I love to go hunting in the mountains. When at home, as a member of the Canadian Coast Guard Auxiliary, I am on call to participate in search and rescue operations. I am an adventurer and always have been. Do not get the impression that to be a Christian and to be involved in warfare means that we have to go around with a long face and a serious countenance, or that we cannot participate in a variety of different pursuits. Life is to be embraced and enjoyed (I know some of you will say a hearty Amen!).

'He delivers me from my enemies'

David expressed praise to God for his great deliverance from all who sought to destroy him. Let us look at a few verses from Psalm 18, although the whole psalm should be read.

'I love Thee, O Lord my strength.
The Lord is my rock and my fortress and my deliverer,
My God, my rock, in whom I take refuge;
My shield and the horn of my salvation, my stronghold.
I call upon the Lord, who is worthy to be praised,
And I am saved from my enemies.

He sent from on high, He took me;
He drew me out of many waters.
He delivered me from my strong enemy,
And from those who hated me,
For they were too mighty for me.
They confronted me in the day of my calamity,
But the Lord was my stay.
He bought me forth into a broad place;
He rescued me, because He delighted in me.

He trains my hands for battle,
So that my arms can bend a bow of bronze.

I pursued my enemies and overtook them,
And I did not turn back until they were consumed.
I shattered them, so that they were not able to rise;
They fell under my feet.
For Thou hast girded me for battle;
Thou hast subdued under me those who rose up against me.
Thou hast also made my enemies turn their backs to me,
And I destroyed those who hated me.

I will sing praises to Thy name.'
(Psalm 18:1–3, 16–19, 34, 37–40, 49)

Never give up!

Chapter 17

The Importance of Proclamation

From the Latin *proclamare*, meaning 'to cry out' or 'to shout aloud', we get the English word 'proclaim'. 'Proclaim' means 'to announce publicly, to declare, to show or indicate plainly, to praise or extol'. Obviously, it is speaking about speaking out.

The words that fill our mouths are like a bit in the mouth of a horse or a rudder to a ship.[1] Words have power to direct and control our lives.

> *'Death and life are in the power of the tongue, and those who love it will eat its fruit.'* (Proverbs 18:21)

That is an extremely important statement – death and life! It should make us carefully consider the words that we speak. To enter into freedom and to maintain freedom, it is crucial that our words are in alignment with the Word of God. If they are not, we may never enter into freedom. If we are enjoying freedom, we could lose it. Paul declares that the righteousness based on faith speaks:

> *'But what does it say? "The word is near you, in your mouth and in your heart" – that is, the word of faith which we are preaching, that if you confess with your mouth Jesus as Lord, and believe in your heart that God raised Him from the dead, you shall be saved; for with the heart man believes, resulting in righteousness, and with the mouth he confesses, resulting in salvation.'* (Romans 10:8–10)

Our salvation has to do with not only believing in our hearts, but also confessing with our mouths.

Jesus Christ – High Priest of our confession

Not only do our words have an impact in the seen world, but also in the unseen world. Jesus sits at the Father's right hand, where He intercedes for us as believers. Our words touch the throne of God and move God to work on our behalf, especially if we are speaking what is right.[2]

> *'Therefore, holy brethren, partakers of a heavenly calling, consider Jesus, the Apostle and High Priest of our confession.'*
> (Hebrews 3:1)

> *'Since then we have a great high priest who has passed through the heavens, Jesus the Son of God, let us hold fast our confession.'*
> (Hebrews 4:14)

> *'Let us hold fast the confession of our hope without wavering, for He who promised is faithful.'*   (Hebrews 10:23)

The word 'confession' in the Greek means 'to speak the same thing, to assent, accord, agree'. We are to be saying what God says in His Word. We are to 'hold fast' our confession; that is, to use strength, to seize or retain our confession, as it is so easy to let a right confession slip away in the midst of adverse circumstances. This right confession is to be maintained 'without wavering', as it is possible to be speaking right one day but not the next; and right the day after but not the one after that. Again, because of adverse circumstances or feelings.

Water is an unstable element. An ocean, for instance, is subject to winds and tides that can cause much up-and-down movement on the surface of the water. Our confession is to be spoken forth in faith, and should not be dictated to by our fickle feelings. No ups and downs! When Jesus was on trial before Pontius Pilate, little of what He said is recorded in Scripture. It appears He did not say much at all, but what He did say was good. Paul says to Timothy that Jesus testified a good confession before Pilate.[3] When Pilate asked Jesus if He was the King of the Jews, He answered that He was. Jesus also stated that His kingdom was not of this world, for if it had been, His servants would be fighting. He said that He had been born into this world to be a king and to bear witness to the truth.[4]

Standing before this ruler, Jesus did not look like a king and in His humanity He would not have felt like a king; yet He held fast a good confession before Pontius Pilate. He knew who He was and

He said who He was, despite adverse circumstances and feelings. He held fast a good confession without wavering! Likewise, despite any negative circumstances or enemy attacks, we are to know what the Word of God says about us in Christ, and to speak it out. We have been born again in this world to bear witness to the truth, as kings and priests unto our God. We are to know who we are and to say who we are in Christ.[5]

In the gospel of Matthew we read that, as we confess Jesus Christ before others, He confesses us before His Father in heaven. In the gospel of Luke, it says before the angels in heaven.[6] Angels are ministering spirits to the heirs of salvation. In the letter to the church in Sardis, we see both the Father and the angels linked in one statement:

> *'He who overcomes shall be clothed in white garments; and I will not erase his name from the book of life, and I will confess his name before My Father and before His angels.'*
>
> (Revelation 3:5)

Something happens at the throne of God when we speak right!

Not as a parrot!

Parrots can be taught to say things. A family I know trained their parrot to repeat a certain phrase. When the father came home from an extended overseas trip, the parrot said to him, much to his surprise, 'Stop your moaning, Dad! Stop your moaning, Dad!' The parrot did not understand what it was saying, even though its words were important for the father to hear and heed. When we speak the word, we are not to just 'parrot' words, even right words. We are to maintain a right proclamation, with understanding and in faith. Also, we are to have faith in Jesus, the High Priest of our confession, and not faith in our confession.

Some think that if they say the right words often enough something good will happen for them. Not at all. If our confession is merely rote, it is devoid of power. It is to be a word of faith that we hold fast. Have you ever met a person who says the right words, but somehow it does not ring true, even though truth is being spoken? Some people can function in a very religious manner. Our proclamation must be made with understanding and in faith. We are not to be like a parrot.

Sword of the Lord

When the Israelites took the land of Canaan they did so by the edge of the sword. Again and again in the book of Joshua we read of them taking city after city by the sword. Again and again we read that they left no survivor.[7] If it should trouble you that God ordered the destruction of the inhabitants of Canaan, then you need to be aware of how wicked the people were in that day.

God takes no delight in judgement, but eventually judgement comes if there is no repentance. This applies to an individual as well as to a nation.[8] The Canaanites and the other tribes in the land were heavily involved in idolatry and evil practices, such as sacrificing their children to the god Molech. Such practices were an abomination to the Lord and provoked His wrath. He chose to use the Israelites as His instrument of judgement, which is why He told them to utterly destroy the Canaanites. If some of the people were to remain in the land, the Israelites might be enamoured by their evil practices and become defiled by them. Actually, this is what happened!

In later years we read of the Philistines lording it over the Israelites. No blacksmith was allowed in the land of Israel lest the Israelites should fashion weapons for themselves. Whenever an Israelite wanted to sharpen his ploughshare, mattock, axe or hoe, he was obliged to go to the Philistines, money in hand, and ask one of their blacksmiths to do the job.

> *'So it came about on the day of battle that neither sword nor spear was found in the hands of any of the people who were with Saul and Jonathan . . . '* (1 Samuel 13:22)

In those days, without swords and spears, the people were unarmed and largely powerless against their adversaries. You have to have weapons to go to war! You have to have weapons to win a war! Isaiah 49:2 says,

> *'He has made my mouth like a sharp sword.'*

When John had a revelation of Jesus Christ years after His resurrection from the dead, he describes the brilliance of His appearance[9] John also wrote,

> *' . . . and out of His mouth came a sharp two-edged sword.'*
> (Revelation 1:16)

In another vision, John saw Jesus going to war to judge those who had lived unrighteously. He again describes the majesty of Jesus and again mentions His mouth:

> *'And from His mouth comes a sharp sword, so that with it He may smite the nations; and He will rule them with a rod of iron; and He treads the wine press of the fierce wrath of God, the Almighty.'*
> (Revelation 19:15)

A sharp sword in his mouth! What is this sharp sword? Ephesians speaks of a sword in relation to the armour of God:

> *'And take the helmet of salvation, and the sword of the Spirit, which is the Word of God.'*   (Ephesians 6:17)

The sword that John saw in the mouth of Jesus was the Word of God. Swords are used in warfare. The Word of God in our mouth is as a sword against demonic powers. As the Word of God is in our mouth, something happens in the ranks of the enemy. The enemy's strength diminishes, his bonds are loosed, his forces driven back.

> *'For the Word of God is living and active and sharper than any two-edged sword.'*   (Hebrews 4:12)

We have a sword, but are we using it?

Some years ago, I was visiting a missionary training school I had been to a number of times. One of the staff, whom I had known for years, described to me how tired she was. For some months she had been troubled at night by demonic attacks, which had taken their toll. She was discouraged and depleted of strength. When she asked if I would pray for her, the Lord spoke to me not to do so. I was surprised, because the woman was in obvious distress. Without telling her that the Lord had spoken to me, I said I would see how the next few days went. Next day she made a further request for prayer, and again I put her off, because the Lord again said not to pray for her. The third day when she requested prayer, I talked to her at length and discovered something that really surprised me. I had asked her if she rebuked the enemy before she slept and claimed the protection of the blood of Jesus. She said she did not. With all the training she had received in spiritual warfare, I did not expect to hear this.

Now I understood why the Lord told me not to pray for her. I could have done so and all the nights I was on the compound she could have slept well. After I left, the attacks could have recommenced and she would not have known what to do. I told her to resist the enemy before she went to bed and claim protection through the blood of Jesus. This she did, and her sleeping problems vanished. When I met her some months later she had had no further problems. In her passivity she was very vulnerable. She needed to go on the attack. The enemy's position is vulnerable – but only to attack! Attack she did, and broke free. By using her sword, the Word of God in her mouth, she prevailed over her enemies.

There are some things we ask God to do that He will not do. He has given us authority over the evil one and we are to exercise that authority. When we do our part, the Lord does His part. There is a time to pray but also a time to say!

Sing it or say it!

A few years ago, Shirley was inspired to write a simple song on proclamation.

We Proclaim

We proclaim the Name of Jesus,
We proclaim His victory,
We proclaim He is exalted,
Over all the enemy,
We proclaim He lives forever,
And His blood has set us free.

Sing it, or say it; shout it, or pray it,
For He has won the victory.

We proclaim the Name of Jesus,
We proclaim Him Lord of all,
We proclaim He'll reign forever,
Every tongue will call Him Lord,
We proclaim He is eternal,
Every knee to Him will fall.

Sing it, or say it; shout it or pray it,
For He has won, the victory.

Proclaiming who we are 'in Christ'

The following are some wonderful truths that we need to acknowledge and declare. This is how God the Father sees us as Christians through His Son, Jesus. The list could be significantly extended.

I am:

1. A new creature in Christ (2 Corinthians 5:17)
2. Redeemed through the blood of Jesus (Ephesians 1:7)
3. Delivered from the domain of darkness (Colossians 1:13)
4. More than a conqueror through Him who loved me (Romans 8:37)
5. A temple of the Holy Spirit (1 Corinthians 6:19)
6. Dead to sin and alive to God in Christ Jesus (Romans 6:2, 11)
7. Strong in the Lord (Ephesians 6:10)
8. An heir of God and fellow heir with Christ (Romans 8:17)
9. A partaker of the divine nature (2 Peter 1:4)
10. Complete in Christ (Colossians 2:10)
11. Healed by His wounds (1 Peter 2:24)
12. Being changed into His image (2 Corinthians 3:18)
13. Seated with Christ in the heavenly places (Ephesians 2:5)
14. Chosen, holy and loved (Colossians 3:12)
15. Led in triumph in Christ (2 Corinthians 2:14)
16. Able to do all things through Christ who strengthens me (Philippians 4:13)
17. Alive with Christ (Ephesians 2:5)
18. An overcomer of the world (1 John 5:4)
19. Free from condemnation in Christ (Romans 8:1)
20. Sealed with the Holy Spirit of promise (Ephesians 1:13)

Focusing on Jesus

This has been discussed already, but bears mention again in conclusion. In the midst of warfare, aware of demonic powers attacking and retreating, our main focus must always be on the Lord Jesus Christ and not on the enemy. It is Christ, the All-conquering One, whom we need to see before us. If we lose focus of Him, then we will find ourselves with a wrong focus and therefore a wrong confession.

> 'If then you have been raised up with Christ, keep seeking the things above, where Christ is, seated at the right hand of God. Set your mind on the things above, not on the things that are on earth.

For you have died and your life is hidden with Christ in God.
When Christ, who is our life, is revealed, then you also will be
revealed with Him in glory.'   (Colossians 3:1–4)

A Psalm of David

'The Lord is my light and my salvation;
Whom shall I fear?
The Lord is the defence of my life;
Whom shall I dread?

When evildoers came upon me to devour my flesh,
My adversaries and my enemies, they stumbled and fell.
Though a host encamp against me,
My heart will not fear;
Though war arise against me,
In spite of this I shall be confident.

One thing I have asked from the Lord, that I shall seek:
That I may dwell in the house of the Lord all the days of my life,
To behold the beauty of the Lord,
And to meditate in His temple.

For in the day of trouble He will conceal me in His tabernacle;
In the secret place of His tent He will hide me;
He will lift me up on a rock.

And now my head will be lifted up above
My enemies around me;
And I will offer in His tent sacrifices with shouts of joy;
I will sing, yes, I will sing praises to the Lord.'   (Psalm 27:1–6)

Biblical References

Chapter 1

[1] 2 Corinthians 4:3–4 [2] John 8:31–32 [3] 2 Kings 6:17 [4] 2 Kings 6:17
[5] 2 Kings 6:18–23 [6] 2 Corinthians 12:1–4 [7] 2 Corinthians 5:1–10;
Hebrews 1:14; Luke 16:22 [8] 2 Corinthians 4:16–18; 5:6–8 [9] Matthew
7:13–14; 16:24–26 [10] Genesis 5:21–24; 2 Kings 2:1–18 [11] Luke 16:26
[12] Hebrews 10:1–14 [13] Isaiah 14:12–15; Ezekiel 28:14–16 [14]Hebrews
9:11–22; 10:19–22; 12:22–24 [15] John 10:11; 17–18; Hebrews 10:1–4
[16] 2 Corinthians 1–8; Colossians 2:13–15 [17] John 3:14–21, 36 [18] 1 Peter
3:18–20 [19] Kevin Connor, *Three Days and Three Nights*, Bible Temple
Publications [20] Leviticus 16:1–19; John 20:17; Hebrews 9:11–26
[21] Ephesians 4:7–8 [22] 2 Corinthians 5:1–9 [23] Matthew 7:13–14; Luke
16:22–23; Revelation 20:11–15 [24] Revelation 20:11–15; Romans 2:14–16

Chapter 2

[1] Revelation 4:11 [2] Luke 12:15; 1 Timothy 6:6–7 [3] Revelation 20:11–15
[4] Hebrews 1:14; Luke 16:22 [5] John 20:19, 26; 1 Corinthians 15:35–57

Chapter 3

[1] Ezekiel 10; Isaiah 6:1–3 [2] Ezekiel 28:11–16 [3] Daniel 10:13, 21; 12:1;
Jude 9; Revelation 12:7 [4] 1 Thessalonians 4:16 [5] Daniel 8:16; 9:21; Luke
1:19, 26 [6] Revelation 5:11–12 [7] Psalm 148:1–5; Job 38:1–7 [8] Hebrews
1:13–14 [9] Luke 20:36 [10] Luke 20:34–36 [11] Daniel 7:9–10; Psalm 68:17
[12] Hebrews 2:7 [13] Isaiah 14:12–14 [14] Psalm 103:20–21 [15] Colossians
1:16 [16] Daniel 10:4–21 [17] 1 Chronicles 21:15–30 [18] Acts 12:1–17
[19] Hebrews 13:2 [20] 1 Timothy 5:21; 2 Peter 2:4; Jude 6, 9 [21] Revelation
12:4; Isaiah 14:12–15 [22] Job 38:7; Isaiah 14:13 [23] 1 Thessalonians 2:18
[24] Ephesians 2:1–2 [25] Titus 3:3–7 [26] Proverbs 14:12 [27] Matthew 4:1–12
[28] 1 Corinthians 10:13 [29] James 1:13–16; 1 John 1:5–10 [30] Titus 1:15;
Matthew 15:11; 17–20 [31] Mark 5:1–5 [32] Revelation 12:9–11
[33] 2 Corinthians 11:3 [34] Luke 13:11; 2 Timothy 2:26 [35] Revelation 9:5
[36] Deuteronomy 28:65–67 [37] John 10:10 [38] Revelation 9:11 [39] 2 Timothy
2:26 [40] 1 Corinthians 2:6–8 [41] Luke 10:18; Genesis 3:14–15; Colossians
2:15 [42] Mark 16:17; Revelation 12:7–9; 20:1–3 [43] Matthew 25:41

Chapter 4

[1] 1 Corinthians 4:3–4; Ephesians 2:1–3   [2] Titus 3:1–3   [3] Genesis 1:26–27
[4] Genesis 2:16–17   [5] Genesis 2:16–17   [6] Genesis 3:6–8   [7] Genesis 5:5
[8] Genesis 3:15   [9] Genesis 3:22–24   [10] Genesis 4:8   [11] Genesis 3:17–19
[12] Ephesians 3:1–3   [13] Genesis 15:12–21; 1 Corinthians 11:23–26
[14] Deuteronomy 30:15–20   [15] Genesis 4:1–8   [16] Genesis 12:1–5   [17] Genesis
12:3; 15:5–6   [18] Genesis 15:12–21   [19] Genesis 16:1–4   [20] Genesis
17:18–19   [21] Genesis 21:1–5   [22] Genesis 27:1–45   [23] Genesis 32:22–32;
Exodus 3:15   [24] Exodus 14:2   [25] Exodus 31:18   [26] 1 Chronicles 16:26
[27] Romans 1:18–23   [28] Exodus 20:1–17; 21–41; Leviticus 1–27   [29] Hebrews
8:1–5   [30] Hebrews 9:1–12   [31] Hebrews 9:1–7   [32] Hebrews 9:1–3
[33] Leviticus 16:1   [34] Exodus 40:36–38   [35] Leviticus 1:1–4   [36] Leviticus 1–7
[37] 2 Kings 10:29–31; 12:1–2   [38] 2 Samuel 12:1–12   [39] 1 Kings 11:6–8
[40] 2 Kings 10:1–10   [41] 2 Kings 17:1–6, 23   [42] Job 1:1–6   [43] Job 1:6–12
[44] Job 1:13–19   [45] Job 1:20–22   [46] Job 2:1–6   [47] Job 2:7–10   [48] Job
42:10–17

Chapter 5

[1] Luke 1:8–23   [2] Luke 1:15–17, 41   [3] Matthew 1:18–20   [4] Luke 1:30–33
[5] Luke 1:39–56   [6] Matthew 1:24–25   [7] Luke 2:1–7   [8] Luke 2:8–20
[9] Matthew 2:1–2   [10] Matthew 2:3–8   [11] Matthew 2:12–15   [12] Matthew
2:16–18   [13] Genesis 3:15   [14] Luke 2:41–52   [15] Luke 1:80, 3:1–6   [16] Romans
6:1–4   [17] Matthew 3:13–17   [18] Luke 3:18–20; Mark 6:27   [19] Matthew 4:1
[20] Matthew 4:1–11; 1 Corinthians 15:45–49   [21] Philippians 2:5–8
[22] Matthew 4:4, 7, 10   [23] Luke 4:14   [24] Luke 4:22–30   [25] Luke 10:1
[26] Matthew 16:24–26   [27] Matthew 4:17   [28] Matthew 15:17–20; John 6:66
[29] Matthew 23:1–36   [30] John 3:1–15; 7:50; 19:39   [31] Matthew 3:2;
Colossians 1:13; Mark 3:23–27   [32] Ephesians 6:12; John 3:23–27
[33] 2 Corinthians 4:3–4   [34] Ephesians 2:1–3   [35] Mark 2:1–12   [36] Matthew
8:16   [37] Matthew 8:16–17   [38] Mark 5:35–43   [39] Acts 10:38   [40] Luke
22:3–6   [41] Luke 22:47–48   [42] Matthew 26:65   [43] Matthew 27:11–14; Luke
23:7–12   [44] Luke 23:17–25   [45] Matthew 27:19   [46] *Westminister Dictionary
of the Bible*, p. 483   [47] Matthew 27:24–26   [48] *Westminster Dictionary of the
Bible*, p. 538   [49] Matthew 27:28–31   [50] Matthew 27:32   [51] Matthew 27:37
[52] Matthew 27:46   [53] John 19:30   [54] Hebrews 10:9–14   [55] Hebrews
10:19–22   [56] John 19:31–37   [57] John 19:38–42   [58] Matthew 27:62–66
[59] Matthew 28:2–4   [60] John 20:19–23   [61] John 20:26–29   [62] Acts 1:1–3
[63] Acts 1:4–8   [64] Romans 8:34   [65] John 12:16   [66] Matthew 24:1–14
[67] 2 Thessalonians 1:7–10   [68] 1 Thessalonians 4:13–17; Revelation 1:7
[69] Matthew 25:31–46   [70] Acts 1:8

Chapter 6

[1] Ephesians 2:1–3; Titus 2:11–15; 3:1–7   [2] Ephesians 2:11–12   [3] Mark
6:12–13   [4] Hebrews 6:1   [5] Matthew 3:7–8; Luke 19:1–8   [6] Revelation 15:3;
17:14; 19:16; 1 Timothy 6:13–16   [7] Romans 10:6–10; John 3:16

[8] Galatians 4:6   [9] 1 Corinthians 12:12–27   [10] Romans 12:2   [11] Matthew 4:4   [12] John 20:22

Chapter 7
[1] Romans 10:11–13

Chapter 8
[1] 1 Corinthians 5:7   [2] Romans 13:11–14

Chapter 9
[1] John 10:10   [2] Galatians 6:7   [3] Mark 16:9   [4] Mark 5:13   [5] Mark 5:15
[6] Deuteronomy 23:2   [7] Proverbs 3:7; 8:13; 16:6   [8] 1 John 1:5–10
[9] Ephesians 4:26, 27   [10] Proverbs 18:21   [11] Isaiah 53:3–5; 1 Peter 2:24

Chapter 10
[1] Exodus 40:34–38   [2] Leviticus 16   [3] The Greek word that translates into English as 'discerning' or 'distinguishing' in many of our English Bible translations, is actually in the plural. The correct translation is 'discernings' or 'distinguishings'.

Chapter 11
[1] Matthew 3:15   [2] Matthew 28:18–20; Ephesians 5:18   [3] Revelation 12:10
[4] Isaiah 53:4

Chapter 12
[1] Acts 13:11   [2] Hebrews 1:14   [3] Daniel 10:4–19   [4] Hebrews 13:2   [5] Acts 12:7–11   [6] Acts 16:6   [7] Acts 16:7–8   [8] Mark 9:17–29   [9] Luke 13:10–17
[10] Acts 16:16–18   [11] Galatians 5:22–24; 1 Corinthians 12:11   [12] Mark 9:21   [13] 1 Corinthians 14:1   [14] Romans 10:17   [15] Acts 2:1–4   [16] Acts 19:1–7   [17] 2 Corinthians 5:7

Chapter 13
[1] Revelation 1:8; John 12:48   [2] Romans 10:12–13   [3] 2 Thessalonians 1:7–10; 1 Thessalonians 4:13–17   [4] 1 Corinthians 2:6–8   [5] Mark 16:17–18
[6] Isaiah 55:10   [7] John 12:49–50   [8] Revelation 1:12–15   [9] Matthew 4:1–11
[10] 2 Chronicles 20:1–30   [11] 2 Chronicles 20:18–19   [12] Acts 1:4–8   [13] Acts 2:14–21   [14] Acts 2:37–42   [15] Acts 2:1–4; 1 Corinthians 14:22
[16] 1 Corinthians 14:14–17   [17] 1 Corinthians 12:28   [18] 1 Corinthians 12:10   [19] Exodus 8:19   [20] Exodus 3:18   [21] 2 Corinthians 3:1–3   [22] Matthew 3:11   [23] Acts 2:1–4

Chapter 14
[1] Mark 16:18   [2] 1 Timothy 5:21, 22   [3] 1 Timothy 4:14   [4] Genesis 48:14
[5] Numbers 27:22, 23   [6] Numbers 27:18, 19   [7] Acts 6:8; 8:4–8   [8] Acts

14:23 [9] Acts 14:26–27 [10] Acts 2:1–4; 10:44–48 [11] James 4:7; 1 Peter 5:1–5 [12] 2 Corinthians 5:7 [13] Matthew 3:11–12

Chapter 15

[1] Acts 6:5 [2] Romans 10:6–10; 2 Corinthians 3:5–6 [3] Romans 8:24–25 [4] Revelation 1:8; Psalm 139:13–16 [5] Luke 11:5–13 [6] Ephesians 1:3 [7] Romans 10:17 [8] Mark 16:19–20 [9] Romans 12:3

Chapter 16

[1] Colossians 2:13–15 [2] Acts 9:1–9 [3] Acts 9:10–12 [4] Exodus 17:8–3 [5] Joshua 9:3–21 [6] Joshua 10–14 [7] Judges 1:1–36; 2:20–23

Chapter 17

[1] James 3:2–4 [2] Romans 8:34 [3] 1 Timothy 6:13 [4] John 18:33–38 [5] 1 Peter 2:9–10 [6] Matthew 10:31–32; Luke 12:8 [7] Joshua 10:28 [8] 2 Peter 3:9 [9] Revelation 1:12–16

If you have enjoyed this book and would like to help us to send
a copy of it and many other titles to needy pastors in the
Third World, please write for further information
or send your gift to:

Sovereign World Trust
PO Box 777, Tonbridge
Kent TN11 0ZS
United Kingdom

or to the '**Sovereign World**' distributor in your country.

Visit our website at **www.sovereign-world.org**
for a full range of Sovereign World books.